Platinum and Palladium Printing

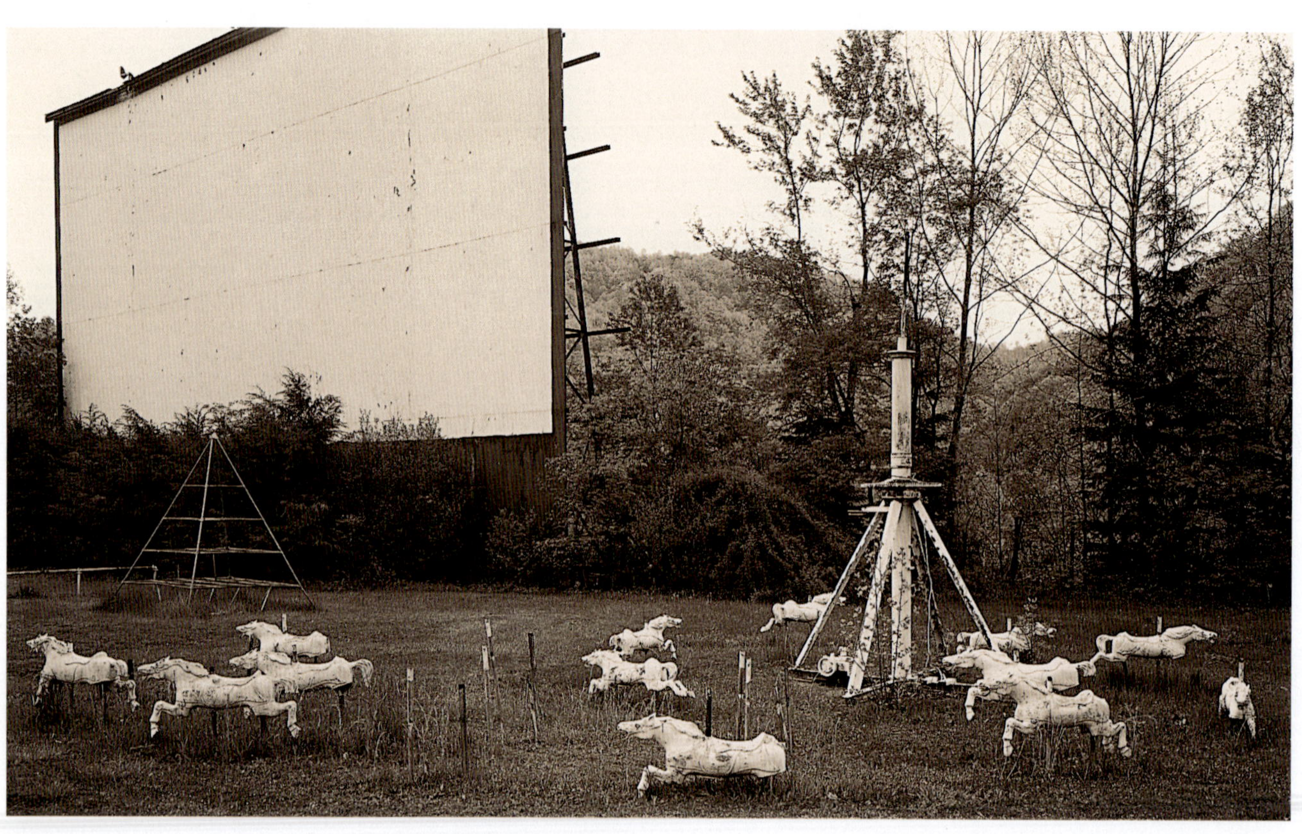

Platinum and Palladium Printing

Dick Arentz

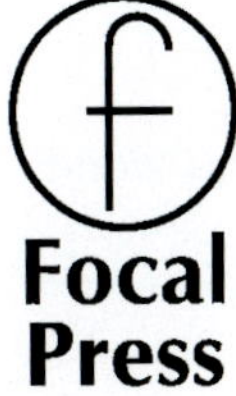

Boston Oxford Auckland Johannesburg Melbourne New Delhi

Photo illustrations by Alan Spiegler.

Focal Press is an imprint of Butterworth–Heinemann.
A member of the Reed Elsevier group

∞ Recognizing the importance of preserving what has been written, Butterworth–Heinemann prints its books on acid-free paper whenever possible.

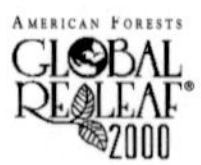

Butterworth–Heinemann supports the efforts of American Forests and the Global ReLeaf program in its campaign for the betterment of trees, forests, and our environment.

Library of Congress Cataloging-in-Publication Data
Arentz, Dick
Platinum and palladium printing / Dick Arentz.
p. cm.
Includes bibliographical references (p.)
ISBN 0-240-80377-9 (pbk. : alk. paper)
1. Photography—Printing processes—Platinotype. I. Title.
TR420.A74 1999
772'.3—dc21 99-28233
CIP

British Library Cataloguing-in-Publication Data
A catalogue record for this book is available from the British Library.
The publisher offers special discounts on bulk orders of this book.

For information, please contact:
Manager of Special Sales
Butterworth–Heinemann
225 Wildwood Avenue
Woburn, MA 01801-2041
Tel: 781-904-2500
Fax: 781-904-2620

For information on all Butterworth–Heinemann publications available, contact our World Wide Web home page at: http://www.focalpress.com

10 9 8 7 6 5 4 3 2 1

Printed in China

Dedication

To Phil Davis
Professor Emeritus, University of Michigan
Teacher, Mentor, and Friend

In 1970, I was an Assistant Professor at the University of Michigan, in a discipline far removed from art or photography. I was also an advanced amateur photographer, having taken a number of Ansel Adams workshops. Phil Davis was, at that time, head of the Department of Photography. One winter weekend, I hitched a ride with Phil and his students to a *Society of Photographic Education* meeting in Rochester, NY. For some reason, Phil and I were billeted at a motel removed from the rest. A typical Rochester snowfall came to bury the city, completely removing parked cars from sight, and confining us to our rooms . . . and the bar. It was there that Phil finally suggested that I knew practically nothing about photography. If, however, I would be willing to make the effort, he would tutor me.

Almost thirty years later, Phil, the source of one of the most significant changes in my life, is still my teacher. A good portion of this text, and the entire basis for Part Two, come from Phil's research, his book *Beyond the Zone System*, and his Plotter Program®. He has read and, mercifully, graciously criticized only those sections of this book.

Contents

Preface and Acknowledgments

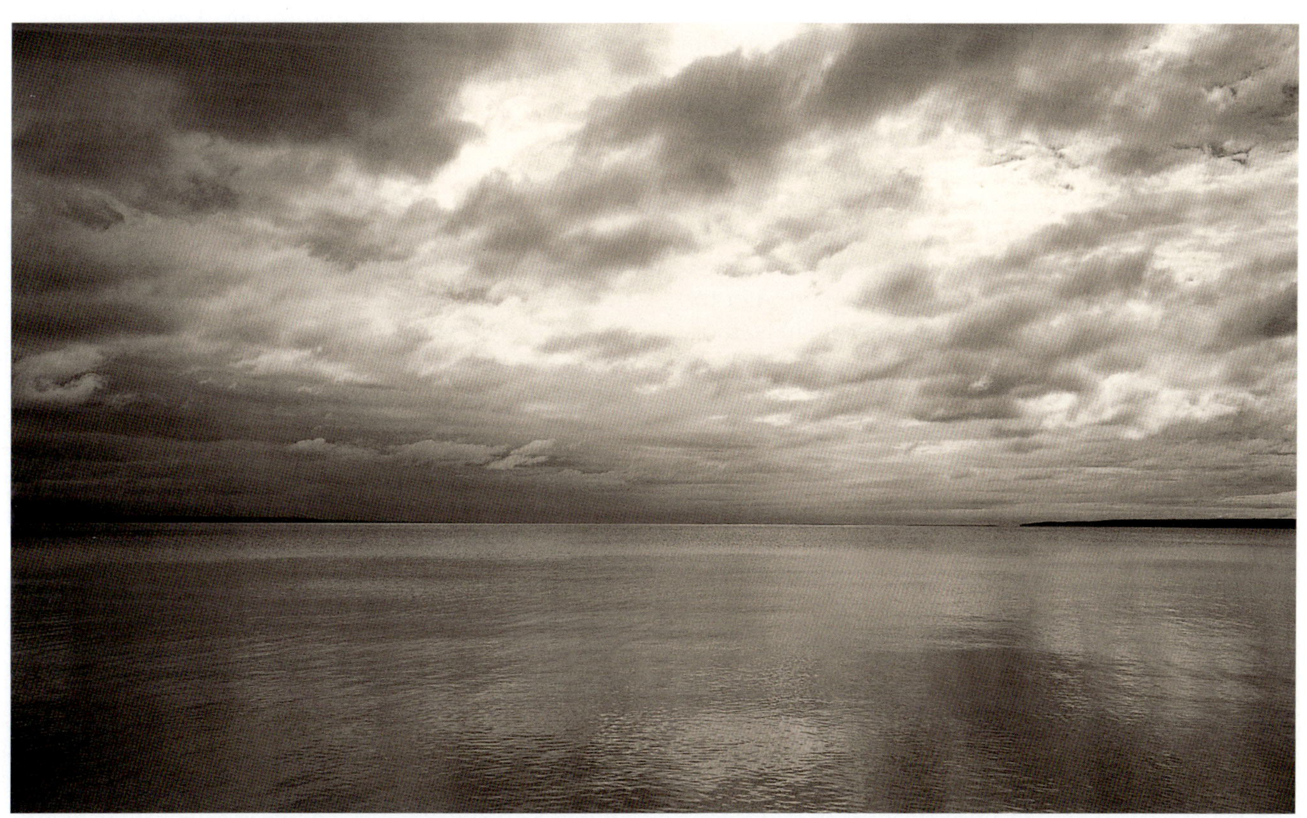

PLATE P.1 Batchawana Bay, Lake Superior, Ontario. 1997 12 × 20 inch Pt/Pd

This is a book is about the *craft* and *science* of platinum and palladium printing. For the most part, creativity or "*Art*" cannot be taught in a text or in the classroom—it must come from within. The teacher can only plant the seed and, if there is any growth, nurture it a bit. My goal, therefore, is simply to provide some of the tools needed for the artist to express and communicate his or her vision to others.

My first tasks in planning this text were the matters of inclusion and exclusion. Although I easily could have included more than I have, a seemingly endless recitation of photographic technology would have defeated the purpose of a practical guide for the platinum and palladium printer. Nevertheless, to exclude vital information out of the fear that some might be scared away by "science" would be a disservice to all who wish to master this unique process.

Here, I was guided by my contact with hundreds of workshop students. Their backgrounds varied from health science professionals and individuals with a Ph.D., to art students with only a minimum of high school science. In response to their questions and needs, the first *Outline for Platinum and Palladium Printing* was written over ten years ago. It is from that *Outline* that this text is constructed. Some presentation of elementary physics, mathematics, and chemistry is essential. It was necessary to find a middle ground—not too complicated, yet not too simplistic. Fortunately, those who are attracted to platinum printing possess the innate intelligence and curiosity to grasp the fundamental concepts quickly.

I also benefited in writing this book from my students. Because of the varied backgrounds represented by workshop participants, I gained as much or more than I imparted. Without their input, I would not have had the temerity to attempt a project of this nature.

Most importantly, I have made the effort to connect scientific subject matter and technique to the ultimate purpose of platinum and palladium printmaking. Consequently, images made using the concepts presented here are reproduced throughout this text.

Platinum and Palladium Printing is divided into two parts. Part One, "The Process," provides the theory and practical applications indispensable to the platinum and palladium printer. Part Two, "Sensitometry for the Platinum/Palladium Process," presents the actions of light on platinum and palladium materials.

For my discussions of platinum and palladium in Part One, I chose to make comparisons to the more ubiquitous silver gelatin process. The platinum/palladium (Pt/Pd) laboratory is different from the traditional photo darkroom, and I have made some effort to cover the distinctions between the two, as well as discussing the equipment that is unique to this form of photographic printmaking. I wish to thank dermatologist Fred McElveen, M.D., for providing me with the practical understanding of the properties of ultraviolet light I have presented.

The making of the photographic negative is an essential part of the platinum/palladium process and is covered in detail. The subject of the pyrogallol negative is one of the more illusive topics in photography. Although we were not able to reach any dramatic conclusions, I am indebted to Bob Herbst, Grant Evans, and Eric Marler for their help in this area.

Of all the sciences involved with photography and photographic printmaking, chemistry is most fundamental. For the optimum practice of this medium, the basic chemical reactions involved should be understood. While I had at one time taken some advanced college chemistry, much had faded away with time. Drs. John P. Schaefer and Richard Foust patiently disassembled my original chapters and offered the necessary suggestions for me to attain a reasonable degree of accuracy. One of the more pleasant experiences of writing this book came when my daughter Pamela Motley, a graduate student in chemistry, invited her old man to her office, and brought him up to speed—at the college freshman level—on the Redox reaction.

Recently, the deleterious effects of many chemical substances have come to be more appreciated. The careless practices of the past are no longer tolerated. Unfortunately, with this surge of new information and regulations, those who have applied indiscriminate interpretation of data to many essentially safe photographic processes have victimized platinum/palladium (Pt/Pd) printmaking. I have made the effort to find a logical middle ground by describing the *Reasonable and Prudent Use* of chemicals. Safe alternatives have been offered in place of the few truly harmful agents used in the Pt/Pd process. One, formaldehyde, has been eliminated in James Hajicek's formula for gelatin paper-sizing.

But perhaps the greatest effort was made in untangling the frustrating problem of finding papers appropriate to this process. I am indebted to Kathryn Clark of Twinrocker, a paper company in Indiana, for her generosity in assisting me in understanding the basics of papermaking in 1988—and allowing me to spend two days making feeble efforts at dipping the mould into the vat of pulp to make paper.

Keith Schreiber, formerly at The Center for Creative Photography in Tucson, was one of my workshop students in 1991. Years later, unbeknownst to me, he had quietly assembled a comprehensive series of paper tests that now serve as the basis for Chapter 5, "Paper," which he also coauthored. Many of his exceptional palladium prints are reproduced in this text. We have presented a list of papers that many will find helpful. We have continued our dialogue with paper companies with the hope that some of the mysteries of papermaking may become decoded.

Chapters 6 through 8 delve into the process of platinum/palladium printing from the simple sun print, to calibration of equipment and the making of the final print. Here I present the many practices that I have accumulated over a twenty-five-year career. Two methods are discussed in detail: the traditional "A+B" method, which utilizes the contrast control ingredient in the paper coating, and the dichromate method of controlling contrast by developer. Two of the fine ammonium-based processes, the Malde/Ware process and the Ziatype are introduced in Appendix D, "The Ammonium-Based Process."

In presenting methods for making a Pt/Pd print, some degree of editorial selection was necessary. Today, hundreds of fine photographers have described dozens of methods of making platinum and palladium prints. Since it would be impossible to cover even a small segment of this information, the reader is encouraged to "surf the net" for discussion groups and Web sites.

In Part Two, "Sensitometry for the Platinum/Palladium Process," the actions of light on platinum and palladium materials are presented for practical application with the inclusion of various exercises. I introduced densitometers in Part One, but they were not required for the making of a Pt/Pd print. In Part Two, the transmission densitometer is presented as an essential tool in the making of *predictable* and *reproducible* platinum and palladium prints. For some, this may be a quantum leap, for it requires some effort and consultation of recommended texts. Even if some of these practices are not completely adopted, reading the section will give the reader a better understanding of the process.

As other helpful information is available, but not necessarily essential to the development of the text, I have included an extensive set of appendices. Most significantly, the making of a large negative is described, either made directly in camera or though photomechanical means. As a large camera user, I have had limited experience in negative enlargement. Rod Klukas, Richard Lohmann, Kevin Martini-Fuller, and Norma Smith shared their knowledge of the photomechanical processes. Since I am also somewhat of a computer illiterate, I am grateful to John Schaefer and Dan Burkholder for providing their input on the subject of negative computerization. As many comprehensive guides to the computerized negative exist in book form, and on the Internet, a complete guide here would be redundant. Instead, I provide an introduction with source material.

I wish to thank Phil Davis, Darkroom Innovations, and Keith Schreiber for sharing the Plotter Program® files used to compile the film/developer combinations listed in Appendix B, "Some Film/Developer Combinations to Produce Platinum/Palladium Negative."

While compiling the basics of the ammonium-based processes, I was in constant e-mail contact with Professor Mike Ware of Buxton, England. Due to his generosity, we have presented an outline of the Malde/Ware process. And during the summer of 1998, Richard Sullivan and Carl Weese supervised me in making my first Ziatypes.

Kevin Martini-Fuller and Alan Spiegler read and provided corrections for the manuscript. In addition to sharing their expertise, Alan Spiegler and Keith Schreiber used their other talents to make the transparencies used for all the photo illustrations and plates. Special thanks to Keith Schreiber for his expertise while reading the page proofs.

Introduction

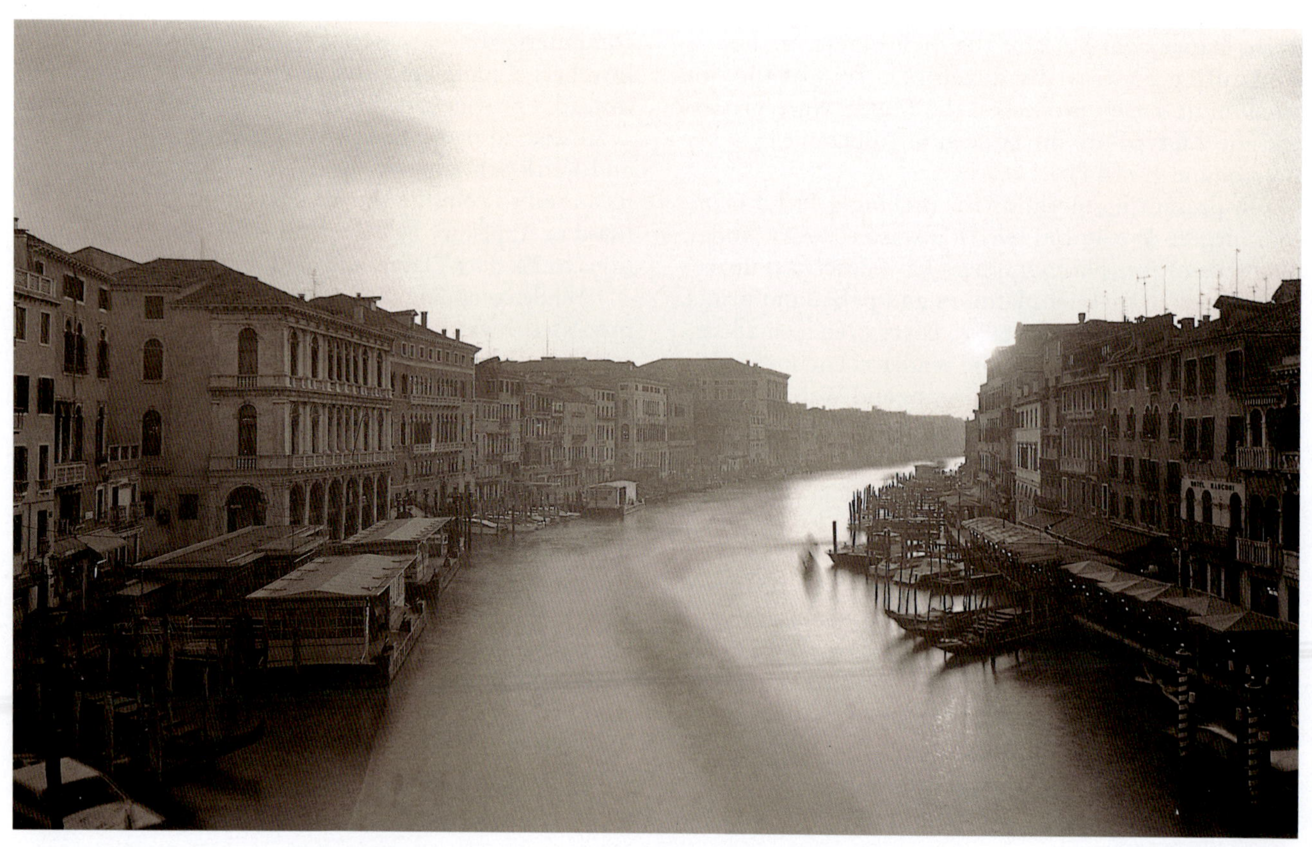

PLATE I.1 Grand Canal, Venice, Italy. 1996 12 × 20 inch Pd

Today, in the field of monochromatic photography, platinum printing has been categorized as one of the alternate processes. With a myriad of other photographic printing methods available today, the application of other nonsilver metals, inks, pigments, and dyes with a bas-relief matrix are now considered an *alternative* to the silver gelatin print.

It was not always so. In the nineteenth century, although Fox Talbot's first photographs were based on the reactions of silver chemicals to light, printing procedures utilizing different materials and techniques soon became available. Within a generation, silver was frequently considered a second choice to the more elegant examples of carbon, gum bichromate, bromoil, photogravure, Woodburytype, and platinum.

At that time, all processes required a large negative for contact printing. By the early twentieth century, however, with the development of faster film for the hand-held camera and enlarging paper—both of which rely on silver emulsions—the silver gelatin print became the predominant printing process in monochromatic photography, a position it still occupies today.

Nevertheless, the nonsilver photographic processes have endured and have recently undergone a resurgence. Some are practiced out of academic interest. A few, including platinum, have resumed their place among the finest of artistic media.

Platinum, as did other early processes, originally required hand preparation of the paper. Then, by the turn of the century, platinum and its sister metal palladium were available in many commercially prepared forms, only to disappear during the next twenty years as styles and techniques changed and the miniature camera gained popularity. Now, with renewed interest, one mechanically coated platinum/palladium paper has reentered the market. However, most platinum printers practice it as it was originally described in 1872—a hands-on printmaking process.

A platinum worker must still contact print with standard commercial silver-based film; if enlarging is desired, it must be done through internegatives or with the aid of computerization. The film is processed for greater contrast than is suitable for modern silver gelatin. Working in low incandescent light, a platinum and/or palladium salt mixed with a sensitizing ingredient is brushed on to a compatible, well-sized paper. Contrast control equivalent to a dozen silver paper grades is achieved through the use of minute amounts of oxidizers. After drying the paper in heated air, a negative is sandwiched between glass and the dried, coated paper. Approximately five minutes of intense ultraviolet light, either directly from the sun or a specific light source, is passed through the negative to the sensitized platinum and/or palladium salt. The print is then developed in a solution of naturally occurring organic salts and cleared in dilute acid or sulfite compounds. Minimal washing is required. The print is allowed to dry on a screen.

The finished hand-coated print consists of pure platinum and/or palladium metal imbedded upon and within the paper at a considerably greater thickness than can be laid on the surface by machine. A well-made platinum or palladium print excels in the delicacy of the tonal scale, image color and depth. Papers of different texture, hue, and weight can be used, so interpretation is not limited to the dictates of a uniformly manufactured product.

Depending on the market costs of precious metals, palladium is more often less expensive than platinum. Contemporary workers frequently combine platinum and palladium metals (Pt/Pd), or print with pure palladium. With a mixture of both metals, the characteristics of a pure platinum print can be essentially duplicated at less cost. Depending on available techniques, the print color of a platinum/palladium print can range from neutral gray to sepia. The midtones, rather than being compressed with modern silver paper, are evenly distributed, allowing for great subtlety in print values.

Pure palladium particularly captures the nuances of the mid- to high-tones. It is frequently possible to print brilliant highlights directly while still maintaining texture. A silver printer might be challenged to include the ball of the sun in a photograph. In palladium, a lightly diffused sun can easily take its place in the planning of an image (Plate I.1).

As one of the most permanent of photographic processes, platinum is also one of the most environmentally safe. The chemicals used are relatively inert metals, common cations (sodium and potassium), iron oxalates (rust), and weak acids. The oxidizing compounds, while hazardous, are used in infinitesimal quantities. For some compounds described in the literature that are now found to be hazardous, satisfactory alternatives exist.

In choosing platinum, the drawbacks must also be considered. It is a process made cumbersome by camera size or negative enlargement. Platinum and palladium salts are expensive. Technical control is necessary to minimize waste. Despite attempts to capitalize on the novelty or "preciousness" of platinum, some imagery does not do well in platinum or palladium. Simply put, platinum does not make bad photography acceptable.

Perhaps, these latter characteristics should be considered the greatest advantage of platinum and other alternate processes. In a way, to do them well, one must return to the inquisitiveness and noncommercial incentives of the nineteenth-century amateur photographer and master a craft for the purposes of personal satisfaction and achievement, attributes that might provide a refreshing counterpoint to some aspects of the contemporary art scene.

Platinum printing is one of the easiest of the nonsilver processes to learn. The platinum/palladium process also offers a number of variations, which the photographer can closely control. The advantage, however, makes the process a bit like chess: it is easy to learn the basic moves, but because of the options available to the skillful player, the complexity increases as the subject is mastered.

This book is flexibly bound with the intent that it be used as a laboratory manual rather than a library text. The step-by-step format is meant to guide the platinum or palladium printer through the multiple sensitometric, chemical, and mechanical tasks that must be mastered for consistent and predictable results. If, in the near future, the pages are dog-eared and liberally marked with notations and various chemical stains, then it will have served its purpose well.

Communication with the author can be done by e-mail at dick.arentz@nau.edu

PART ONE

The Process

CHAPTER 1

Platinum and Palladium

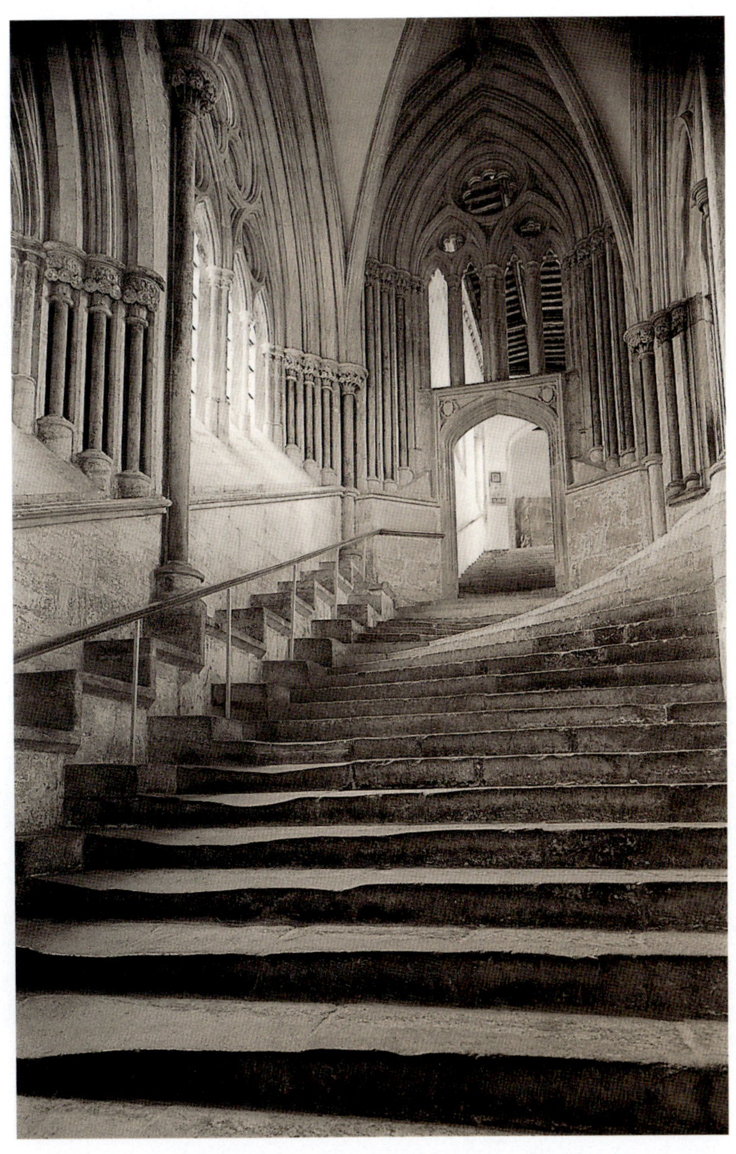

PLATE 1.1 Wells Cathedral, England. Homage to Frederick Evans. 1990 12 × 20 inch Pd. Among the platinum printers at the turn of the century, Frederick Evans was the premiere practitioner of the art.

Platinum Printing in the Twentieth Century

The first patent for the platinum process was obtained by William Willis in 1873. Improvements and modifications followed during the remainder of the nineteenth century (Abney, 1895; Pizzighelli and Hubl, 1886; Nadeau, 1994; Sullivan and Weese, 1998).

By 1900, dozens of commercially made platinum and palladium papers were available in England and the United States. However, within two decades, as the result of two unrelated occurrences, platinum printing was brought to the verge of extinction. First of all, World War I started in 1914. The need for platinum in the manufacture of munitions (it was used as a hardener for the tips of cannon shells) caused the market price of the element to reach astronomic highs during that time. Manufacturers discontinued the papers. Secondly, recent developments in photography allowed for an increase in the speed of lenses and film. Similar increases in the printing speed of silver paper led to the design of a practical enlarger. Smaller hand-held cameras could be used; the photographer could later enlarge the image to any size desired. Platinum, as with most of the nonsilver processes, did not have light sensitivity to react to the relatively dim light of the enlarger. Many elegant nineteenth-century processes, as well as the traditional tripod mounted camera, fell into disuse.

By 1920, no commercially made platinum papers were available in the United States. Some photographers, such as Laura Gilpin, imported their paper directly from England.

In the mid-1960s a resurgence in platinum printing began. Since no commercially prepared papers had been available since 1941, photographers went to the literature to repeat the processes described by Willis, Pizzighelli, and others. By 1970, Irving Penn and George Tice were making hand-coated platinum and palladium prints. With the explosion of university photography programs at the time came a renewed academic interest in all nonsilver processes. Also, with photographic education, a new, sophisticated audience for fine art photographs was born. Galleries restricted to the sales of photographs to connoisseurs and collectors opened throughout the country. Custom printers now discovered that established photographers in the fields of fashion, advertising, portraiture, and photojournalism wanted their images rendered in platinum and palladium.

For a brief period, following this major entry of photography into the art markets, platinum, with other recently reintroduced processes, was judged more by its status as a novelty than by its content. Today, platinum printing has found its proper place. It is practiced by hundreds of photographers, covering the spectrum from the amateur to the significant photographers of our time.

The Platinum/Palladium and Silver Processes Compared

Most significantly, silver gelatin paper is a manufactured item. Minute particles of silver are imbedded into a microscopic layer of gelatin. The glossy or semigloss

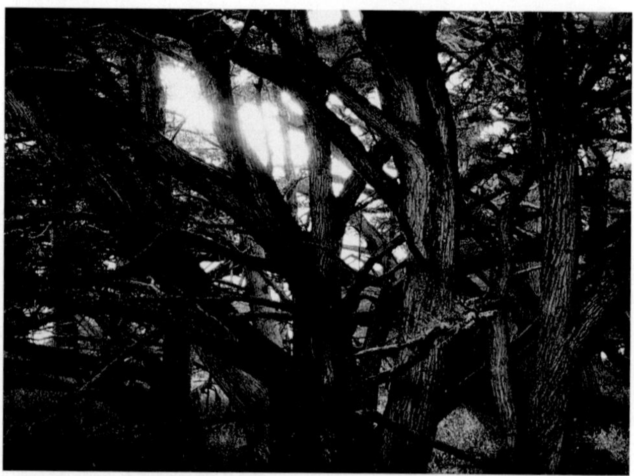

PLATE 1.2 Cypress, Point Lobos, California. 1977 10 × 12 inch Silver Gelatin. Note the predominance of low and high tones, with little facility to record the effects of the harsh backlighting. The image color would be more toward the blue-black scale than depicted by the inks used in duotone printing.

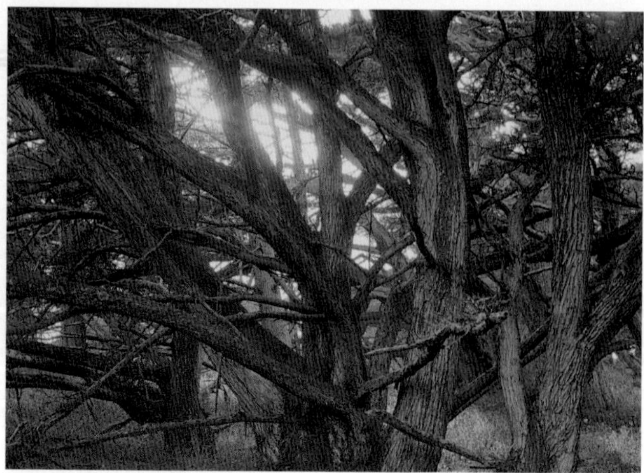

PLATE 1.3 Cypress, Point Lobos, California. 1977 5 × 7 inch Pt/Pd. The tones of the print have been more evenly distributed. Because of the pronounced ability to separate high values, the backlighting is now more assimilated into the image.

silver print is capable of reflective densities greater than any matte finish, hand-coated process. Also, the amount of detail or "sharpness" is enhanced by the slick, thin surface of the paper.

Pt/Pd printing, when practiced as a hand-coated procedure, has a surface of metal granules many times thicker than any mechanically made paper. As such, it takes on many of the characteristics of the hands-on printmaking processes.

Considering the many unique properties of each process, the platinum or palladium print is no more superior to that of silver than the cello is to the violin; it simply has characteristics that make it different. With certain imagery, the platinum or palladium print offers a refreshing, complimentary change from the traditional monochromic silver print. To carry the analogy a step further, some music will be amenable for transposition from one instrument to the other, and some may not be. Similarly, in imagery, some images can succeed in either media; most will work in only one.

When compared to commercial silver papers, the Pt/Pd process has some attributes:

1. It is one of the most stable of the photographic processes—as stable as the paper it is printed on.
2. It has a delicate response to highlights.
3. The midtones of the print are more evenly distributed, creating a distinctive "platinum" image.
4. The process of hand-coating allows the printer to increase the depth of metal particles, resulting in an image with extreme physical presence.
5. There is a wider exposure range of paper contrast, allowing the use of a rich, "contrasty" negative.
6. There is considerable choice of papers, allowing for variations in image tone, paper hue, and texture. As a hand-coated process, platinum or palladium can also be placed on materials other than traditional artists' paper.

Despite some deterioration in manufacturing techniques, silver has a distinct set of advantages that have made it the most popular of the monochromic printing processes. When compared to platinum, silver exhibits the following:

1. It is less expensive than platinum or palladium. (A typical small Pt/Pd print will cost $5.00 in materials.)
2. A silver print can be made from an enlarger, utilizing a much smaller negative. The printing speed of platinum or palladium is much slower; consequently, a projected image cannot be used for printing. A contact print is required. Unless the negative is reprocessed to a larger size, the size of the platinum or palladium print is determined by the format of the camera.
3. The maximum reflection density (depth of black) is much greater with silver than with platinum.
4. Optical detail or "sharpness" is greater on commercially prepared silver paper than what may be found in any hand-coated process.
5. Because of the myriad of commercial materials specifically made for the silver gelatin process and the use of the enlarger to compose and expose, silver printing is generally easier to learn and practice than the Pt/Pd process.
6. Silver is capable of producing a "black," "cool," or "bluish" black not possible with traditional platinum images. (For an exception, see the Ziatype in Appendix D, "The Ammonium-Based Processes.")

As you can see, no process is "superior." With the beginning photographer in particular, I believe that many nonsilver processes should be explored in addition to platinum. If a decision is made to concentrate on a process other than silver, taking into account the added difficulty and expense, it should be made based on factors other than the desire to be different. In many ways, silver is still the most versatile and effective medium for photographic expression.

Platinum and Palladium Compared

For many years, my "platinum" prints have actually been equal parts each of platinum and palladium. My tests have shown little discernible difference between a platinum and a Pt/Pd print. (See the section "Image Color" in Chapter 9, "Advanced Technique.") The pure platinum print is cooler and more amenable to certain toning techniques; however, the tone of a print made from both metals can be controlled by the choice of developer. The cost advantage of this technique is usually significant. Most "platinum" prints made today are actually a combination of platinum and palladium.

Platinum and palladium are both relatively inert noble metals of great similarity. With minor variations, the mixing, coating, and developing is identical. The prints produced by each of the metals are similar but have some individual differences.

When compared to platinum/palladium, palladium is:

1. Usually less expensive (approximately one-quarter the cost)
2. Warmer (more sepia) in tone

3. More easily solarized (true solarization, as compared to the Sabattier effect) (see Solarization with Palladium, Chapter 10, "Problems")
4. More susceptible to bleaching in the clearing process, unless care is taken
5. Characterized by a greater latitude (a more contrasty negative is needed)
6. Deeper blacks and a higher *Dmax* can be obtained compared to those of platinum alone or a platinum/palladium mixture.
7. With a given paper and contrast range, the palladium print often exhibits smoother tones.

Printing with pure palladium may be precarious, but it is often worth the effort. If well done, it is the most exquisite of printing processes.

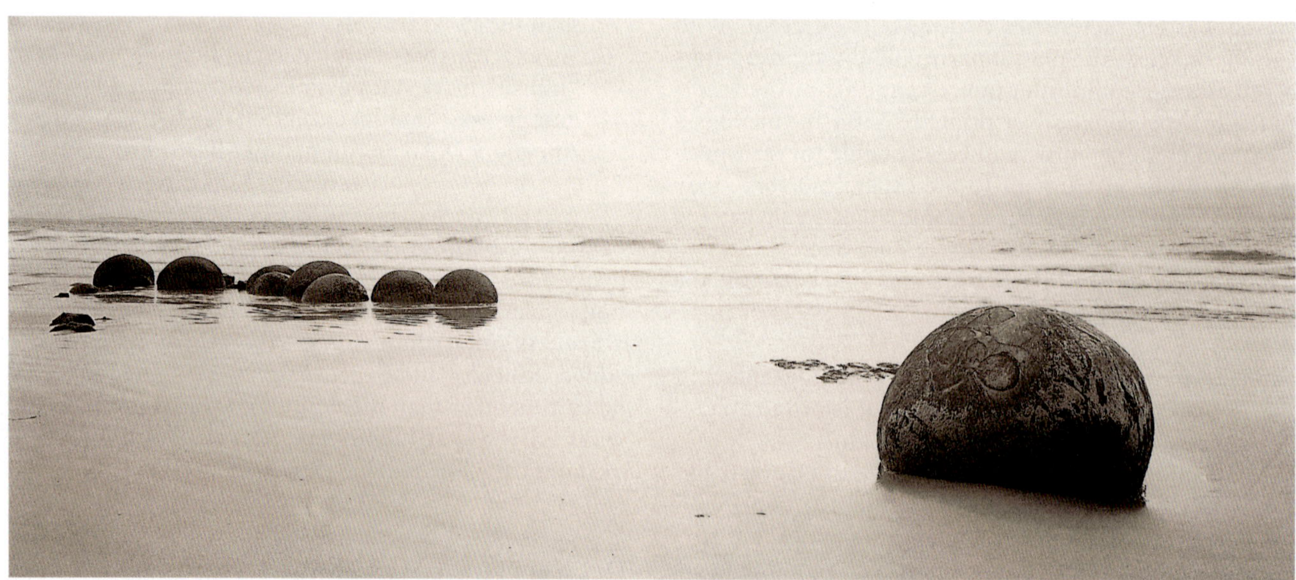

PLATE 1.4 Moeraki Boulders, NZ. 1995 18 × 20 inch Pt/Pd

CHAPTER 2

Setting Up a Laboratory

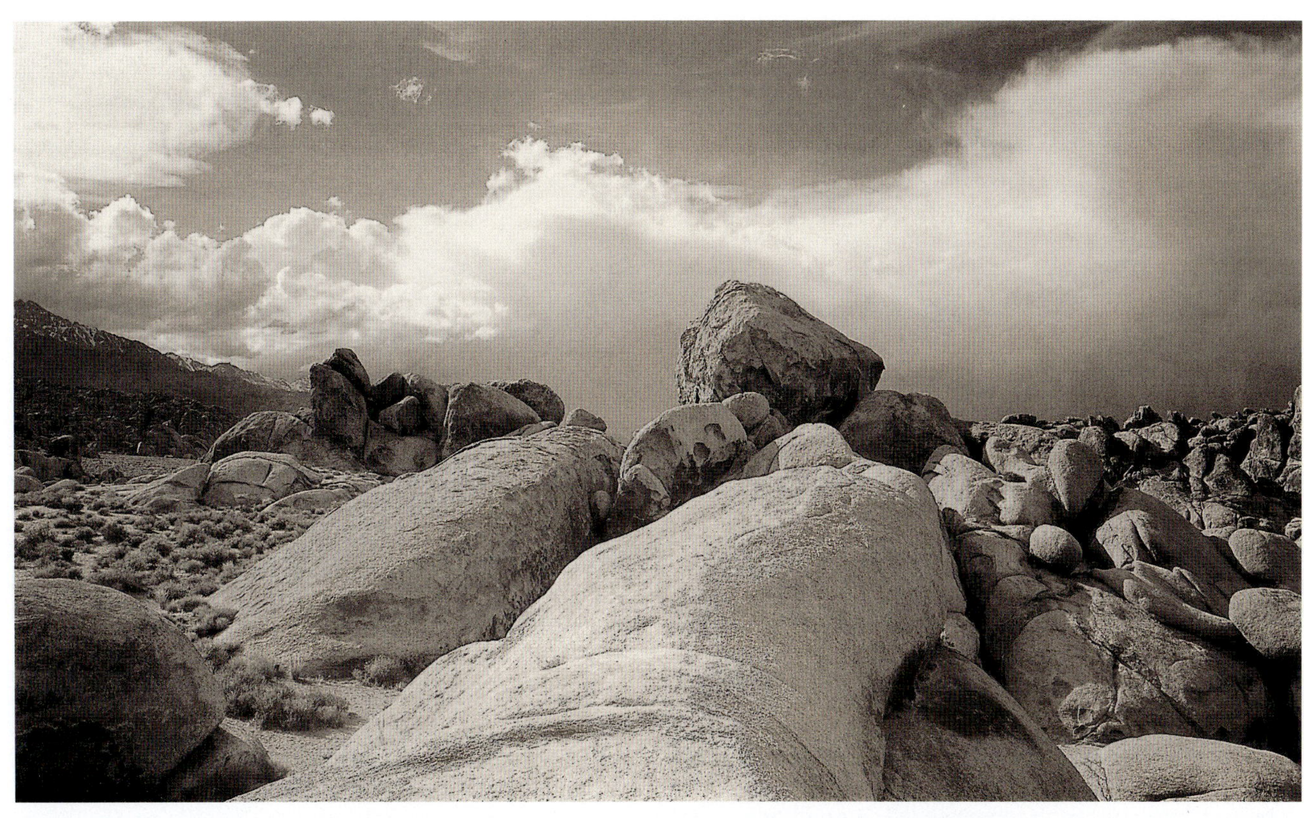

PLATE 2.1 Alabama Hills, California. 1997 12 × 20 inch Pt/Pd

It is best that a separate, well-ventilated space be planned for any photographic process, including platinum printing. For designing a laboratory, the following guide is recommended: *Kodak: Building a Home Darkroom* (Publication KW-14, 1986). Calumet Photo, Inc. has extensive choices for sinks, plumbing, filters and temperature control units, and exhaust systems. *(Source: CPI)*[1]

In designing modifications in a typical photographic laboratory for the purpose of platinum and palladium printing, the decision must be made as to whether silver or color printing is contemplated for the present or future. If not, considerable changes in the design normally recommended for a darkroom may be incorporated.

Most significantly, unless photomechanical enlargement of negatives is planned, safelights or an enlarger are not needed. Since the actual exposure is best done in another space, the "wet" area of the laboratory can be mostly occupied by the working sink, designed to accommodate the largest negatives and prints you think you might make. (Plan ahead; do not be disappointed when your sink will not take the 12 × 20 trays.) An adequate flat surface for coating the platinum and/or palladium solutions onto the paper should be set aside in this room.

The Wet Space and Coating Area

While the platinum/palladium process can be done in low incandescent light, negative development requires a light-tight environment. If using tubes or a JOBO® processor, a small light-tight space need only be provided for the loading of tubes and film holders. (See Appendix A, "The Large Negative.")

The wet space and coating area are ideally situated in the same room. Both coating and processing are done under the same low incandescent light source. Since a humidity of 40 to 60% is recommended for coating, in most climates, the "wet" area of the laboratory can maintain more consistent humidity than most other rooms. A hygrometer is recommended. A good one is the Airguide 112 that sells for about $70. *(Source: VWR)*

In extreme climatic situations, a humidifier or dehumidifier may be needed. The solutions used for platinum, and the coating and storage area for paper, should both be located at room temperatures of 65 to 70°F. The coating area should be far enough away from the sinks to avoid any contact with water splashes (Figure 2.1) Any water droplets on the paper before or after coating will permanently ruin the print. If a coating rod is to be used, a perfectly flat piece of tempered plateglass must be provided as a coating surface.

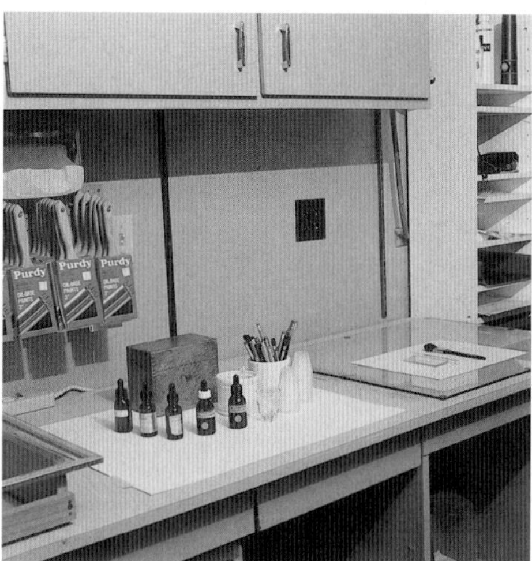

FIGURE 2.1 The Coating Area

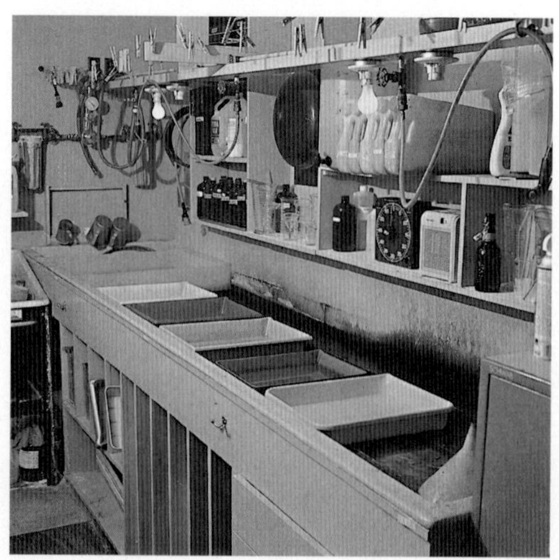

FIGURE 2.2 The Wet Space

A flat sink large enough to take at least four trays and a washing tank is necessary (Figure 2.2). An additional laundry tub is valuable for mixing solutions.[2] Two light sources are recommended: a set of 40 Watt bulbs at least four feet from the coating area and

[1] Sources of materials will be referred to by a designated abbreviation, found in the section "Sources."

[2] For mixing from powder, a stir and heat plate is highly recommended (Figure 2.3). Potassium oxalate developer works best at 90°F. The heated plate can maintain that temperature. Most importantly, however, the magnetic stirring function allows you to be distanced from the powder and fumes during mixing. *(Source: TS)*

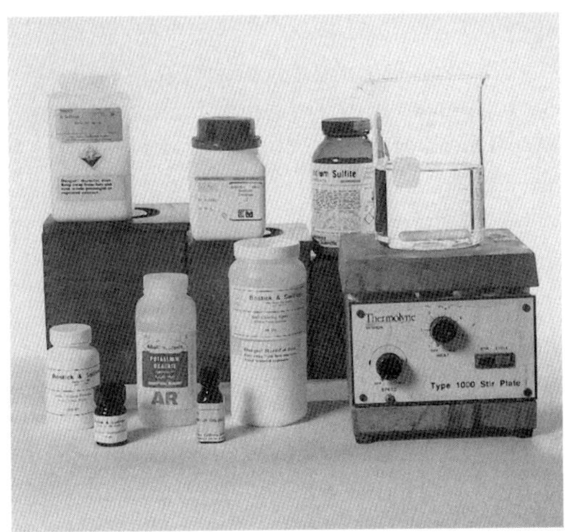

FIGURE 2.3 Chemicals and Stir Plate

developing trays, and a standard fixture with adequate wattage to view prints after development.

Since most of your time in the darkroom will be spent standing, purchase antifatigue rubber mats.

The Drying and Exposure Area

Ideally, the wet and dry areas should consist of two rooms. Practically, many do not have the available space or means to construct such a facility. A compromise can be achieved by dividing the laboratory into two distinct areas, utilizing a room divider, for example. The following recommendations are based on "ideal" circumstances.

Drying is usually done with the use of a hair dryer. Since particles of the coating may conceivably be blown into the air, a larger more open space is recommended. Also, continuous use of a hair dryer in a confined space will alter temperature and humidity. For smaller prints, if budget and space allows, a drying cabinet is a preferable alternative. A specific paper dryer for platinum and palladium prints is available from Edwards Engineering. *(Source: EE)*

Also, see Chapter 9, "Advanced Technique," for a description of the *drying apparatus*.

The light source, unless well shielded, will emit ultraviolet rays beyond the print to be exposed (usually 3 to 15 minutes). Freshly coated paper or chemicals used for coating are best protected from ultraviolet light. Antiactinic glasses should be worn for eye protection, and children should be kept away. A curtain composed of light-blocking drapery material can be constructed. Then, if the exposure unit is on a timer, additional prints can be coated while another is "cooking" under the light source.

This drying and exposure room is the best room for the handling of negatives. A light table and densitometer can be situated here, as well as a vault for storage of negatives. Fiberglass drying screens and a retouching table can also be located in this room. (See Figures 2.4 and 2.5.)

- I use both sides of the film holder for identical exposure of each image. To supply "insurance" in case of a scratch, light leak, or blunder in developing, I produce an extra set of negatives. The original set is stored in a fire-retardant cabinet. The extra set is kept in another building.

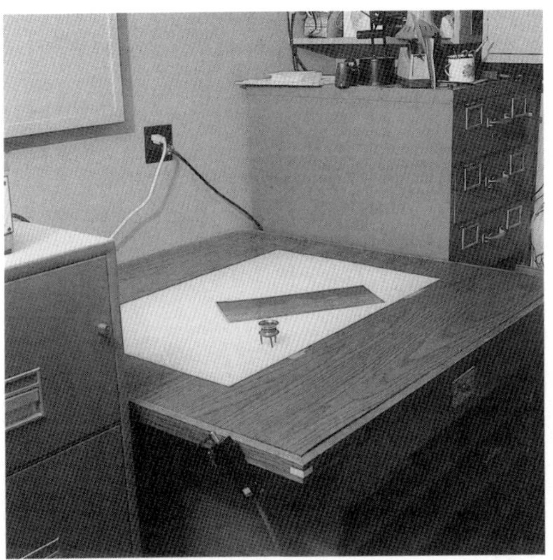

FIGURE 2.4 The Light Table

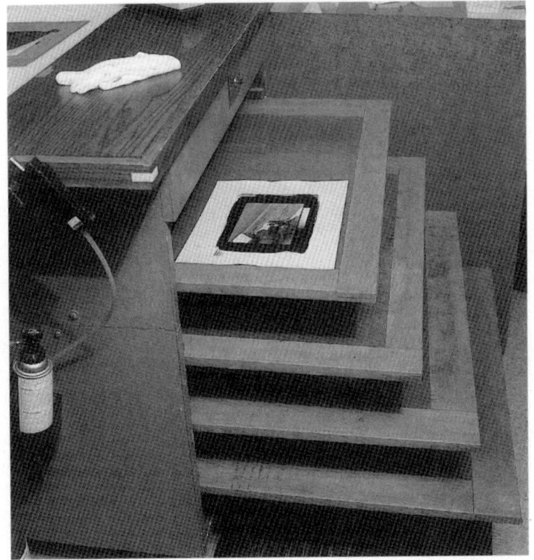

FIGURE 2.5 The Drying Screens

- *For any lab, provide for escape in the event of fire.* If there are no windows, consider putting one in, covering it with thin Masonite, and keeping a tool accessible for rapid removal. In the event of a home sale, the presence of a window will increase the value to a nonphotographer. For those spaces in a windowless area away from the main living area, check with the fire department for remote access to smoke alarms.

Materials

The Wet Area

PHOTO SUPPLIER

Clean towels

Clock timer

Five ml measuring graduates (3)

Hot plate (Use wire-mesh insulator over coils if a glass container is used)

Latex gloves, lightly lubricated with Silicon

Print tongs not previously used for other process

Sponges

Stirring rods

Trays not previously used for silver, at least one size larger than print paper

Two-liter stainless steel or Pyrex container for developer

The Coating Area

ART SUPPLY

Black felt-tip marking pen

Drafting tape

Plastic pushpins

Scissors

Single-edged razor blades

Photo Supplier

Camel hair negative dusting brushes, one- and two-inch

Clean blotters

Pharmacy

One-ounce dropper bottles (at least 4)

One-ounce plastic medicine cups

Cotton applicators

Hypodermic syringes for rod coating. (In some states, you may need a prescription from a doctor.) Discard the needle after securing it in the plastic cover.

Chemical Supply House

Chemical balance (optional)

Stir-and-heat plate (optional)

Filter paper, student grade

Funnel, glass (for filtering metal salts)

Hygrometer *(Source: VWR)*

pH 0-14 paper strips *(Sources: VWR, LI, TS)*

Specialty Supplier

Antistatic solution *(Source: MD)*

Coating rods *(Source: BS, EE)*

One sheet of tempered double-thickness glass

pH pen *(Source: LI)*

Anti-actinic glasses *(Source: Ski shop, PS)*

The Exposure and Finishing Area

SPECIALTY SUPPLIER

Printers' Rubylith® material (from printing shop)

Step tablets (discussed in Chapter 7) *(Sources: DI, GAS, BS)*

Photo Supplier

Air syringe or canned air

Cotton gloves

Beauty Supplier

Hair dryer (buy a professional model). Diffuser is optional.

General Supply

11 × 14 thick corrugated cardboard

Art Supply

#000 fine camel hair brushes

Light Table

Watercolors: Ivory black, Burnt umber (tubes), Titanium white (powder)

Watercolor dish

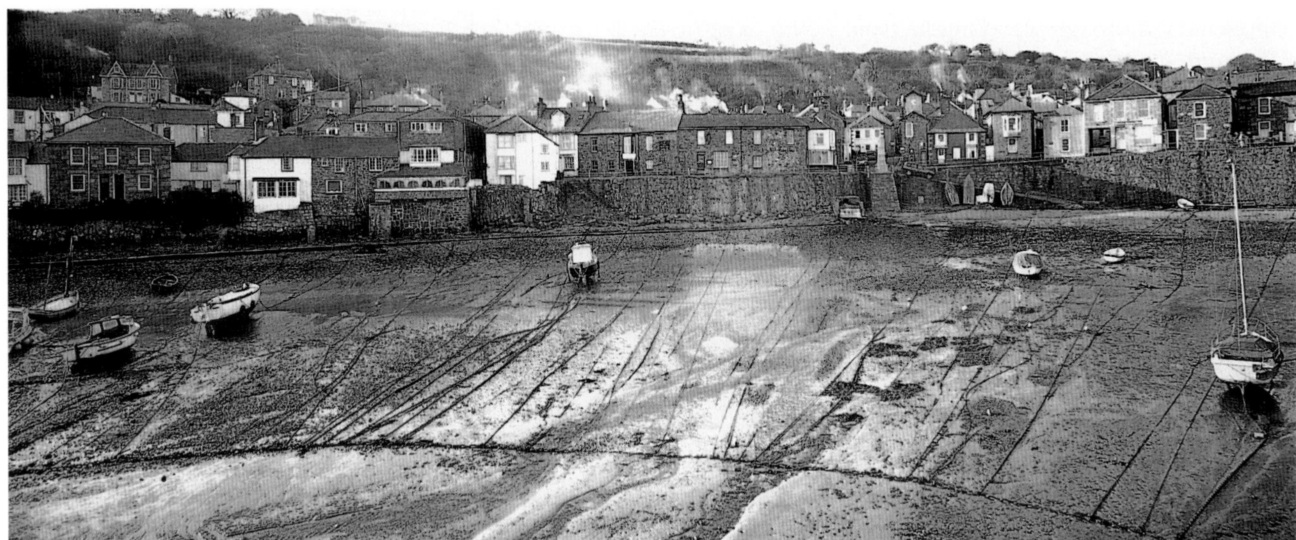

PLATE 2.2 Mousehole, England. 1998 8 × 20 inch Pt/Pd

Contact Printing Frames

There are alternatives to using a contact printing frame. A vacuum easel is superior. If the light is coming from above, a heavy sheet of plate glass over foam rubber is quite adequate.

If you use a contact printing frame, choose one of high quality. Most frames available from photo supply houses are inadequate: the springs are not strong enough, and the inexpensive wood flakes off between the negative and glass. (On the sky in the photograph, of course.) The older ones are best. Check catalogues of used photo equipment. Otherwise, good sources exist for new and better contact printing frames. (See Figure 2.6.) *(Sources: GB, BS)*

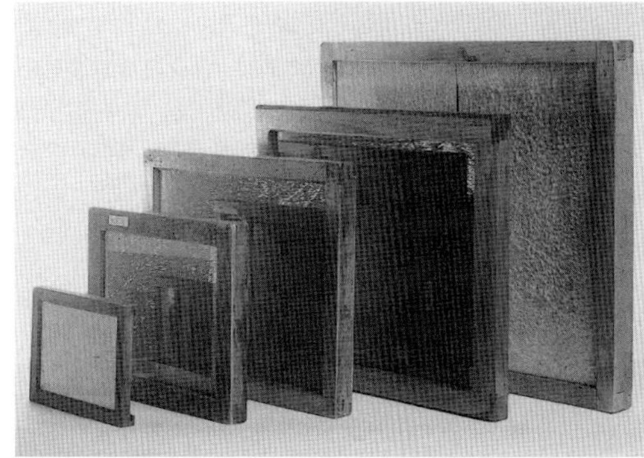

FIGURE 2.6 The Contact Printing Frames

The Ultraviolet Light Source

The light needed to convert the sensitized salt used in platinum/palladium printing, is in a rather narrow region of the ultraviolet (UV) spectrum. Light from other spectra is inadequate or useless. Frequencies of light waves are measured in *nanometers*. A nanometer (n) is one-billionth of a meter. The ultraviolet spectrum is defined as the range of emissions from 200 to 400 nanometers, although wavelengths from 100 n exist in a vacuum. (See Figure 2.7.) UV light is further divided into bands of UV-A (320 to 400 n), UV-B (290 to 320 n), and UV-C (200 to 290 n). The actinic conversion of the iron salts used for platinum and palladium printing occurs most often in the UV-A and the upper ranges of the UV-B spectra. Fortunately, the health hazards of UV light are less at these higher frequencies, whereas the nanometer range of UV-C and the lower UV-B is highly destructive to the skin and is carcinogenic. Equally fortunate, most of it is filtered out by the atmosphere. For personal protection, the UV sources used in platinum printing are such that severe measures need not be taken. Sunglasses used for skiing help to cut the annoying glare and some of the UV spectrum. Shielding of the eyes with the use of glasses specifically designed for the UV spectrum[3] is a better choice if there will be continuous contact. Further covering of the light source is advisable, particularly if others will be in the vicinity.

The following types of ultraviolet light sources are available. Most will need a printing frame or heavy glass to hold the negative and coated paper in register. Some of the more expensive commercial "plate burners" come with a vacuum easel.

The Sun

The sun was the first light source for all photographic printing and remained so for most of the nineteenth century. Because sunlight contains all of the spectra, more portions of the sensitized salts darken to form a distinct "provisional" image. Utilizing a hinged printing frame, one can, with practice, gauge the exposure process by opening one side of the back, keeping the negative in register. A well-made platinum or palladium

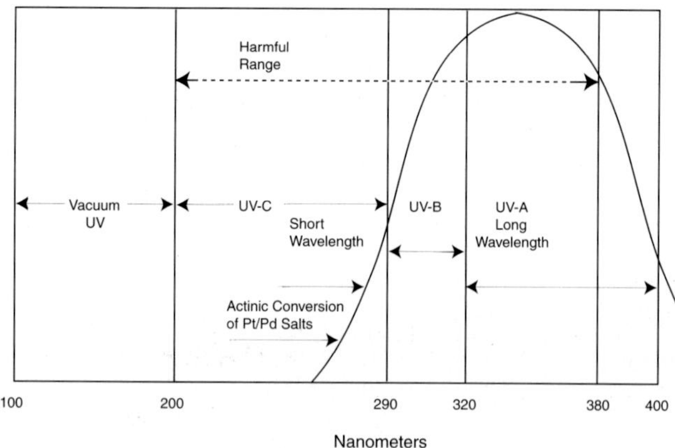

FIGURE 2.7 The Ultraviolet Spectrum Showing the Actinic Range at Which Salts used for Platinum and Palladium Printing are Converted

print will require from five to fifteen minutes of direct midday sun. (See Chapter 6, "The First Print.")

Obviously, the amount and type of sunlight is contingent upon climate, atmospheric conditions, season, and time of day. While these variables are fascinating while learning the platinum/palladium printing process, eventually a more dependable source of light will be needed.

Mercury Vapor Lights

Mercury vapor bulbs or "yard" lights, used for outdoor lighting, emit ultraviolet light as part of their function. At a proper distance, each is capable of exposing a platinum print within the same period of time as required for a sun exposure. Mercury vapor lights are available from any lighting store. Some come with a timer that must be disconnected. With this light source, particularly when larger negatives are used, one must set the distance to the print without vignetting.

UV Fluorescent Tube Box

A bank of 24- or 48-inch UV fluorescent tubes can be laid side by side in an exposure box (Figure 2.8). The lights are available from many specialty lighting stores. The types are listed here in order of increasing efficiency: BL (Black Light) (least), SA (Super Actinic), and AQA (Aquarium) (most). They emit UV light in the 350 to 750 nanometer range, so much of the visible light is ineffective. Nevertheless, they do the job. They should be spaced as closely as possible, while still leaving enough finger room for replacement. The base should be covered with a reflective material. A complete

3. Solar Specs®, designed specifically for protection from the UV spectrum of light, are manufactured by Psoralight Corporation. They are available as clear (1081PC) and gray (1082PC). They sell for $8.50 each. *(Source: PS)*

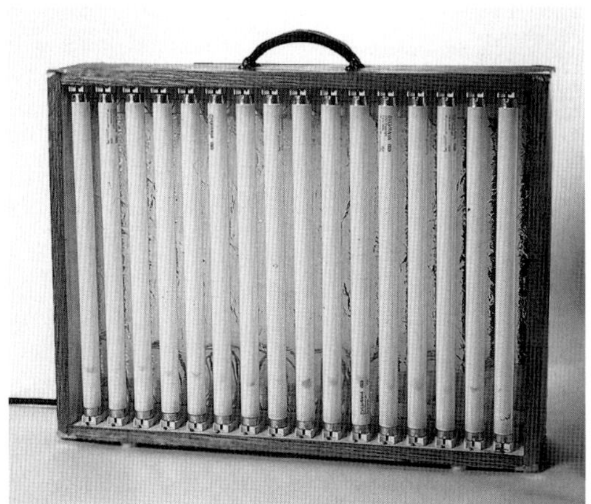

FIGURE 2.8 The Homemade Light Source

description for do-it-yourself construction can be found in Luis Nadeau's *History and Practice of Platinum Printing*, and Richard Sullivan and Carl Weese's *The New Platinum Print*. Some of the older Palladio instruction manuals contain instructions.

Following the general plan presented by the literature, some parts can be found from inexpensive sources. Buy as many cheap four-foot fluorescent light fixtures as needed to provide the necessary outlets. Disassemble them, leaving the ballasts wired. Anchor the fixtures to your light box. The sides should allow the printing frame to come to within three inches of the bulbs. If you cannot drill into the receptacles for anchoring them, pin them between sets of large-headed wood screws.

You may need the advice of an electrician for wiring the entire apparatus into a parallel circuit. If possible, plan the box so that it works directing the light downward onto a flat surface. In your calibration of the source (discussed in Chapter 7, "Calibration"), various paper-to-light distances must be tested to find the ideal. Usually, it will turn out to be three to four inches.

Either the light box can be suspended over adjustable shelves, or legs can be modified to suit. Additional advantages are that dodging and burning in can be done by placing printers' Rubylith material on the glass. Heavy glass plates can be substituted for the printing frame. Due to uneven lighting, many homemade fluorescent light source will produce scalloping effects on skies. Simply move the printing frame sideways every few minutes to avoid this.

With either the mercury vapor lights or fluorescent tubes, it is advisable to allow considerable warm up time before use. After that, leave it on for the entire printing session.

UV Light Boxes

It is possible to purchase manufactured UV light boxes. Some are available with vacuum easels. Sources of well-made professionally constructed light boxes are listed. *(Sources: AR, EE, BS, PC)*

Sizes are from 11 × 14 to 20 × 24. Prices vary from \$400 to \$3,000.

Commercial Plate Burner

The commercial plate burners used in the graphic arts industry—if one is within your budget—are the ideal choice. (See Chapter 8, "The Platinum and Palladium Print," Figure 8.17.) Many come with a vacuum easel. The light is collimated from a reflecting surface to give even distribution over the entire field. Most come with light integrators: timers based on units of light, so fluctuations in current do not affect printing times. They draw considerable 110-volt power and, therefore, require a separate circuit breaker. Be sure to specify a mercury vapor model.

A perfect choice is the nuArc 26-1K table model, which comes with a 24 × 26 inch vacuum easel, for approximately \$1,700.[4] *(Source: NA)*

Densitometers

Densitometers read either transmission or reflective densities. More costly models come with both modes, as well as a bank of filters for color separation work. To maintain controls in this costly process, many platinum printers eventually find that they need a transmission densitometer. However, unless research is contemplated, a reflection densitometer is not needed, nor are the filters.

You can locate a densitometer in your area, usually at a print shop, and rent it during their slow hours. To familiarize yourself with a transmission densitometer, read a batch of negatives. After a while, you get a sense of the characteristics of good, not so good, and unprintable negatives. Then, particularly after delving into Part Two, "Sensitometry for the Platinum/

4. nuArc has come out with a metal halide model 26-1KS. Analysis of the published data indicates that it will work in the 200 to 400 n range, and most likely be adequate for conversion of Pt/Pd salts, perhaps requiring less exposure time. To standardize at 400 units of light, as recommended for calibration, it might be necessary to adjust the light integrator. If that is not possible, it may require standardization at 200 units. It will be priced at about \$2,200. The mercury vapor model (26-1K) will still be made on special order.

Palladium Process," you might consider a purchase, or at least share one with a photographer friend.

Modifying a Light Meter

Using the instructions in Phil Davis' *Beyond the Zone System*, you can convert a Pentax or Minolta 1° spot meter to both a transmission and reflection densitometer.

Inexpensive Table Models

Transmission densitometers from $400 to $1,500 are available from Calumet Photo. Some are quite flimsy. The German-made Heiland TRD 2 is both a transmission and reflection densitometer for $895. *(Source: DI)*

A table-model transmission densitometer has been released by Absolute Photographic Company. The Mantis Densitometer is specifically designed for monochromatic negatives and sells for $595. The measuring throat length is four inches, allowing use with negatives of only up to 8 × 10. *(Source: AP)*

Hand-Held Densitometers

X-Rite makes portable, battery operated units:

Transmission Model 331.	$845
Reflection Model 400.	$1,045

These are quite convenient, but they come only with a six-inch arm that makes the reading of ultralarge negatives difficult. Because of this compactness, the reading circle is quite small. At times, it is hard to position the area to be read (Figure 2.9). *(Source: DI)*

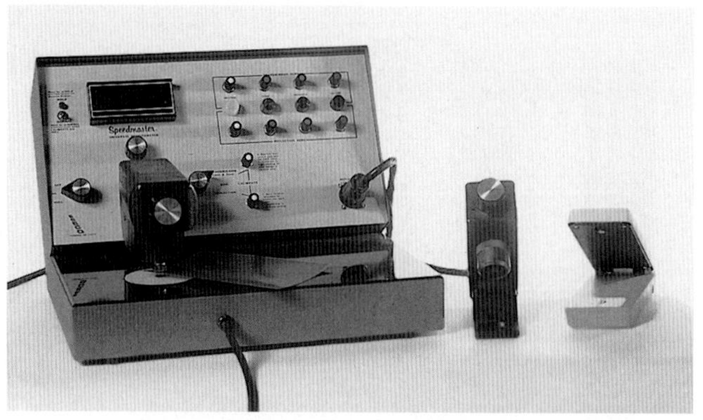

FIGURE 2.9 The Professional and Hand-Held Densitometers

The Professional Models

Eseco Speedmaster leads the industry (Figure 2.9). The units come with extensive warrantees, as well as an efficient support service. Models starting from $500 attach to your computer. Their table models are more expensive, but they are worth every penny. I recommend the Model T-85D at $1,850. They are made so well, that if you can find a used one—particularly the TRC-60D dual model—snatch it up. *(Source: ES)*

Older MacBeth models can also be found in the used market. They are excellent.

CHAPTER 3

The Negative

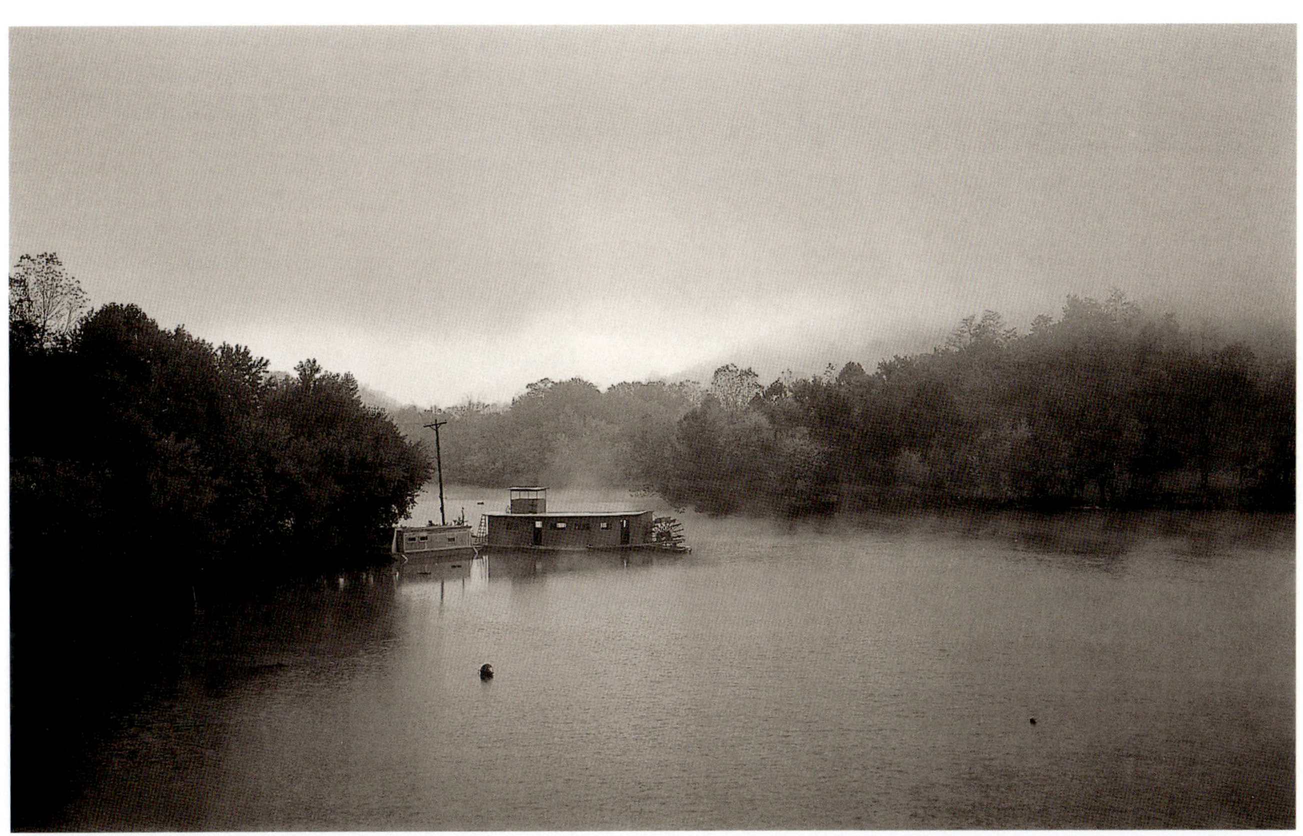

PLATE 3.1 Red Oak Creek, Ripley, Ohio. 1989 12 × 20 inch Pt/Pd. For the negative positive printing process, Ansel Adams used a musical analogy to refer to the negative as the *score* and the print as the *performance*. No amount of technical skill or virtuosity can redeem a poorly written musical composition, and the same can be said for photography. In the language of our times, we can use the computer term "garbage in, garbage out" to convey the same meaning.

Becoming a successful platinum or palladium printer demands that the production of negatives be under control. Unless one is into more avant-garde methods of expression, or relying on a totally computer-generated negative, there are no shortcuts to this. A basic knowledge of the properties of light-sensitive materials is required. This involves a working knowledge of *photographic sensitometry*. While the very concept may be intimidating to some, the principles needed for the basic practice of photography are surprisingly simple.

The printing speed of hand-coated platinum/palladium (Pt/Pd) emulsion is approximately one million times slower than modern silver paper. No practical enlarging units are capable of producing enough light to properly expose Pt/Pd paper. It is, therefore, a contact printing process. Unless steps are taken to produce an enlarged copy negative (Appendix A, "The Large Negative"), the size of the finished print is determined by the format of the camera used.

The Pt/Pd process shares another characteristic common to the nineteenth- and early-twentieth-century photographic printing processes. The negative densities to produce both shadow and highlight print values must be of a greater range then required by modern silver gelatin paper. The Pt/Pd paper, therefore, has a greater *exposure scale* (ES) than silver gelatin paper (Todd and Zakia, 1969; Crawford, 1979; Davis, 1998; Kodak, 1998).

As the print is the final product of the negative positive photographic process, the exposure and development of the negative must be tailored to fit the exposure scale of the paper. The relative amounts of light passed through the negative during the exposure of the paper is measured in multiples or divisions of two. This concept is also used during the exposure of the negative to light, since camera settings of the length of exposure and aperture are spaced in the same intervals. The *range* of light transmitted by the shadow and highlight portions of the negative is the *density range* (DR).

NOTE: *For a full tonal range print, the density range (DR) of the negative must match the exposure scale (ES) of the particular paper grade to be used.*

An appeal: One of the pitfalls in the study of any photographic science is the tendency to produce some "techno-fascists" who are more interested in manipulating materials than engaging in visual expression. If we keep sight of the purpose of our endeavors—to produce photographic images by the exercise of the right side of our brain—we can allow the left side to help out without taking over.

Photographic Sensitometry

Photographic sensitometry is the science related to the reaction of light-sensitive materials to exposure and development. Anyone who pushes the button on a camera engages in the application of sensitometry. If one were to go into the collection archives of any great photographic museum and choose six photographers at random, the chances are overwhelming that each has mastered the sensitometry necessary for their art. As with accomplished painters, sculptures, and musical artists, each has studied and become proficient with the characteristics of their materials, be it paint, structure, or the timbre of the musical instrument. Strangely, some photography students, particularly if they have not had some basic math and chemistry courses, are reluctant to learn the technical aspects necessary for control of light-sensitive materials. Fortunately, most young photographers, as they become immersed in their forms of expression and are confronted by the cost of wasted materials, will learn sensitometry indirectly by problem-solving.

The following is a rather elementary discussion of the principles of sensitometry as applied to the Pt/Pd process. Purists may find that some of the information presented is not entirely accurate. But photography when practiced as an art form is an imprecise science. Most of the materials and equipment that we use are only accurate within tolerances of plus or minus 10%. (Check the guarantee of the shutter speeds of your lens.) It is our goal to control the process to the best of our ability, so that the errors inherent in the process are not compounded. For this, it is highly desirable to have a *working knowledge* of sensitometry.

Definitions

Average Gradient ($\bar{G}$): One of the measurements used to determine the slope of the characteristic curve made by plotting the transmission density of a film in relation to the amount of exposure to light. Other methods used are the *Contrast Index* (CI) and *Gamma* (γ). They are discussed in the recommended texts (Davis, 1998).

Base plus Fog (B+F): The transmission density of portions of the negative unexposed to subject light.

Subject Brightness Range (SBR):[1] The range of reflected light produced by the subject to be photographed. It is generally determined by the use of a spot meter measuring the limits of textured shadow values and highlight areas. The difference is normally expressed in stops or logs (multiples of 0.3). When measured as a ratio, it is referred to as the *Subject-Luminance Ratio.*

Density Range (DR): The transmission densities of a negative, which represents the image to be exposed to photographic paper. It is determined by subtracting the shadow density from the highlight density.

Effective Film Speed (EFS): The optimum film speed when adjusted for variations in development.

Exposure Scale (ES): When applied to photographic paper, it is the range of light needed to produce a *full tonal scale print* for a particular process and contrast grade. It is also referred to as *exposure range* (ER).

ISO (International Organization for Standardization): A value for film speed assigned by the manufacturer relating to exposure at a given subject brightness range. Replaces *ASA* (American Standards Association).

Lens Flare: The effect of extraneous light within the photographic image caused by lens elements and reflected from within the camera. The flare effect, added to base fog, determines the beginning of minimum useful shadow density of a negative.

Logarithm (log): An exponent of the number 10.

Transmission Densities

The amount of light passed through a negative can be measured quite simply with a *transmission densitometer* (Figure 2.9). The portion of the negative to be read (usually a one millimeter circle) is placed over a pin-sized light source, and a button is pushed. A number is given, either by dial or digital readout. Numbers are given, relying on the *Logarithmic System of Measurement.*

1. The use of a spot meter to identify and place "Zones" is beyond the scope of this text. Nevertheless, unless one is photographing in a set lighting system (i.e., a studio), some method must be used to accommodate varying lighting conditions. Most often, this involves reading selected areas of reflected luminance with a spot meter. These values are "placed" in values of black, gray, and white to plan the finished print; this is the process of *previsualization*. Differences in the range of reflected light (SBR) will dictate development times and concentrations, so that a standardized, usable negative can be made (Schaefer, 1998; Davis, 1998).

- A good transmission densitometer can be obtained for the same amount as a good enlarging lens. (See "Sources.") Its use allows technical controls to greatly cut down on prints that are destined for the "round file." If one delves into Pt/Pd for any period of time, the savings will shortly pay for a transmission densitometer.
- For those not inclined to purchase a densitometer, a "Visual Comparison Densitometer" can be utilized. This is simply a portion of dark cardboard through which a small round hole has been punched. It is used for assessing transmission densities by using a step tablet for reference (see Chapter 7, "Calibration," Figures 7.4 and 7.5).

The Logarithmic System

If density range and exposure scale were to be expressed in actual arithmetic numerical values, such as 2, 4, 8, 16, 32, 64, 128, and so on, the numbers would soon become unwieldy. We use the shorthand system of logarithms or *logs*. A logarithm is a *power* of 10 rather than a numerical value.

For example, we know that 10 times 10 is 100. This is 10 *squared* and is expressed in logs as 10^2. Also, $10 \times 10 \times 10 = 1{,}000$, which is 10 *cubed*, or 10^3. The superscript number is the *exponent* or *power.*

If decimals are used to denote fractions, a number can be found to represent multiples of two:

That number is $10^{.3}$. The numerical value is 2.
$10^{.6}$ is twice the value of $10^{.3}$ and, therefore, equals 4.
$10^{.9}$ is three times the value of $10^{.3}$ or 8, and so on.

If we now drop the 10, logs can be expressed in a simpler manner:

$10^{.3}$	becomes 0.3
$10^{.6}$	becomes 0.6
$10^{.9}$	becomes 0.9
$10^{1.2}$	becomes 1.2

Using this system, large numbers such as 10,000 can be expressed as 4.0, and 100,000 as 5.0. Note that to multiply or divide 2, one simply *adds* or *subtracts* 0.3 to or from the log.

A lens aperture or *stop* of f/5.6 lets in twice the amount of light as f/8, F/11 lets in half the amount of light as f/8, and so on. Thus, in photography, the word *stop* is also used to represent multiplications or divisions of 2.

Following this system, paper exposure scales and negative density ranges can be expressed in logs. The ES

TABLE 3.1 The Log Equivalents

Log	*Numerical Value*	*Stops*
0	0	
0.3	2	1
0.6	4	2
0.9	8	3
1.2	16	4
1.5	32	5
1.8	64	6
2.1	128	7
2.4	256	8
2.7	512	9
3.0	1,000	10
4.0	10,000	100
5.0	100,000	1,000

of grade 2 silver paper expressed in logs is approximately 1.1 or 3 and 2/3 stops. Therefore, the shadow areas of the paper require 3 and 2/3 the amount of light as the highlights. The ES of grade 3 paper may be 0.9 and requires three ranges of stops. The DR or *contrast* of the negative must match these values to produce a full tonal value print.

The Density Range for a Platinum or Palladium Negative

Platinum or palladium paper has a greater exposure scale. The average or "grade 2" equivalent paper has an ES of 1.4 for a Pt/Pd mixture and 1.65 for pure palladium. Therefore, to make a full tonal value print, we must match the negative DR to the paper ES. As with silver printing, a less contrasty negative will require a higher grade paper, and a more contrasty negative a lower grade.[2] It is better, however, to make a negative suitable for a middle grade of any paper, only using the other grades to compensate for the many variables in photography that may account for a less than "perfect" negative.

Negative Contrast versus Negative Density

Exposure

The working negative contrast is derived by subtracting the shadow values from the highlight values. The inherent transmission density of the Estar base of a negative and the minute portions of the unexposed silver salts reduced at development, is called base plus fog (B+F). This will be found at the edges outside the image frame.

Within the image area, *lens flare* must be added to the inherent B+F density of a negative. At the instant the image is projected onto the film, lens flare from reflections within lens elements and the camera body, adds a diffuse halo of light to that of the image. The amount of lens flare is dependent on the lens and camera design. View cameras and lenses contribute enough flare that it must be taken into account. Once the film becomes sensitized to where the silver salts become reactive to increases in light, the actual image projected by the lens begins to register, a *Threshold* is reached. It is at this point that useful *shadow density* begins.

Base + Fog,	Usually 0.1 to 0.2
+ Lens Flare Factor	Usually .02 to .04
Threshold for Shadow Density	Usually 0.15 to 0.25

Since B+F and lens flare contain no information, for most imagery, they are not considered in planning a print. Depending on film and development, it is not until a shadow density of 0.2 to 0.4 is reached that it becomes useful. Since this "magic number" determines printing time for both silver and platinum, it should be our goal. This is accomplished by proper exposure in the field or studio. Correcting shadow areas by altered development techniques is difficult to impossible. Too little exposure results in the valueless areas just discussed; too much will result in lengthy printing times. For the purposes of this text, we have chosen 0.3 to be an ideal shadow density.

NOTE: While silver paper exposures are measured in seconds, platinum exposures are calculated in minutes. A two-stop error in the exposure of a platinum negative may easily result in a forty-five-minute printing time!

Development

It is in the highlight areas that negatives are "constructed" by selective development for the chosen print media. As all photographers learn, this is accomplished by changing developing time and concentration.

Increasing development time and developer concentration will increase the transmission densities of negatives.[3] The thinner shadow densities will be less

[2] Over fifteen platinum and palladium "paper grades" can be achieved by varying the concentrations of restrainer and the combinations of metal.

[3] This will be discussed in more detail in Chapters 11 to 13 in Part Two, "Sensitometry for the Platinum/Palladium Process." You may, however, wish to peek ahead if you are more curious about this phenomenon.

affected. The more dense, or highlight, areas will be changed far more significantly. (See Appendix A, "The Large Negative," and Appendix B, "Some Film/Developer Combinations to Produce a Platinum/Palladium Negative.")

If a film is given a series of developer/time combinations, the changes can be plotted to produce a *Family of Curves* (Figure 3.1).

Note in Figure 3-1, as the development times increase, from 4 to 20 minutes, the lower shadow areas remain relatively unaffected. The more dense highlight areas change considerably. By increasing development over that usually used for silver, we achieve the contrasts necessary for the platinum and palladium negative. (Courtesy of Phil Davis Plotter Program®)

The Negative Density Range

In addition to the advantage of faster speeds, modern films allow control over the density range by either decreasing or increasing the normal development procedure. In densitometric terms, lesser development will produce a lower contrast, or *Average Gradient.* This is done to compensate for a subject brightness range of more contrast (from 8 to 12+ stops). Conversely, a negative made from a "flat" subject with a range of 4 to 6 stops can be structured to fit photographic paper by overdeveloping. This is the basis of *Zone System* photography.

NOTE: A word about the Zone System: Ansel Adams did not invent photographic sensitometry. He and his colleagues simply implemented a language to measure the reflective values of the subject matter that will be translated by way of a negative to the reflected grays of a monochromatic photographic print (Schaefer, 1998).

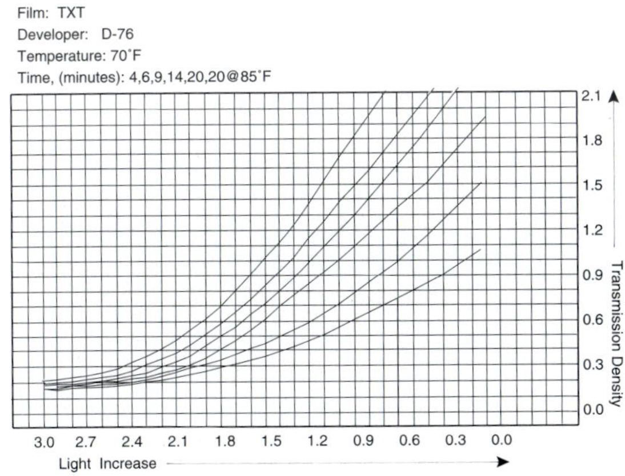

FIGURE 3.1 A Family of Curves Appropriate to Platinum/Palladium Paper

In calculating negative values with a transmission densitometer, both the useful highlight (Zone VIII) and the useful shadow densities (Zone III) are measured. After simple subtraction, the difference is determined, which represents all the intermediate values. This is the *Density Range* of the negative.

> Useful Highlight Density – Useful Shadow Density = Density Range (DR)

While the "ideal" silver negative may be 1.4 – 0.3 = 1.1, the Pt/Pd negative will be 1.7 – 0.3 = 1.4. The negative for a palladium print should be 1.95 – 0.3 = 1.65. Note that regardless of the process and negative requirements, the shadow densities should remain approximately the same.

Over- and Under-Exposed Negatives

The negatives discussed have proper *contrast* for the paper to be employed. If, in the construction of a Pt/Pd negative, shadow values are overexposed, and then the film is subjected to the increased development necessary for greater contrast, the minimal effect noted by development on shadow areas will rapidly become significant. A totally dense or "bulletproof" negative may result. This negative may be worthless, even using reduction techniques. Conversely, a grossly underexposed negative, contrary to the claims made by manufacturers, cannot be "pushed" to the point where shadow values become adequate.

Using a Portion of the Paper Scale

Until now, we have been discussing the requirements to make a negative that will exploit the complete range of values available for each particular paper: the "full tonal value" print. For more accomplished photographers, this may not be their goal, and they may plan accordingly.

Many subjects, particularly portraits, can be better expressed using only a portion of the tonal scale. Platinum and, in particular, palladium are quite adaptable to images that occupy the elegant high- and mid-values that the paper is capable of rendering. For this, the density range of the negative may be less than the exposure scale of a particular grade of platinum or palladium paper. A DR of a typical negative for silver paper (1.1) or less can be used with exquisite results. (See "Using

Portions of the Paper Curve" in Chapter 12, "Using the Print Curves.")

Exposing and Developing the Platinum or Palladium Negative

Manufacturers of photographic film have determined that the brightness range of a typical outdoor subject is seven stops or a logarithmic value of 2.1, or a Subject-Luminance Ratio of 128:1. When transferred to a transparent negative, the range must be compressed to match the photographic paper to be used. For modern silver paper, the compression must be extreme, down to a density range of 0.9 to 1.05, or an opacity range of 11:1 (Davis, 1998; Kodak, 1998; Schaefer, 1998). See Figure 3.2.

- The subject is measured in stops, Subject Brightness Range (SBR), or Subject Luminance Ratio.
- The resultant compression of the negative is measured as stops, Density Range (DR), or Opacity Ratio.
- The final print is measured as Reflective Density Range or Reflection Opacity Ratio.

Note that the negative must be constructed to match the exposure scale of silver gelatin paper. In this case, it is contrast grade 2. The reflective density[4] of the final silver gelatin print is 1.8 (six stops), considerably more than can be obtained with Pt/Pd. Under certain conditions, and with toning, a silver gelatin print can be brought to a reflective density of 2.1!

For a typical platinum or palladium paper with an exposure scale of 1.4, the required opacity range of the negative is 30:1. (See Figure 3.3.)

- As the exposure scale of Pt/Pd paper is greater than that of silver gelatin, a negative of more contrast is required. At a given subject brightness range, proportionately more development is needed.
- Because of the greater density range of the negative, the values of transmission densities are spread over a greater useful portion of the negative silver emulsion. This allows for more subtlety of tones to be transferred to the paper. This is seen in the final print as a smoother distribution of midtones and

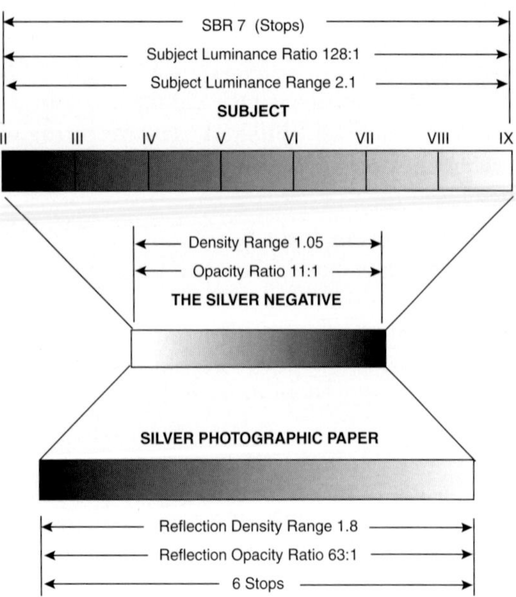

FIGURE 3.2 The Silver Gelatin Print. Compression and Reexpansion of Brightness Ranges from Subject to Negative to Final Print

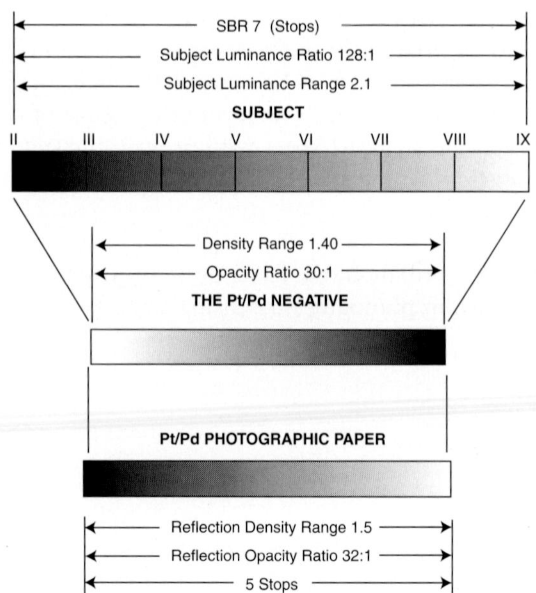

FIGURE 3.3 The Platinum/Palladium Print. Compression and Reexpansion of Brightness Ranges from Subject to Negative to Final Print

4. The reflected grays of a photographic print can also be measured with a *reflective densitometer*. This machine is considerably more expensive than its transmission counterpart. Unless one is doing studies of photographic papers, a reflective densitometer is not necessary, as the human eye is much more sensitive and can be trained to identify reflected values. (For a discussion of this phenomenon, consult Chapter 7, "Calibration.")

whites. Also, because of this property, the medium-low and midtones of the subject (Zones IV and V) are more accurately placed in the Pt/Pd print. (They tend to be depressed in the silver gelatin print.)

- At best, the reflective densities of platinum or palladium paper is two to three stops less than that of the silver gelatin print. This characteristic is more than compensated for by the depth of the hand-coated image and the qualities described above.

NOTE: Minor White, teacher and photographer, used the term *convincing black* to describe maximum paper blacks. When seeing a monochromatic print, the viewer interprets all tones in comparison to the others. Thus, a well-printed black will be seen by the mind as "black," even though it might register poorly on a machine (Todd and Zakia, 1969; Adams, 1981).

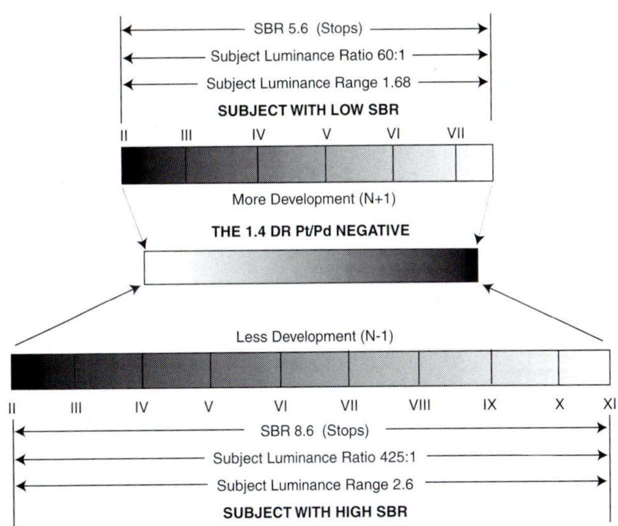

FIGURE 3.4 Selective Development of the Negative Based on Subject Brightness Range

Zone System Development Compared to Subject Brightness Range

For those using the Zone System, there may be some confusion regarding the "N" designation and the subject brightness range (SBR). With N development, N = SBR 7. Some, however, might conclude that N+1 would be synonymous with an SBR of 6 (6 → 7 = N+1). That is not the case. With expansion development, one zone is simply not kicked into the next. All zones are expanded proportionally. Therefore, the SBR for N+1 development is somewhat lower than 6. If N+1 development is indicated, the actual modification would be SBR 5.6 → 7. For N+2, it would not be 5 → 7, but SBR 4.2 → 7.

With contraction development, the same principles apply. N–1 development is not 8 → 7 = N–1, but SBR 8.6 → 7. An N–2 is SBR 10.5 → 7. N–3 is SBR 12 → 7. A more complete presentation may be found in Davis, *Beyond the Zone System* (1998).

Development for Subject Brightness Ranges

The low 5.6 SBR requires more development than the normal 7 SBR to make a negative with a 1.4 DR. In Zone System terms, this is a N+1 development (see Figure 3.4). The high 8.6 SBR requires less development (N–1) than does the normal 7 SBR to make the same negative. With proper technique, both extremes of subject brightens range can be managed to produce negatives with essentially identical transmission characteristics.

The Low Subject Brightness Range

We have referred to platinum printing as the art of adapting today's materials to a historical process. With all its remarkable characteristics, contemporary film does not have the silver content exhibited in older films. Therefore, many films that are perfectly adapted for modern silver paper cannot be expanded sufficiently by development to produce negatives in the 1.4 to 1.7 density ranges necessary for platinum or palladium printing. These films reach a *gamma infinity* where further development only increases overall density rather than DR. A list of recommended films may be found in Appendix B, "Some Film/Developer Combinations to Produce a Platinum/Palladium Negative."

The High Subject Brightness Range

Because of the broader scale of the negative needed, it is less of a challenge with Pt/Pd to manage a high-contrast subject by using less development. Exposing at an effective film speed and using diluted developer, subject brightness ranges as high as 14 can be recorded on the Pt/Pd negative (see Plate 3.2 and Plate B.1).

Average Gradient

A most effective measurement of quantifying the effect of development is to calculate the slope of the film curve. As indicated in the section of definitions provided earlier, a number of methods may be used. Comprehensive coverage of such methods is beyond the scope of this text; however, I will make some reference to the *average gradient* to compare the effects of altering film development.

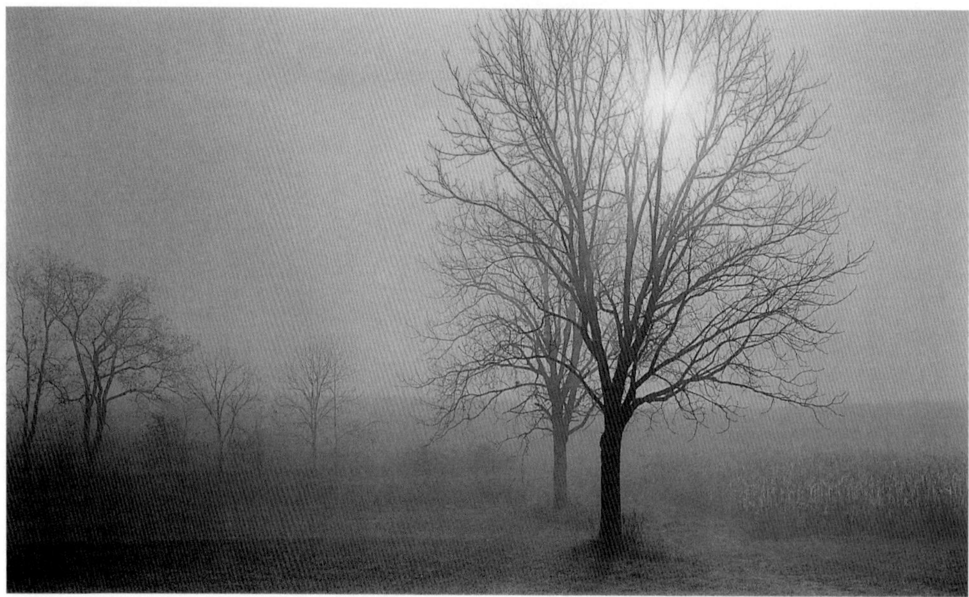

PLATE 3.2 Bedford Co., Pennsylvania. 1989 12 × 20 inch Pd. To capture the ball of the sun, a SBR of 11 was calculated. The ISO for TXT film is normally 320. Here, it was given an effective film speed of 50 and developed for only 8 minutes in diluted D-76.

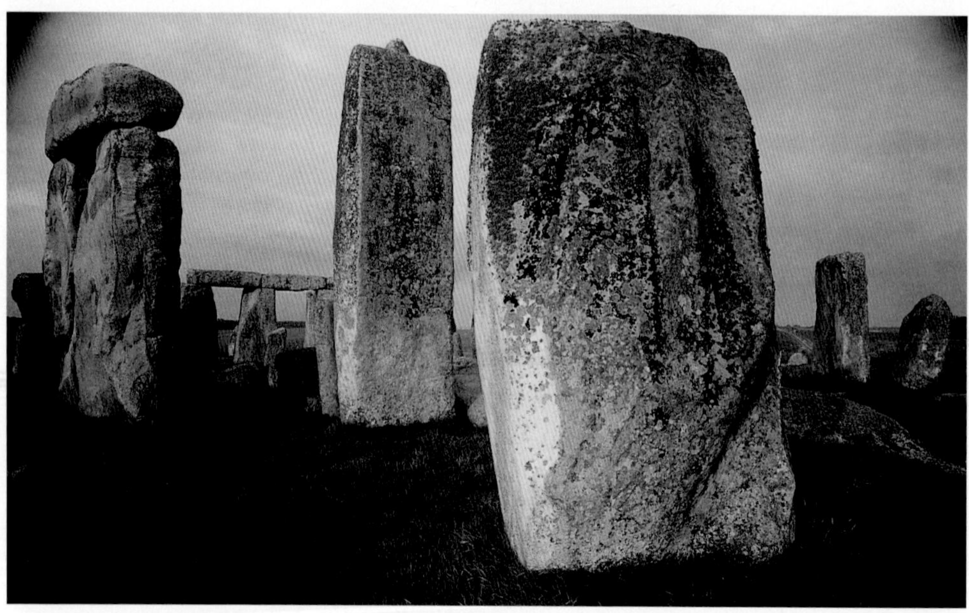

PLATE 3.3 Stonehenge, England. 1986 12 × 20 inch Pd. This low-contrast subject required maximum development and Selenium toning of the negative.

Increasing development steepens the slope of the curve and increases the average gradient. (Figure 3.1). If one were to refer to average gradient numbers to compare slopes of the curve, a typical negative developed for silver paper would be at approximately .60. Platinum or palladium paper requires an average gradient of .70 to .80. If one needed to tailor an overdeveloped "N+2" negative for platinum, an average gradient of 1.10 might be needed! Few film/developer combinations can accomplish this. Some cannot be developed to N+1.

Graphic reference to this will be provided in Part Two, "Sensitometry for the Platinum/Palladium Process."

Effective Film Speed

Manufacturers assign each film an ISO. This ISO is only applicable when the film is developed for a seven-stop subject brightness range for *silver gelatin paper.* If the film is overdeveloped to increase or decrease the slope of the curve, shadow density is also affected. It happens to a lesser extent, but since shadow density determines printing time, small changes may be critical.

As seen in Figure 3.5, a slightly diagonal line was plotted to identify the portion of the film curve where enough changes occur relative to light increases to cause textured shadows (at about a transmission density of 0.3). As development times are changed to compensate for various subject brightness ranges, exposure must be modified to keep shadow densities under control. This is most easily done by assigning an *effective film speed* (EFS) other than the ISO determined by the manufacturer.

NOTE: ISO is set by the manufacturer at a specific Subject Brightness Range (SBR) and development time. If either is changed, a new value of film speed, the effective film speed (EFS), must be used.

Overdeveloping film can increase the shadow values to over one stop. This must be taken into account. For overdevelopment, shadow densities are controlled

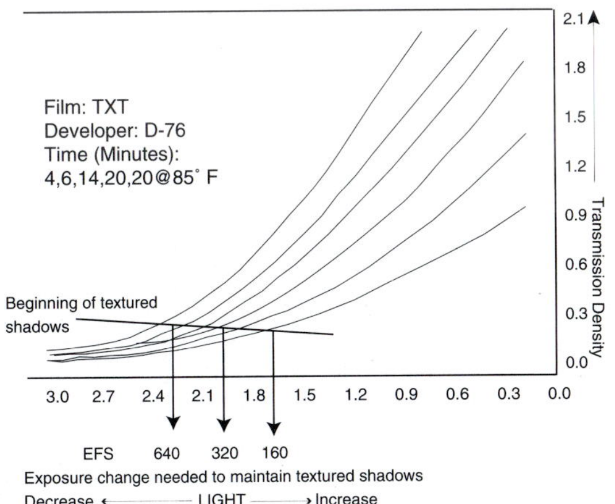

FIGURE 3.5 A Family of Film Curves Showing Exposure Changes for the Various Development Times Necessary to Maintain Optimum Textured Shadow Values

by *decreasing* the exposure. This is best accomplished by *increasing* the ISO. The new value is referred to as effective film speed (EFS). Therefore, for example, while the ISO of Tri-X Pan Professional Film (TXT) is listed as 320, it must be understood that this value does not apply to the increased development needed for a platinum or palladium negative. For that processing, an EFS from 400 to 600 may be needed.

At a high SBR, exposure must be increased to prevent the shadows from falling on the horizontal portion of the film curve (and producing no separation of values). With TXT, an EFS of 160 may be necessary. While some films may not require such pronounced changes, the principles apply. Over- or underexposure as much as one stop can significantly affect the Pt/Pd image. The extent of the film speed change needed is largely dependent on the film used. (See Tables B.2 to B.9.)

NOTE: A simple rule to make a platinum negative is to increase development one and one-half times over what is required of a negative for silver paper. Concurrently, an EFS of one-third to two-thirds over the published ISO is required to control shadow value by reducing exposure. For a palladium negative, double both the development and the ISO.

Characteristics of the Platinum/Palladium Negative

We have discussed some of the difficulties of making Pt/Pd negatives and the measures that must be taken to produce them; however, when a Pt/Pd negative of the desired density range is produced, most of the other characteristics that often plague silver photographers become relatively negligible.

Sharpness

Many platinum photographers will eventually find that a larger camera is more suitable to their needs. Large cameras require lenses of longer focal length, frequently with extended image circles to allow for view camera movements. Unless one is willing to pay a small fortune for a monstrous piece of glass, less resolution and more aberrations are generally found in direct proportion to the length of the lens. Moreover, for satisfactory depth of field, small apertures of f/45 to f/90 are frequently used, further increasing the degree of aberrations.

NOTE: Some process lenses work remarkably well at apertures from f/64 to f/128. Their maximum apertures, however, are usually quite small, in the f/9 to f/11 range, making focusing difficult. For my big cameras, I use a Fresnel lens. Good, inexpensive varieties can be found at Edmund Scientific (ES). Placing it behind the ground glass will not significantly affect the focus at small apertures, and this will protect the glass from breakage as well.

Fortunately, with the increase in negative size, less enlargement is practiced, negating the visual effects of these aberrations—particularly when the final presentation is in one of the nonsilver processes.

Platinum and palladium printing when practiced as a hand-coated, printmaking process produces an image that becomes wedded to the structure and characteristic of the paper. Sharpness, or lack thereof, is not generally noticeable, except through magnification. Even if it is, the other qualities previously described do not rely on mechanical sharpness to convey a message.

Graininess

At the smaller apertures needed for large format photography, a faster film is needed if one wishes to avoid longer exposures—and the resultant reciprocity failure. For camera sizes of over 5 × 7 inches, the use of higher speed films of ISO 320 or over is desirable. The structure of the silver halide emulsion in films of higher ISO affect the graininess. Also, the high-energy developers and increased concentrations and time we must use to produce a platinum negative further increases the "grain."

With a hand-coated process, the increase of size and clumping of silver particles responsible for increase of film grain are simply not discernible under normal viewing conditions. Visible film grain is also related to the degree of enlargement. Platinum and palladium printers do not enlarge, unless internegatives are made from smaller negatives. Even in that case, the qualities described in the previous paragraph more than compensate for the graininess produced by the negative.

Graininess from the negative should not be confused with granularity found in the platinum or palladium emulsion. This can be a serious problem, to the point of degrading certain images. Methods to avoid this are covered in Chapter 9, "Advanced Technique," and Chapter 10 "Problems."

Scratches and Pinholes

It is best to avoid scratches and pinholes by handling film carefully and keeping the camera as free of dust as possible. However, if either a scratch or a pinhole occurs, one further appreciates the many advantages of contact printing. Since these defects will not be enlarged, covering the pinhole with Crocein Scarlet will take care of all but the most severe. (Its use is discussed in Chapter 9, "Advanced Technique.") When using enlarged internegatives and positives, the problem may be acute, as each adds a new layer of blemishes.

The Circle of Confusion

The ability to discern "sharpness" and "grain" is related to the ability of the naked eye, at a certain distance, to distinguish a circle from a point. This is called the *circle of confusion* (Stroebel, 1993). As the distance from the viewer to the print increases, this distinguishing ability is diminished. Studies have shown that, in an exhibit space, viewers tend to establish a distance twice that of the diagonal dimension of the artwork. It is from this position that (it is hoped) the content of that work becomes more significant than the degree of technical perfection.

The Use of Selenium Toner to Increase Negative Contrast

Negative density range can be increased by 0.1 to 0.3 by selenium[5] toning without an appreciable effect on shadow density. This may be enough to bring a marginal negative into platinum range, or move a Pt/Pd negative into palladium range (Plate 3.3).

After washing, immerse the wet negative in a 1:3 solution of Rapid Selenium Toner to distilled water. Agitate constantly for five minutes and rewash. Take care before subjecting an unread negative to selenium toning. A wet negative viewed through a ceiling bulb looks a lot thinner than it will eventually test after drydown. Injudicious selenium toning may blow the negative even beyond the capabilities of palladium paper. Until considerable experience is obtained, it may be more prudent to study the dried negative before selenium toning. Simply soak it in water for five minutes before toning. The effect may not be as pronounced as immediately following development, but it is much safer.

5. Selenium is a toxic heavy metal. Use only in a well-ventilated space. The use of rubber gloves or print tongs is strongly recommended.

Pyro Development for Platinum and Palladium Negatives

The use of pyrogallol for developing negatives is at least as old as the platinum process. The yellow/green stain produced is approximately that of the complementary color used to selectively block transmission to the blue sensitive paper. Consequently, negatives of much less development can be used over the unstained counterpart. Since less density is required in highlight areas, graininess is diminished. Pyro negatives are also said to produce more edge sharpness.

The negative, when developed in a solution containing both pyrogallol and the conventional Metol developing agents is doubly developed. The transmission density is produced by both the selective reduction of silver particles as well as a "tanning" effect produced by pyrogallol. In the thinner areas of the negative, little effect is noted, but as the midtones and highlights are reached, the yellowish stain adds as much as 50 to 100% more effective transmission density (Hutchings, 1991).

Because of the extreme sensitivity to UV light, Pt/Pd paper has been said to be even more susceptible to the pyro stain than silver gelatin. Bob Herbst, Grant Evans, and I have done limited studies on adapting densitometric methods to the pyro negative. While most of our findings are beyond the scope of this text, by using the standard blue filter found in better densitometers, we were able to roughly quantify some of the transmission characteristics of the yellow stain when used with Pt/Pd paper. These are summarized in Chapter 7, "Calibration" (Table 7.3) using a *converted density range* in place of the effective DR found with standard film developers.

One must bear in mind, however, that a properly developed negative made by more traditional means may accomplish the same purpose. Nevertheless, in low SBR, the pyro stain may more efficiently bring a negative into the Pt/Pd printing range. In an extreme N+2 situation when even more strenuous development may be required, pyrogallol staining may solve the problem.

Sullivan and Weese have discussed a more distinctive distribution of tonal values when using a pyro negative with the Pt/Pd process (Sullivan and Weese, 1998). But Pt/Pd and, in particular, palladium, have extensive tones, giving almost limitless textures in the highlight areas. With a hand-coated process, grain and acuteness are not as significant a factor as with commercially manufactured paper.

The final assessment as to the superiority of pyrogallol must remain in the hands of the photographer. For some, the use of the pyrogallol negative is their route to effective image making.

Pt/Pd printers who use pyro may wish to explore some of the limited controls for that process presented in this text and are welcome to correspond with the author for more information.

However, those just investigating the Pt/Pd process are urged to first spend sufficient time learning to effectively use one of the appropriate film/developer combinations (see Appendix B "Some Film/Developer Combinations to Produce a Platinum/Palladium Negative"). Once an effective film/developer combination is found using standard developers, pyro can be investigated for comparison. Many Pt/Pd printers, the author included, have found that with Pt/Pd printing, many of the reported advantages of pyro development can be duplicated using more traditional methods.

CHAPTER 4

Chemicals

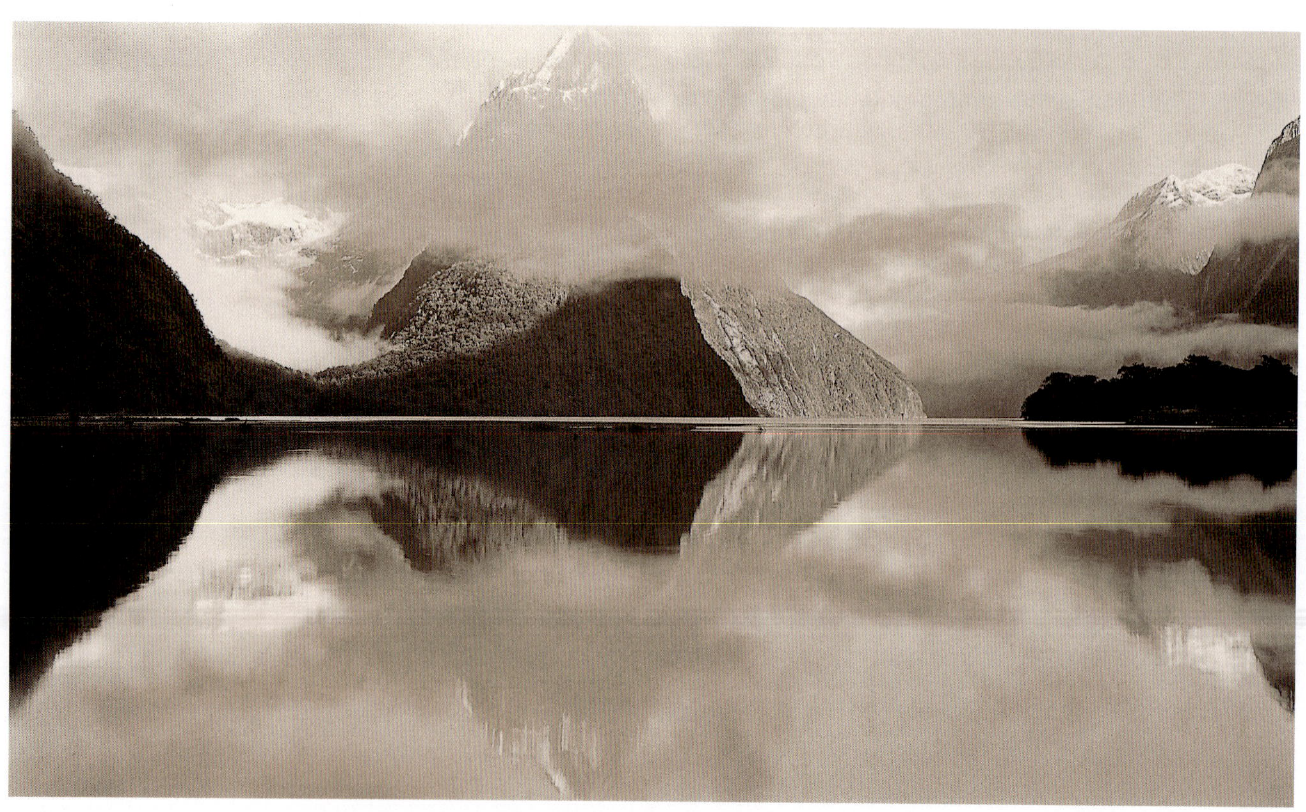

PLATE 4.1 Milford Sound II, N.Z. 1995 12 × 20 inch Pt/Pd

The Reasonable and Prudent Use

Chemical safety is based on a *reasonable and prudent use* of chemicals. Platinum/palladium printing is one of the safest of all the photographic processes. The chemicals used in significant quantities are inorganic salts, oxalates, and high dilutions of weak acids. More hazardous compounds are used in infinitesimal amounts, most often measured by eyedropper. For the most dangerous substances listed in the literature, satisfactory substitutes exist.

The Material Safety Data Sheet (MSDS)

Each chemical is accompanied by a *Material Safety Data Sheet (MSDS)*. While the information therein is of considerable value to the Pt/Pd printer, *it is from the indiscriminate use of this data that many of the "scare" tactics about our process have been formulated.* If each chemical used in Pt/Pd photography is intelligently analyzed with the category of photographic practice in mind, safe guidelines can be set up individually without a "one solution fits all" mentality.

WARNING AND DISCLAIMER

The following material in no way constitutes a recommendation to deviate from standard regulations and requirements for the safe handling of chemicals. It represents the author's own personal philosophy and procedures. All of the chemicals described in this text can be potentially harmful, particularly if misused. The reader is advised to inform him or herself in advance of any dangers and to take appropriate precautions. Such information can be obtained from the Material Safety Data Sheets (MSDS) or by consulting any reference manual on chemical safety. Furthermore, for any person to be in contact with these chemicals, a thorough review of personal health should be obtained to rule out allergies and to be aware of possible teratogenic effects in the case of pregnancy. With chronic smokers, many of the natural defense mechanisms of the body are seriously impaired, aggravating the effects of exposure to chemicals. It is also assumed that children and irresponsible adults will be shielded from contact with these agents.

The author hereby denies liability for any subsequent injuries resulting from the use of the information contained in this text.

Four categories of potential hazards are outlined in the MSDS information:

Health: Toxic effects of a substance if inhaled, ingested, or absorbed.

Flammability: Tendency of a substance to burn.

Reactivity: Potential of a substance to react violently with air, water, of other substances.

Contact: The danger a substance presents when it comes into contact with skin, eyes, or mucous membranes.

Of these categories, the platinum printer will be most concerned about the following. The numbering system from 1 to 4 is used in MSDS data to designate the degree of hazard.

Health

0. No hazard
1. Slight hazard
2. Moderate hazard
3. Severe danger
4. Deadly, life threatening

Contact

0. No contact hazard to normal, healthy tissues
1. Slight hazard: irritant to sensitive tissues
2. Moderate hazard: irritant to sensitive tissues; damages tissue
3. Severe danger: destroys tissue, including skin
4. Extreme danger: life threatening

In addition, the chemicals are indexed by relative toxicity: the lower the LD50 (which is the oral dose that will kill 50% of laboratory animals) for a particular chemical, the more the potential risk.

Here is a helpful classification and summary of the MSDS system and categories that uses the MSDS and other data available for chemicals:

MSDS 1—Those that under normal usage are basically harmless.

MSDS 2—Those that require some degree of caution in handling.

MSDS 3—Those that can cause considerable harm through some or all the routes by which a chemical can enter the body.

MSDS 4—Extremely dangerous. It is recommended that they not be used in the Pt/Pd process.

As each chemical group is discussed in this text, these classifications will appear with pertinent information and precautions. If questions exist, the reader is encouraged to check the data for specific chemicals.

Monochromatic Film Developing Agents (MSDS 2)

While not specifically part of the Pt/Pd process, some discussion is in order regarding monochromatic film developers. It is beyond the scope of this text to list all of the organic agents used for this purpose; therefore, generalities must be made.

The most common agents are *Metol* (*Elon*, monomethyl para-aminophenol sulfate), and *Hydroquinone* (para-hydroxy benzene). Many similar phenolic and benzene compounds are also found in developing agents.

> *As a group, monochromatic film developing agents represent more cause for concern than most of the chemicals used in the Pt/Pd process. Contact with skin should be avoided. In the slightly alkaline film developers, surgical gloves are quite effective (see Appendix A, "The Large Negative"). It is entirely possible, following continued skin contact, that a contact dermatitis may develop, in many cases necessitating a change to other agents. Full-time workers should consider the use of tube or JOBO® methods (see Appendix A).*
>
> *In some literature, Pyrogallic acid (pyrogallol, 1,2,3-trihydroxybenzene), has been listed as more toxic than it may actually be. Utilize the same precautions as listed above. A Rollo Pyro is now available from Bostick and Sullivan (BS), which can be used with a JOBO processor.*

For a brief description of the chemical reactions involved in the Pt/Pd process, see Appendix C, "Principles of the Developing and Clearing Process."

About Measurement Units

The platinum/palladium processes were developed in England, so it is natural that many measurements are expressed in the British as well as U.S. units of measurement. Some formulas have retained the British units; however, for ease of mixing and determination of concentrations, the metric system is superior, and has been used here whenever possible. A short guide to the more common conversions is presented (Anchell, 1994).

Weight	Volume
16 ounces = one pound	32 ounces = one quart
454 grams = one pound	1 quart = 0.95 liters
2.2 pounds = one kilogram	1 gallon = 3.78 liters
1 ounce = 28.35 grams	1 ounce = 29.5 milliliters
1 gram = 0.03527 ounces	

Temperature	C = Celsius	F = Fahrenheit
Boiling at sea level	100°	212°
Freezing	0°	32°
	20°	68°
	38°	100°

(C × 9/5) + 32 = degrees F (F – 32) × 5/9 = degrees C

The Metric System

The metric system encompasses measurements of weight, volume, and length. All terminology is interrelated and expressed in units of ten. In the case of distilled water,[1] for example:

1 cubic centimeter (cc) of distilled water = 1 milliliter (ml) and weighs 1 gram (gm)

1,000 gms = 1 liter (l) = weighs 1 kilogram (kg)

1 gm or 1 ml = 0.001 or 1/1,000 of a liter or 0.001 of 1 kg

A simple, but effective way of determining concentrations, is to work in units of 1,000 ml (1 liter). Realizing that a percent is units/100, simply put the weight in grams of volume in milliliters over 1,000, and remove one zero from each side of the equation. For example:

1,000 gms = 1,000 ml

$$\frac{100\text{ gms}}{1{,}000\text{ ml}} = \frac{10}{100} \text{ or } 10\% \qquad \frac{50\text{ ml}}{1{,}000\text{ ml}} = \frac{5}{100} \text{ or } 5\%$$

This method, although not exactly precise, is adequate for most photographic processes.

For a more chemically correct method, the formula is:

$$\% = 100 \times \frac{\text{Weight of Compound}}{\text{Total Weight of Solution}}$$

[1] As solutions are mixed, variations between volume and weight measurements occur; however, for most photographic processes they are negligible.

Purity of Chemicals and Water

Chemicals are available in differing grades of purity. For those used in coating paper and toning techniques, reagent or analytic grade should be used. It is recommended that these be obtained from specific suppliers of platinum and palladium materials. For the chemicals used in larger quantities for developing and clearing, technical grades may be used.

Distilled water should be used for the mixing of coating agents and developers. If tap water is relatively free of impurities, it can be used for the clearing agents and wash. If you have significant impurities in the water supply, consider a water softener, as conventional photographic filters may not do the job.

Sizing of Paper

Presently, a wide choice of papers are available that do not need sizing (see Chapter 5, "Paper"). For those who wish to experiment with papers not completely amenable to the Pt/Pd process, many undesirable characteristics can be overcome with starch or gelatin sizing. The starch used is simple arrowroot starch (MSDS 1).

For gelatin sizing, Knox gelatin is used. *It can burn severely if allowed to contact skin when at high temperatures.* More significantly, Formalin has been used in the past for a final "fix" to harden and make the gelatin impervious to microbial growth. Chrome alum can be used as a substitute. See Hajicek's formula for gelatin sizing in Appendix E, "Sizing of Paper."

Formaldehyde 23% (Formalin) (MSDS 3-4)

> *Formaldehyde is extremely caustic to skin and respiratory tract. Other alternatives exist. Do not use.*

Solutions Used for Paper Coating, Developing, and Clearing

For those unfamiliar with the Pt/Pd process, see Table 8.1, "Algorithm for Platinum and Palladium Printing," for a brief summary of steps in the making of a platinum or palladium print.

The Coating Solutions

For the paper coating, equal parts of sensitizer (ferric oxalate) and metal salts are combined. In addition, a restrainer (oxidizer) may be incorporated to control contrast.

The most common method is to place minute amounts of restrainer into a second solution of sensitizer. By varying the proportions of pure ferric oxalate (A) and a similar solution with restrainer (B), over thirteen contrast grades are possible. One may also control contrast by putting the restrainer in the developer, thereby eliminating the use of sensitizer B.

The metal salts (C), are either platinum, palladium, or a mixture. Most "platinum" prints made today are actually a mixture of platinum and palladium. Pure platinum salts are not entirely amenable to a ferric oxalate sensitizer, but may work better with ferric ammonium oxalate in the presence of moisture. Since print tone or color is largely determined by the choice of developer (see Chapter 9, "Advanced Technique"), for most practical purposes, a mixture of platinum and palladium salts will be indistinguishable from a pure platinum print. A further advantage of combining metal salts lies in the cost of materials: depending on market prices, palladium is usually approximately one-fourth the price of platinum.

A print made with pure palladium is unique in tone and character. It is best developed in potassium oxalate and is most responsive to restrainer placed in the sensitizer. In this text, only pure palladium printing and 50% combinations of platinum and palladium will be covered in detail. Reference is made to varying proportions of platinum and palladium in Chapter 9, "Advanced Technique." A special section on the Malde/Ware and Ziatype processes is also provided in Appendix D, "The Ammonium-Based Processes."

Developers

Several developing agents are available: potassium oxalate (warm tones) and ammonium citrate or Sullivan's cold tone developer (cooler tones). In some processes, Ethylene Diamine Tetraacetic Acid (EDTA) and sodium citrate can be used for development.

Clearing Agents

Phosphoric acid, EDTA (with or without sodium sulfite), hypo clearing agent, and oxalic acid can be used in dilute solutions for dissolving and removing the metallic salts. Most early literature discusses hydrochloric acid as a clearing agent; however, because of the danger in handling this caustic material, I believe there are satisfactory alternatives.

COATING SOLUTIONS

SENSITIZERS (MSDS 2-3)

FERRIC (FERROUS) OXALATE 27% $Fe_2(C_2O_2)_3 \cdot 5H_2O$

FERRIC AMMONIUM OXALATE $(NH_4)_3Fe(C_2O_4)_3 \cdot H_2O$ (MALDE/WARE PROCESS, ZIATYPE)

Sensitizers are salts of unstable iron compounds, some containing oxidizing agents. While it is possible to make your own ferric oxalate,[2] it can be a hazardous procedure. It is safer to buy it already formulated. The salts can be quite toxic, but are used in minuscule quantities; consequently, absorption of significant quantities through any route is unlikely. They can also be purchased premixed, but shelf life is limited. In powdered form, they last indefinitely.

Solution A Ferric oxalate 27%

Ferric oxalate	15 gms
Oxalic acid[3]	1 gm
Water at 150°F	55 ml

Continuous mixing and heating may be required.

Solution B Ferric oxalate with 0.6% restrainer (oxidizer).

Solution A	55 ml
Potassium chlorate $KClO_3$.	.33 gm (will need custom scaling)

NOTE: This makes 0.6% potassium chlorate. It is used for Pt/Pd. Pure palladium has a longer exposure scale. If you want to simulate the Pt/Pd sensitometry, use 0.66 gms for a 1.2% solution (Bostick and Sullivan ferric oxalate No. 2 Pd). If you want to take advantage of the longer printing scale, as I do, use the 0.6% solution (BS ferric oxalate No. 2 Pt).

[2] For making your own ferric oxalate, 30% hydrogen peroxide H_2O_2 is used. It is highly reactive in concentrated form. Do not use. Purchase ferric oxalate already formulated from platinum supplier. Hydrogen peroxide is also used at 3% for contrast control. At this concentration, it is quite safe. Buy it premixed from the pharmacy.

[3] I use 2 grams of oxalic acid per 55 ml. When mixing ferric oxalate from powder, the extra oxalic acid facilitates getting the powder into solution. Also, it decreases printing time. (Be careful of fog.)

THE RESTRAINERS (OXIDIZERS) (MSDS 3-4)

POTASSIUM CHLORATE $KClO_3$

POTASSIUM DICHROMATE $K_2Cr_7O_7$

SODIUM DICHROMATE $Na_2Cr_7O_7$

The restrainers are powerful oxidizing agents used for contrast control in the coating material or developer. They are highly toxic by ingestion or inhalation. Under certain conditions, they can be extremely reactive and explosive. They are used in minute quantities and highly diluted in the Pt/Pd process (0.6 to 1.2%). It is advisable to purchase restrainers in premixed liquid form or to have the powder quantities preweighed and placed in gelatin capsules by a lab utilizing a ventilation hood. Restrainers are a human carcinogen. They are fatal if inhaled.

THE METAL SALTS (MSDS 2-3)

POTASSIUM CHLOROPLATINITE 20% K_2PtCl_4

SODIUM TETRACHLOROPALLADATE 15% Na_2PdCl_4

PALLADIUM CHLORIDE $PdCl_2$

The platinum and palladium are salts used in conjunction with a sensitizer for coating. In powdered form, platinum and palladium salts are unstable, reverting to the metallic state. Use the same precautions as listed with the sensitizers. When drying in heated air, avoid close contact. Note the commercial print dryers in Chapter 2, "Setting Up a Laboratory," or see the drying apparatus in Chapter 9, "Advanced Technique."

Solution C

To make 20% potassium chloroplatinite, mix:[4]

Distilled water at 100°F	50 ml
Potassium chloroplatinite powder	10 gms

Or . . .

To make 15% tetrachloropalladate, mix:

Distilled water at 100°F	55 ml
Palladium chloride	5 gms
Sodium chloride	3.5 gms

[4] Technically, this is not a 20% solution; however, it has been listed as such in the literature for over 100 years—and it works.

NOTE: Both Pt and Pd salts are mixed to a near-saturated solution. Prior to their use, *do not stir or shake*, as particulate metal may be transferred to the image.

The Use of Metal Utensils

It is difficult to determine when and where the caveat that "*metal" shall not be in contact with platinum materials* started. The type of metal is not specified; nonetheless, the same adage is repeated in much of the platinum literature. It undoubtedly refers to the potential for iron and platinum metals to go into solution and plate on to one another.

Today, most good laboratory equipment is made of stainless steel, a substance considered essentially inert for many photographic processes. If, with high-quality stainless steel, any metallic elements escape the bounds of your utensils, it would be in such infinitesimal amounts as to be insignificant. I have used the same stainless steel beaker and brushes with metal ferules for twenty years. I suspect that they are well plated with platinum and palladium. I would not, however, push the phenomena by developing prints in stainless steel trays. I use plastic trays or those of baked enamel.

Developers (MSDS 1-2)

Formulas

Ammonium citrate $(NH_4)_2HC_6H_5O_7$ *(MSDS 1)*

Sodium citrate $C6H_5NA_3 \cdot 2H_2O$

Since relatively large amounts (1 to 3 liters) are used, take precautions regarding skin contact and inhalation. Use in well-ventilated areas. A standard surgical mask will not prevent inhalation of vapors from exposed liquid form.

Potassium oxalate $K_2C_2O_2$ *(MSDS 2-3)*

Potassium oxalate is mixed from powder to 35% solution. In some literature, its use has been discouraged because of toxicity; however, with normal precautions, it presents no more hazards than the more benign developers. This chemical occurs naturally in leafy green vegetables, particularly spinach. Decomposition products of carbon monoxide and carbon dioxide may be formed. Use only in a well-ventilated area. Skin contact should be kept to a minimum.

Potassium oxalate

Potassium oxalate	66 gms
Distilled water at 120°F	200 ml

Or . . .

Potassium oxalate	454 gms (1 lb)
Distilled water at 120°F	1,350 ml

NOTE: Developer is never discarded. The developer that is absorbed by the paper or evaporated is simply replaced with fresh developer solution. As with sherry, a portion of the original mixture, no matter how old, remains. Paul Anderson used "30-year-old" developer. My developer age is approaching 20 years.

Ammonium citrate

(Available in solution from BS)	
Ammonium citrate	200 gms
Water at 15°C	100 ml
Make syrupy, add to water,	1,500 ml

Sullivan's cold bath developer

(Available as solution)	
Potassium oxalate	150 gm
Potassium monobasic phosphate	75 mg
Water to make	1 liter

Sodium citrate, potassium sodium tartrate, and sodium acetate are also used as developers (Nadeau, 1994).

NOTE: An interesting observation is that image color is influenced by the content of metallic ions in the developer. If, for example, a Pt/Pd print is made following a previous session of palladium printing, the image color will be slightly warmer. The reverse is true going from platinum to palladium. Some may object to this. I find it desirable. Pt/Pd is a printmaking process. I limit my work to editions of fifty. Each print is identified and distinct. I would not prefer the mechanical perfection obtained by some other photographic processes.

The pH

The pH is defined in simple terms as the acidity or alkalinity of a solution. The pH progresses from the most acid (1) to neutral (7) to the most alkaline (14).

pH 1	pH 7	pH 14
Acidic ←	Neutral	→ Alkaline

Each whole number change represents an increase or decrease of a factor of 10. The issue of pH cannot be ignored, as many reactions in the Pt/Pd process are altered by changes in pH. It is recommended that pH 0-14 paper strips be used to monitor and record the pH of solutions.

NOTE: It is possible that, with an alkaline developer, insoluble crystals of iron hydroxide may form to participate on the paper. For that reason, it is wise to monitor the pH of the developer, particularly if stains are found on the print following clearing. Citric or oxalic acid can be occasionally added to bring the developer to a slightly acidic state. For those who use an acidic alum-rosin-sized paper, the internal paper sizing in the developer usually keeps it at a pH of 6.5.

Filtering of Developer

Eventually, if developer is reused, crystals and undissolved debris can form in the solution. If the developer is stored for a period in a glass jug, particularly at cooler temperatures, large crystals may form that cannot be removed through the opening. As developer is close to a saturated solution, this is to be expected. It is not significant. Try heating and agitation. Eventually, pour off the liquid into a new container. The sludge can now be dissolved in a weak acid (clearing bath) and discarded. Some Pt/Pd printmakers occasionally filter the developer before use. In that case, a coarse coffee filter can be used. Instead of filtering, I simply carefully decant at the first print of the day and throw out the sludge.

Temperature of Developer

The early literature refers to a heated developer. I have found that, with potassium oxalate, a temperature of 90°F results in a quick reduction of the image with a pleasing tone. Regardless of the temperature, it should be consistent; higher temperatures result in faster printing speeds and a slight loss of contrast. The reverse is true for developers used at room temperature. Image color can be greatly modified by developer temperature (see Chapter 9, "Advanced Technique"). Care should be taken with extreme temperatures. Cold developer may result in granularity. Hot developer (over 120°F) can affect the internal sizing of some papers and produce mottling of tones.

Clearing Agents

The Dilute Acids (MSDS 2-3)

The acidic clearing baths are composed of highly diluted acids. Hypo clearing agent (sodium sulfite) and EDTA can also be used. Both are less hazardous; but if proper precautions are taken with the acids, the differences are largely academic. Even hydrochloric acid, once mixed in its 1% concentration, is relatively safe. While in the concentrated form, all clearing agents should be handled carefully.

Phosphoric acid H_3PO_4:[5] *Comes in a 85% technical grade solution. Take reasonable care. Add acid to water. Protect eyes when mixing. If some acid gets in contact with skin or clothing, immediately rinse. 85% phosphoric acid will not burn unless held against skin for an extended period. The 2 to 4% solution used for clearing is safe unless carelessly used.*

Oxalic acid $C_2H_2O_4$: *It is mixed from powder to a 1% solution for clearing. It is also used in minute amounts in ferric oxalate sensitizer. The powder is relatively safe unless allowed in contact with skin or inhaled. In solution, it is dilute enough to be harmless unless carelessly used. Do not splash on skin or clothing.*

Citric acid $H_3C_6H_8O_7 \cdot H_2O$: *A powder that is mixed in dilute form for clearing and developing. Found in citrus fruits.*

Hydrochloric acid HCl (MSDS 4)

Hydrochloric acid is mentioned in historic and contemporary literature and is still used (1%) by many as a clearing agent. It is extremely caustic. It burns skin, eyes, and clothing. When fumes are inhaled, it damages the cilia of the respiratory track and the covering of the bronchioles in the lungs. It will also corrode the stainless steel in your darkroom. I do not use it.

WARNING:

In mixing any dilute acidic clearing agent, always add acid slowly to water. Protect skin and eyes. Adding water to acid may cause a splattering of concentrated acid when it comes into contact with water (as adding a drop of water to hot grease does).

5. Using phosphoric acid and hypo clearing agent (sodium sulfite) in the same sink or drain may release sulfurous acid and caustic sulfur dioxide gas. The noxious odor is quite unmistakable, as the eyes water and the bronchioles contract. Evacuate the lab until the air clears; then, run water into the sink and drain.

EDTA and the Sulfites (MSDS 1)

Ethylene diamine tetraacetic acid (EDTA) 3 to 8%: Chelating agent used for developing and clearing. Found in foods. Contact with powder to eye or inhalation can be harmful. Ingestion of large quantities can be harmful.

Hypo clearing agent: Sodium sulfite Na_2SO_3 *is the active ingredient in hypo clearing agent. Mixed 20% with water. Avoid skin contact with powder.*

Clearing agents release and dissolve the remaining iron salts from the paper. Failure to adequately clear paper results in a yellowish stain in white areas. This represents contamination and will shorten the archival life of the print. See the section on fog versus stain in Chapter 10, "Problems."

Choosing a Clearing Agent

Choosing a clearing agent is best done by testing with a step tablet (see Chapter 7, "Calibration"). Pay particular attention to the clearing action with coating that contains little or no restrainer; it is the last to clear. Palladium is more difficult to clear. Use only enough concentration and time for the whites produced by the step tablet to match the uncoated paper white. Too much of either may cause bleaching of the image, particularly with pure palladium.

The use of any clearing agent is similar, for each requires three baths of five minutes each with intermittent rinses. When the first bath becomes cloudy (not more than 2 to 3 prints), discard, mix fresh agent, and move to the third position. When using the EDTA sulfite baths, thoroughly rinse the print in running water between the developer and each clearing bath.

TABLE 4.1 Relative Efficiency of Clearing Agents. This property varies with choice of paper and developer.

Weakest	⇑	EDTA 8%
		EDTA 8% with sodium sulfate
		Hypo clearing agent
		Citric acid 1%
		Phosphoric acid 2%
		Oxalic acid 1%
Strongest	⇓	Hydrochloric acid 0.5 to 1%

Formulas

Phosphoric acid 2%[6]

Phosphoric acid (85%)	24 ml
Water	1 liter

Oxalic acid 1%

Oxalic acid	10 gms
Water	1 liter

Oxalic acid is a fine alternative to phosphoric acid. It does come in powder form, however, and may be difficult to get into and maintain in solution. If it crystallizes, it is hard to wash off the finished print.

Citric acid $C_6H_8O_7$

Citric acid	30 gms
Water	1,500 ml

Hydrochloric Acid 1%

Water	1 qt
Hydrochloric acid 37%	1/2 Oz

Use 1/2% with pure palladium.

EDTA 8%

EDTA	1 tablespoon (30 gms)
Water	750 ml

Our (the author and Keith Schreiber) research has shown that EDTA alone does not work well with potassium oxalate developer with some papers, particularly with palladium prints. However, if sodium sulfite is added, it is quite satisfactory for most papers.

EDTA 8% with sodium sulfite

EDTA	1 tablespoon (30 gms)
Sodium sulfite	0.5 tablespoon (25 gms)
Water	1 liter

Hypo clearing agent

Follow directions to mix Kodak Hypo Clearing Agent from powder to stock solution. Dilute stock solution 1:4.

Or mix stock solution from chemicals:

Water at 125°F	750 ml
Sodium sulfite, anhydrous	200 gms
Sodium metabisulfite	50 gm
Water to make	1 liter

6. A 4% solution may be needed to clear palladium salts.

Hypo clearing agent is a good clearing agent. It is relatively safe. With some papers, it is the most effective choice (see Chapter 5, "Paper"). With some developer/paper combinations it is inadequate. Use with care, as it may bleach the pure palladium image.

A Matter of Print pH

While the print may be free of iron salts after clearing and washing, some acidic clearing agents may effect the pH of the finished print. This is best checked by using a pH pen on the dried print. As the debate over the necessity of "acid-free" platinum paper continues (see Chapter 5, "Paper"), the photographer can take measures in the laboratory to raise the pH of the finished print. My studies have shown that if you are using an acid-clearing bath, a final treatment in a buffering solution will give the finished print a quite respectable pH of 6.5.

Buffering Solutions

Sodium carbonate Na_2CO_3 (MSDS 1)

Sodium acetate $NaCH_3OO$ (MSDS 1)

Used as buffering agents; similar to household sodium bicarbonate.

Sodium carbonate 3%	30 gms
Water to make	1 liter

Or . . .

Sodium acetate 1%	10 gms
Water to make	1 liter

After clearing, soak the print with agitation for 3 to 5 minutes.

While buffering may be a satisfactory solution, my studies have further shown that using one of the nonacidic clearing baths may ensure a final print with an alkaline pH. It seems reasonable that if a nonacidic bath will pass your tests, why not use it? If purchased in bulk form, the EDTA, sulfite, and hypo clear formulas are no more expensive than acids (see "Sources of Chemicals" at the end of this chapter).

Toners

Negative Toning for Contrast

Selenium (MSDS 3)

Avoid inhalation and skin contact. Use only in well-ventilated area.

Selenium is a heavy metal used for negative toning and marketed as Rapid Selenium Toner, containing sodium selinite, ammonium thiosulfate, and sodium sulfite. To increase negative contrast, it is used 1:3 with water (See Chapter 3, "The Negative"). When direct positive copy film is used to enlarge negatives, it is used 1:30 for archival permanence.

Print Toning

Print color can be modified by a number of procedures, including the combination of metals and the type and temperature of the developer (see Chapter 9, "Advanced Technique"). Nevertheless, particularly in the historic literature, compounds containing gold, lead, mercury, uranium, silver pyrogallic acid, and copper are described.

Gold chloride (MSDS 2)

$H(AuCl_4)$. Gold: Gold salt used for toning. Can be purchased as 1% or 5% solution. Because of the concerns expressed above for lead and mercury, I consider gold to be the safest and most efficacious of toning methods.

Gold chloride toning intensifies the image and gives it a cool bluish tone. Gold chloride can be placed in the sensitizer, as a separate bath, or brushed on through a film of glycerin (see Chapter 9, "Advanced Techniques").

Gold chloride 5%	1 gm
Distilled water	26 ml

For a separate bath, see Sullivan's gold tone in the BS catalogue. The formula is not presented here. It contains sodium formate and is more conveniently purchased premixed with instructions (Sullivan and Weese, 1998).

Glycerin $C_3H_5(OH)_3$ (MSDS 1)

Glycerin is an oily substances used for selective development of platinum or palladium image. Harmless by any route. Can be ingested.

Lead oxalate oxide ($Pb\ H_2O_4$) (MSDS 4)

Extremely toxic by all routes. Use with care, or do not use at all. It is used 0.65% for toning. As a heavy metal, doses will accumulate in the body over repeated exposures.

Mercuric chloride $HgCl_2$ (MSDS 4)

WARNING:

Extremely toxic by all routes. The most hazardous of chemicals used in the platinum/palladium process. Use with care, or do not use at all. Avoid all contact. It is used 10% for toning. As a heavy metal, doses will accumulate in the body over repeated exposures.

Sources of Chemicals

The coating agents used in the Pt/Pd must be of reagent quality and must be recently compounded. It is recommended that they be purchased from specialty suppliers. Developing and clearing agents need not be of high purity, so industrial grades may be used. These can be found in chemical supply houses and university chemistry stores. Prices vary between suppliers, so shop around using this guide.

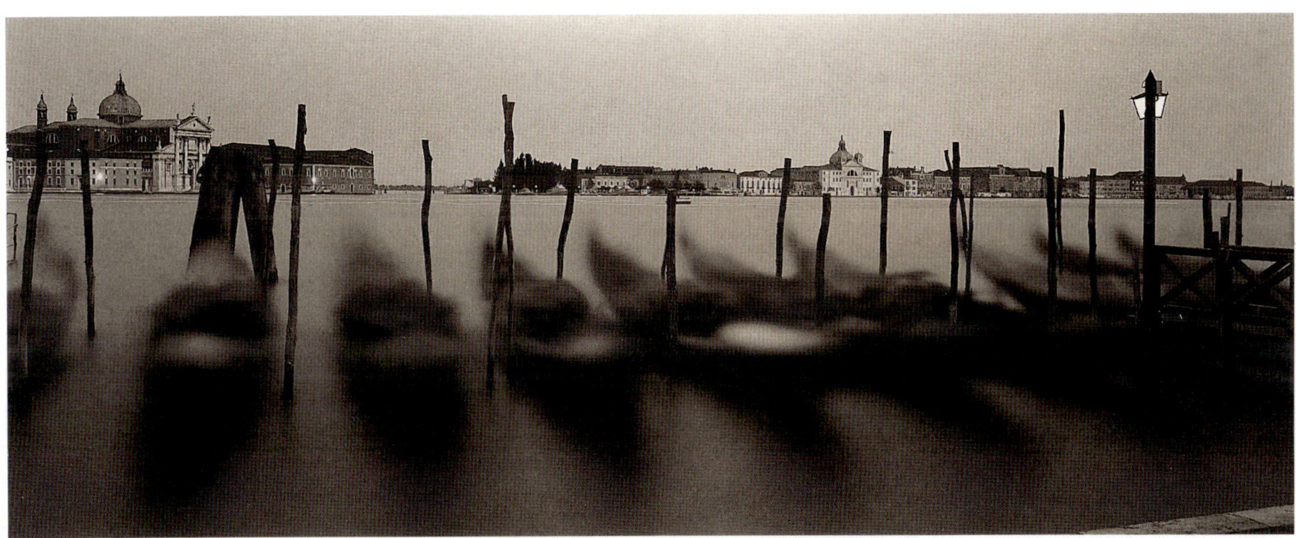

PLATE 4.2 Gondolas, Venice, Italy. 1992 7 × 17 inch Pt/Pd

TABLE 4.2 Sources of Chemicals Used in the Platinum/Palladium Process

Chemicals	*1998-99 Price Range*	*Source*[a]
Metal Salts		
Potassium chloro-platinite 20% Platinum soln. #3	$112.00 / 25 ml $315.00 / 100 ml	BS, PF, AC, FR
Potassium chloro-platinite (powder) 10 gm makes 50 ml	$175.00 / 10 gm $475.00 / 50 gm	BS, PF, AC, FR
Sodium tetrachloropalladate -15% Palladium soln. #3	$32.50 / 25 ml $99.50 / 100 ml	BS, PF
Palladium chloride (10 gm makes 110 ml of sodium tetrachloropalladite)	$5.50–9.50 / 10 gm $350.00–400.00 / 50 gm	BS, PF, FR BS
Ammonium tetrachloroplatinate(II) 25% Ammonium tetrachloropalladate(II) 20% (50% each for Malde/Ware Process)	5 ml / $23.95 to 50 ml / $169.95	FR, QC
Gold chloride 5% Gold chloride powder	$45.00 / 25 ml $39.95 / 1 gm	BS, PF, AC
Sensitizers		
Ferric oxalate 27% (also dry pack) #1 Without restrainer #2 Pt 0.6% potassium chlorate #2 Pd 1.2% potassium chlorate	$7.25 / 25 ml $23.20 / 100 ml $23.20 / 100 ml $23.20 / 100 ml	BS, PF BS, PF BS, PF BS
Ferric oxalate (powder)	$30.00 / 50 gm $54.00 / 100 gm	BS, PF BS
Ferric ammonium oxalate (powder)	$9.00 / 50 gm $12 / 100 gm	BS, QC, FR
Developers		
Ammonium citrate	$6.45 / 100 gm $31.40 / 1,000 gm $13.20 / qt	BS
B and S cold bath	$14.30 / qt	BS
Potassium oxalate (powder)	$7.03 / 100 gm $34.20 / 1,000 gm $18.00 / 1 lb	BS BS AC
Sodium citrate	$7.95 / 1 lb $12.00 / qt.	PF, AC BS
Clearing Agents[b]		
Citric acid	$3.99 / 100 gm $19.40 / 1,000 gm $28.00 / 5 lbs $95.00 / 20 lb	BS BS AC PF

Chemicals	*1998-99 Price Range*	*Source*[a]
EDTA	$5.12 / 100 gm	BS
	$24.90 / 1,000 gm	BS
	$21.00 / 1 lb	AC, PF
Hypo Clearing Agent	$4.75 / 1 gal	AP
(Stock. Mix 1:4 with water)	$20.00 / 5 gal	AP
Oxalic acid	$3.93 / 100 gm	BS
	$18.70 / 1,000 gm	BS
	$6.90 / 1 lb	AC, PF
Phosphoric acid 75%[b]	$7.95 / pt +$14.00 hazard fee	PF
Sodium sulfite	$61.90 / 1,000 gm	BS
(Active ingredient in hypo clear)	$55.00 / 50 lbs	BL
Sodium metabisulfite	$3.25 / 100 gm	PF
(Used in hypo clear)	$15.00 / 5 lb	PF
Oxidizers		
Potassium dichromate	$16.00 / 100 gm	BS
Potassium chlorate	$6.68 / 10 gm + scaling fee	BS
Starter Kits (containing sensitizers, metal, clearing agent, sizing, and restrainer)		
Platinum kit		
(15 ml platinum)	$95.00	PF
(25 ml platinum)	$138.00	BS, PF
Palladium kit		
(15 ml palladium)	$47.00	PF
(25 ml palladium)	$66.60	BS, PF
Ziatype Zia exploration	$120.00	BS
Malde/Ware Process	4 × 5 kit 39.95 8 × 10 kit 67.95	QC
Miscellaneous		
Glyoxal 40%	$7.20 / 100 ml	BS
Glycerin	$4.86 / 100 ml	BS
	$21.31 / pt.	PF
Polyvinyl alcohol	$5.00 / 100 ml	BS
Pyro PMK (Kit)	$32.00	BS, AC, PF
Rollo Pyro (Kit)	$41.00	BS

Continued

TABLE 4.2 Sources of Chemicals Used in the Platinum/Palladium Process *(continued)*

Chemicals	*1998-99 Price Range*	*Source*[a]
Sodium acetate	\$5.96 / 100 gm	PF
	\$15.95 / 1 lb	PF
Sodium carbonate	\$14.90 / 5 lb	PF
	\$39.00 / 20 lb	PF
Sullivan gold toning kit (Contains 25 ml 5% Gold chloride)	\$47.20	BS
Tween 20 (Polysorbate 10%)	\$3.90 / 25 ml	BS, FR

[a] See "Sources" for abbreviations of suppliers.

[b] If you live in a metropolitan area, buy directly from a supplier. Shipping costs for acids are very high.

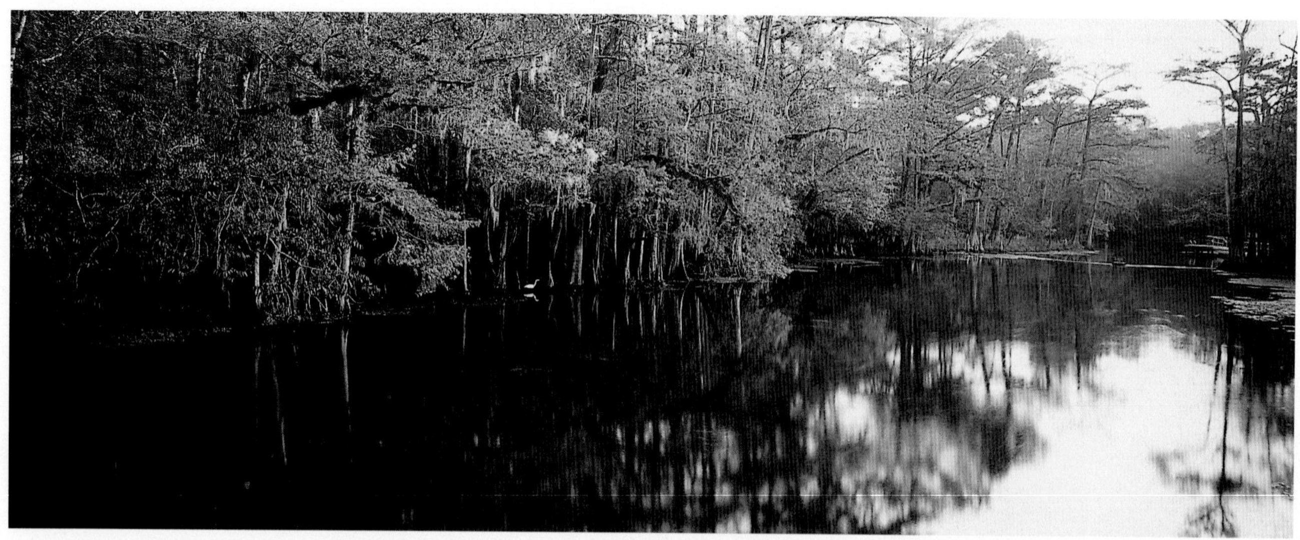

PLATE 4.3 Suwannee River, FL. 1992 7 × 17 inch Pt/Pd

CHAPTER 5

Paper

Dick Arentz and Keith Schreiber

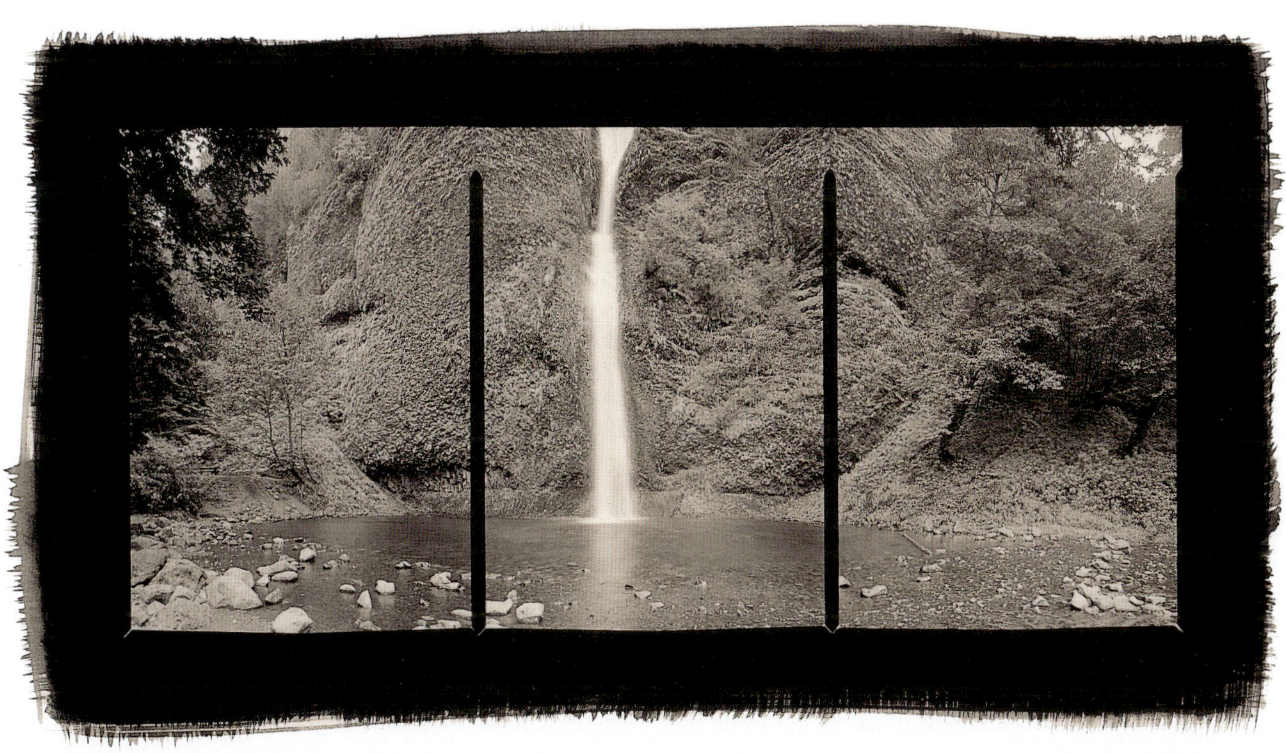

PLATE 5.1 Horsetail Falls, OR. 1994. Three 5 × 7 inch panels. 7 × 15 inch Palladium Print. Printed on Simili Japon paper (© Keith Schreiber)

Most artist's papers are composed of relatively long, uniform fibers of plant cellulose. In Western countries, cotton and linen (flax) are the most common choices; however, many other plant fibers can be utilized, including hemp, jute, and gampi. Treated wood pulp can also be used for good papers. In this case, the wood pulp is processed so that only the high alpha fibers remain.

For true *rag* paper, new cloth cuttings or "rags" are used. Now, however, portions of the cotton plant left over from thread-making, called *linters* are often substituted. Linters of varying quality are available. The quality (and cost) of a paper is, in part, based on the amount of cotton or linen and/or the quality of the linters used.

Until the nineteenth century, all paper was *handmade*. Today, although the process of handmaking paper continues and has hardly changed from its historic processes, most contemporary papers are either *mouldmade* or *machinemade*. Nevertheless, the handmade process existed for centuries before mechanization and is responsible for most of the principles of papermaking and its nomenclature (Airey, 1996; Hunter, 1974). Handmade paper is still used by artists who demand the best papers available. Unfortunately, at this time, only a few handmade papers may be adaptable for the Pt/Pd process, and most have been replaced by mouldmade or machinemade varieties.

The Platinotype Papers

When you are considering materials for purposes other than those intended (see Chapter 10, "Problems"), finding suitable papers for platinum printing remains a continuous challenge. While it may be fascinating to visit an artist supply store and examine the lovely texture and patina of the finer papers, you must keep in mind that few paper manufacturers intend that their products be immersed in chemicals and water for over an hour! Moreover, it hardly occurs to paper designers that less than 1% of their purchasers will place an acid salt on their papers to react unfavorably with the "acid-free" alkaline surface.

At the time of publication, only one paper is made expressly for platinum printing: Arches Platine. Fortunately, many other papers are adaptable for our process. Most platinum printers prefer a 100% cotton paper. Excellent papers are made from cotton linters. The treated alpha cellulose wood papers are considered to be archivally sound and are used for commercial photographic paper.

Prior to 1985, some of the best Platinotype papers were internally sized with an alum rosin material making a slightly acidic (pH 4.5) paper. Combined with a good external sizing of starch or gelatin, this paper took a coating of platinum/palladium salt and sensitizer (pH 1-2), maintaining a creamy consistency that produced the continuous tones desirable in some platinum prints (most noticeable in the areas of skies and flesh tones).

Then, around 1985, paper manufacturers began to follow the trend toward "acid-free" products. The internal sizing was changed to an alkylketone dimer product, sometimes with carbonates added. Many of these "neutral" or alkaline papers, in our opinion, react with the acid platinum coating to produce a typical acid-base reaction with precipitation that causes a reticulation or "flocculation" to produce a granularity in the image. The alkalinity also tends to neutralize the ferric oxalate in the sensitizer.

In early 1990 the paper situation was dismal. Many papers used in the past were worthless for platinum as well as many other processes. At that time, Dick Arentz convinced the Crane's Paper Company to do a special run of pH 4.5 alum-rosin-sized paper. It has proved satisfactory and is presently available from Bostick and Sullivan, marketed as Platinotype.

As of 1998, the situation has improved. Many papers have now regained usefulness for the palladium/palladium process due to improved quality control and the adjustment of internal sizing.

Still, the platinum printer is in a bit of a quandary. While archival "permanence" is desirable, the sacrifice of image quality for permanence, hardly justifies the use of an unsatisfactory neutral or alkaline paper. For many, it is a tradeoff. Up to now, our studies have shown that, with some exceptions, the best papers for the process have tested acidic. Many most likely have alum rosin internal sizing.

When deliberating the choices we must make, it is heartening to consider that the "acid-free" tenets are a recent concept, and that many papers made centuries ago of good materials—and properly stored—remain in excellent condition. One must also consider that, unlike media where the pigment or ink is laid onto the surface, the Pt/Pd process alters the chemistry of the paper significantly. Most likely, after processing an acid paper, much of the internal sizing, either acid or buffered, still remains. However, most of the surface sizing has been removed. If a neutral or alkaline paper was used, the carbonate buffers, if present, may have been partially dissolved.

If, after processing, an acid-free print is desired, certain procedures during the clearing cycle can be followed. When an acid clearing bath is used, the print can be placed in a buffering solution of sodium carbonate before washing. Our studies have shown a respectable pH of 6 following this practice. A better procedure may be to avoid acid clearing baths entirely. In the testing of papers, it was shown that most cleared satisfactorily in hypo clearing agent, and some in a bath of EDTA and sodium sulfite. For these, the pH after drying was considerably alkaline. (See Chapter 4, "Chemicals.")

The proprietary "secrets" held by some paper manufacturers have made the search for suitable papers even more perplexing. Our most recent tests have indicated that other properties besides pH may influence compatibility with platinum printing. Some pH neutral papers tested well; others did not. Those well into the alkaline range tested poorly. We suspect that the presence of a calcium carbonate buffer interferes with the platinum coating material. Perhaps the formation of the cellular fibers (the size and configuration of fibers) and the character of the surface sizing are significant factors. Certainly more "dwell time" in the sizing tub, and pH adjustment of the surface sizing, can be significant. As we continue to understand the characteristics of a good platinum paper, we may be able to specify papers that are both superb and archival.

Practical Matters

As indicated, there are considerable variables involved in producing hand-coated photographic prints, many of which we cannot control. Most art papers are simply unsuitable and are best left for other processes. Some can be made useful by sizing (see Appendix E, "Sizing of Paper").

If the platinum printer finds a suitable paper, slight changes in the manufacturing processes between lots can have serious ramifications on its continued use for platinum printing. A change in pH or sizing or any number of other factors from one batch to the next may render your favorite paper useless, or at least force you to make changes in your printing methods. It is, therefore, advisable to record lot numbers on all paper purchases. If a good paper is found, buy up what you can. There is no assurance that the next run will be the same.

Local climatic conditions and tap water chemistry can also have significant effects on the printing characteristics of different papers. A myriad of "personal variables" can also play a role in whether a paper will work or not. Some papers work better with brush coating, others with the rod. Some give equal results with both coating instruments. Many of the heavier papers and/or alkaline pH work better with double coating. It is possible that the first coat of sensitizer and metal helps to acidify the surface, allowing for a smoother second coating. (See Chapter 9, "Advance Techniques.") The choice of clearing agent is often dependent on the paper used. (See Chapter 4, "Chemicals.") Some do not clear in acidic solutions, but respond well to hypo clearing agent.

NOTE: The Time from Coating to Heat Drying: Each paper appears to have an optimum time during which the paper is allowed to air dry before subjecting it to heated air. See Chapter 8, "The Platinum and Palladium Print."

Platinum printers are versatile people and, in spite of the difficulties, they are producing exceptional prints with the materials available. Each successful printer seems to have his or her own formula and paper. Many size their own paper, some double coat, experiment with temperature and humidity, manipulate the surface, and so on. Some do not work with continuous tone images, so granularity is not noticeable. No doubt, considering the popularity of the platinum/palladium process, dozens of papers that we have not tested are presently being used to produce excellent platinum and palladium prints. In the near future, other papers will be found by diligent Pt/Pd printers to be amenable to our process.

Some Characteristics Required of a Platinum/Palladium Paper

1. A firm surface is required with enough "tooth" to hold the emulsion. The coating tends to slide off of slick or glossy papers. Choose a vellum[1] surface.
2. Permanence is required, usually 100% rag cotton.
3. The paper must be adequately sized.
4. It must not be multiplyed, unless you plan to separate the sheets during processing.
5. It must hold up after at least thirty minutes of immersion in water.

A Word about Paper Weight Measurements

The standard unit to measure the weight of artist's papers is expressed in *gram weight*: the weight of one square meter of the paper. It is expressed in grams/meter^2 or g/m^2. It can also be abbreviated as gsm.

Unfortunately, there is another standard using the English system of measurements, expressed as pounds/ream, which is the *basis weight*. A ream consists of 500 sheets of paper. What size? The size is expressed as *basis*

1. The term "vellum" should accurately be *vellum-like*. True *vellum* is made from calfskin.

size. To complicate matters, each type of paper has defined its own basis size: Bond is 17 × 22 inches; Text is 25 × 38 inches; Cover (a common category for many platinum papers) is 20 × 26 inches. Therefore, a ream of Platinotype paper that is listed as 250 g/m^2 may exhibit a sticker on the package indicating that it is a 90-pound paper. Watercolor papers, many of which are listed here, vary so much in size, that they are mercifully listed as grams/meter^2.

Selected Platinotype Papers and Their Characteristics

Realizing that only a small percentage of art papers would prove to be useful for the platinum/palladium process, Dick Arentz and Keith Schreiber (at the Center for Creative Photography in Tucson, Arizona) resumed the testing of papers in 1996. Of those chosen for testing, many were eliminated at the first run. Approximately forty papers were subjected to further testing. It became apparent that fifteen examples not only met the required criteria but exhibited distinctive qualities to allow for considerable choice in weight, texture, color, and other more subtle characteristics (Table 5.1). Certain other excellent papers, exhibiting less than optimum tonal values, were listed separately (Table 5.2).

Because of the rapid changes and irregular manufacturing techniques, by the time of publication, many of those listed may no longer be suitable, while others may have entered the market or become modified to be of value for this process.

Other methods, such as Sullivan's Ziatype or the Malde/Ware ammonium printing out method, may have very different paper requirements.

Testing Techniques

pH

Papers were tested prior to exposure utilizing the pH marking pen marketed by Light Impressions. Based on indicator colors, papers were identified as at or below pH 6 (A), at pH 7 (N), and at or over pH 8 (B).

Step Tablet

All papers were exposed with a 21-Step Stouffer 4 × 5 inch step tablet.

Coating Solution

Papers were tested with a 50/50 mixture of platinum and palladium, and with 100% palladium, using a coating mixture of 50% metal salt and sensitizer, and 1:1 solutions of A and B. (See Chapter 7, "Calibration.")

Surfactin

After printing with the standard coating solution, each paper was tested with one drop of 10% Tween 20®, a surfactant and spreading agent, per 2 ml of coating solution. (This may not be the optimum amount of Tween 20 for any given paper.)

Coating Instruments

All papers were coated by brush. Those with a smooth enough surface were also coated with a glass rod. All papers were subjected to single and double coating. Few improved with double-coating techniques. They are identified in "Notes on Suitable Papers for the Platinum/Palladium Process" later in this chapter.

Drying

Papers were allowed to air dry two minutes before being subjected to heated air.

Exposure

Exposure was done with the nuArc 26K mercury vapor commercial printer.

Developer

All test prints were developed in potassium oxalate at 90°F.

Clearing Agents

Most papers cleared well in either Kodak Hypo Clearing Agent (HCA) or phosphoric acid. (H_3PO_4). Notable exceptions were Arches Platine and Twinrocker Watercolor. Both cleared well in HCA. Other similar products (e.g., Perma Wash and Ilford Archival Wash Aid) may also be effective.

Reading

The smoothness of tone was assessed by visual inspection. Crane's Crest Natural White Wove (Platinotype) was used as a standard and assigned the number 10. Other papers were assigned values from 10 to 1. Those below 8 were listed separately.[2] With few exceptions, a

[2] If the printing of imagery does not require smooth tones, or if the printer wishes to deliberately add granularity to the image, a number of suitable papers are available (Plates 5.4 and 5.5). These are listed at the end of the summaries, and are evaluated as to tone smoothness with values from 7 to 3. As the process of paper manufacture continues in its unpredictable way, many may exhibit better tonal values in the future.

coating mixture of pure palladium produced smoother tones than a 50/50 platinum/palladium mixture.

Reflection densities were read using a Speedmaster T-85D. Maximum black (Dmax) and 90% of maximum black (IDmax) were recorded. Exposure scales between papers were found to vary too little to be of practical use.

Printing speed was assessed and compared to Platinotype paper. With some papers, particularly the thicker varieties, printing speed was significantly slowed. This is cited in "Notes on Suitable Papers for the Platinum/Palladium Process" below.

The Actual Print

While testing techniques may be interesting, much data simply does not translate when a platinum or palladium print is made from a camera negative. We gave all papers this final assessment and incorporated our observations into our survey.

Notes on Suitable Papers for the Platinum/Palladium Process

Arches *Platine*

Mouldmade in France of 100% cotton, *Platine* has a neutral pH, hot-pressed surface, and a pure white color. Its weight is 310 gsm (grams per square meter). Sizes are 30 × 44 inches with four deckled edges and 22 × 30 inches with two deckled and two torn. Martin Axon worked with Arches to design this paper specifically for platinum printing. For many printers, however, *Platine* has proven to be somewhat difficult to work with. It does not clear well using traditional acid bath methods, but three trays of hypo clearing agent (regular working strength) with intermittent water rinses, will usually be sufficient. Double coating seems to be beneficial; however, some printers have reported good results with a single heavy coat on a well-humidified sheet. Some have found the addition of Tween 20 to the coating solution to cause spots, while others have found it to be useful.

Bienfang Graphics 360

A very thin U.S. made 100% rag translucent marker paper, *Bienfang* is available in fifty-sheet pads in sizes 8 1/2 × 11 inches, 11 × 14 inches, 14 × 17 inches, and 19 × 24 inches. It is machinemade, smooth, white, and slightly acidic. *Bienfang* is a favorite of well-known platinum printer Lois Conner. It clears easily, but coating should best be done with a brush, since it quickly expands and wrinkles as it absorbs the solution. Tonal quality is excellent, but maximum density can be a bit weak. Tween 20 may further lower Dmax.

Crane's *Kid Finish*

Machinemade in the U.S. of 100% cotton fiber, Crane's *Kid Finish* is found as 32-pound white (AS8111) or ecru (8116), as well as a variety of other shades and patterns, in 8 1/2 × 11 inch with cut edges. Larger sheets (21 × 33 inch) are available from Bostick and Sullivan. The pH is slightly acidic. This fine writing paper, found in many stationery stores, is often recommended as a good paper to start with in exploring Pt/Pd and other hand-coated photographic processes. It is very easy to work with, but a small watermark scattered throughout each sheet about 6 to 8 inches apart can be problematic when printing negatives larger than 5 × 7 inches. The use of Tween 20 may lower Dmax.

Crane's *Parchmont*

Crane's *Parchmont* is machinemade in the U.S. of 100% cotton. It is 65 pounds and 22 × 30 inches with a white, smooth wove (vellum) surface, cut edges, and a neutral pH. Easy to work with, if rather nondescript, *Parchmont* has watermarks similar to that of *Kid Finish*, though not as many. It is easy to coat with either brush or rod and clears easily. The use of Tween 20 has no effect.

Crane's *Platinotype*

Machinemade in the U.S. of 100% cotton, *Platinotype* is creamy white, 250 gsm and 23 × 29 inches, with a smooth surface, cut edges, and slightly acidic. Dick Arentz worked with Crane's to design the specifications for this paper, which replaced Crane's *Artificial Parchment*. This paper is the standard or baseline to which we compared all the others. It is marketed by Bostick and Sullivan as *Platinotype*, though the label on a factory-packaged ream reads *Crest Natural White Wove*.[3] Although both sides appear to be hot-pressed before wetting, after the print has dried, one side has noticeably more texture than the other does. The use of Tween 20 has little to no effect. Using more than a minuscule amount of Tween 20 (over one drop of 1%

[3] At the time of publication, we have noted some problems with the consistency of the Crest Natural White Wove paper runs. We will continue to work the Cranes Company, however, it is advisable that sample sheets be tested, and batch numbers recorded, before ordering a large amount of paper.

per ml of coating solution) may penetrate the surface sizing to cause water marks on diffuse areas of the print.

NOTE: All platinum and palladium prints reproduced in this text were made on Crane's Platinotype unless otherwise indicated.

Fabriano Murillo

Mouldmade in Italy of 25% cotton with 100% high alpha cellulose, it is available as 360 gsm, 27 × 39 inches and 19 × 27 inches, with rough texture, cut edges, and slightly acidic. It is available in cream from Daniel Smith or a range of twelve colors from New York Central Art Supply. The use of Tween 20 has no effect.

Fabriano Perusia

Handmade in Italy from 100% cotton, *Perusia* is a laid sheet with a cold-pressed surface and distinctive griffin watermark. Its color is cream. The size is 19 × 26 inches and the weight is 100 gsm. It has four deckled edges and a neutral pH. This is a paper of strong character, which can easily overwhelm an image. It must be coated by brush due to the texture and needs about 50% more coating solution than normally used. Tween 20 has little or no effect.

Gampi (Gampi Torinoko)

Handmade in Japan from 100% gampi fiber, *Gampi* has a pearlescent satiny smooth surface (Plate 5.2). This 96 gsm, 20 × 30 inch sheet with four deckled edges is available in white or cream. In the Daniel Smith catalog it is called *Gampi*, while New York Central calls it *Gampi Torinoko*. Though described as being "acid free," our test showed the pH to be slightly acidic. *Gampi* is another paper with a lot of character. Its long swirling fibers make tearing problematic. Drawing a bead of water along the tearbar to soften the fibers makes it much easier. Coating can be done either by brush or rod. A single coat yields excellent results. It is rather expensive, however, at around $10.00 per sheet. A drop of Tween 20 per 2 ml coating solution will greatly improve coating smoothness and also increases Dmax.

Lenox

Lenox is machinemade in the U.S. from 100% cotton by the Parsons Paper Company (Plate 5.3). The *Lenox* from Daniel Smith is a slightly creamy white, 250 gsm sheet, available in 22 × 30 inch, 26 × 40 inch, and 38 × 50 inch sizes. It has four trimmed edges and a slightly acidic pH. It has a fairly smooth surface, but with a bit more tooth than *Platinotype*. It yields perhaps the smoothest tone quality of any paper tested. Tween 20 may be used but is not necessary. Tween will give a slightly smoother coating but with slightly lower Dmax.

Masa

Machinemade in Japan of 100% sulfite pulp, *Masa* is a bright white, 70 gsm, available in 21 × 31 inch sheets or

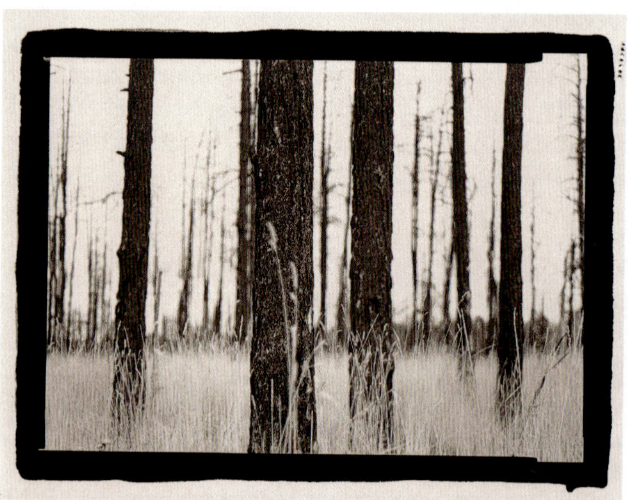

PLATE 5.2 Mogollon Rim, AZ. 1992 5 × 7 inch Pd. Printed on Gampi (© Keith Schreiber)

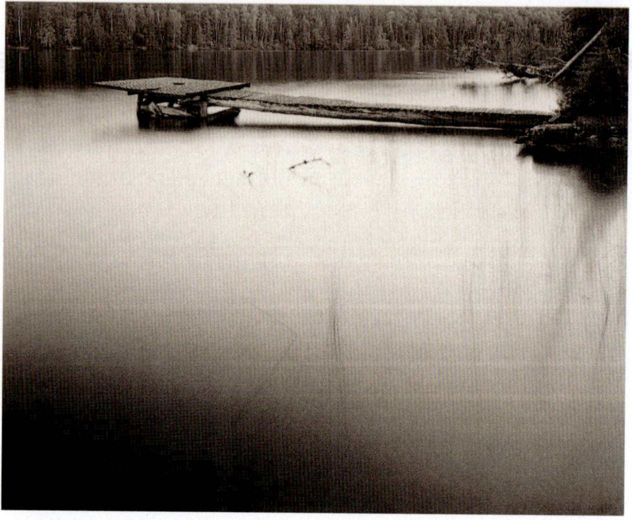

PLATE 5.3 Birch Lake, MN, 1996 8 × 10 inch Pd. Printed on Lenox (© Keith Schreiber)

42 inch × 30 yard rolls (Plate 5.4). One side is smooth and the other is cold-pressed. It has an acidic pH. *Masa* has a very soft surface and is prone to wrinkling when wet. It is best coated by brush. It clears easily, but has poor wet strength. Either side may be used, each having a distinctive look. Tween 20 helps to even out the absorption.

Rising Drawing Bristol

Machinemade in the U.S. of 100% sulfite pulp, *Rising Drawing Bristol* is white, 121 gsm, 22 × 30 inch, with vellum or plate surface and cut edges; it has an acidic pH. The use of Tween 20 improves the coating.

Rising Gallery 100

Machinemade in the U.S. of 100% cotton, *Gallery 100* comes as white, 245 gsm, 23 × 29 inch and 26 × 40 inch vellum or plate finish with cut edges (Plate 5.5); it has an alkaline pH. *Gallery 100* has been a favorite of many printers; however, we have found it to be inconsistent. The use of Tween 20 improves the coating.

Strathmore *Bristol Series 500*

Machinemade in the U.S. of 100% cotton, *Bristol Series 500* is white, 125 gsm (1 ply), 23 × 29 inch and 30 × 40 inch, plate or vellum (kid), no deckles, and has an acidic pH. Tween 20 may improve coating but lowers Dmax.

Twinrocker Watercolor

This paper is handmade in Indiana of 100% cotton and cotton rag. It comes as white, 200 or 400 gsm, in a wide range of sizes from 6 × 8 inch to 30 × 40 inch, hot- or cold-pressed, with four deckled edges that are regular or exaggerated "feather" deckle. It has a neutral pH. The use of Tween 20 improves both coating and Dmax. Like *Gampi* and *Perusia, Twinrocker White Feather Watercolor* is a paper with a lot of character, primarily due to the exaggerated deckled edges. It is available in a wide range of sizes. Small sizes such as 6 × 8 inch and 9 × 12 inch, make it particularly useful for smaller prints using the entire sheet (see Chapter 9, Plate 9.6). The surface can be susceptible to abrasion, so brushing should be kept to a minimum. Clearing should be done using hypo clearing agent.

This paper should be coated by brush, using about 50% more solution than normal. With Twinrocker papers, printing times may be 50% longer. Tween 20 gives much improved absorption and Dmax.

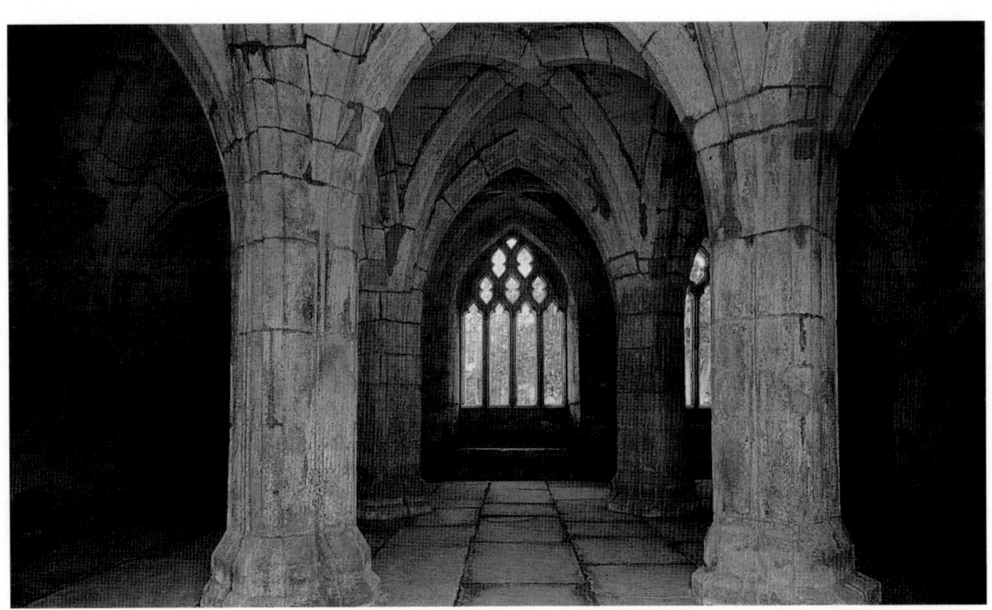

PLATE 5.4 Chapter House, Valle Crucis, Wales. 1985 12 × 20 inch Pd.
The rough surface of Masa paper was used to create a texture for the stone.

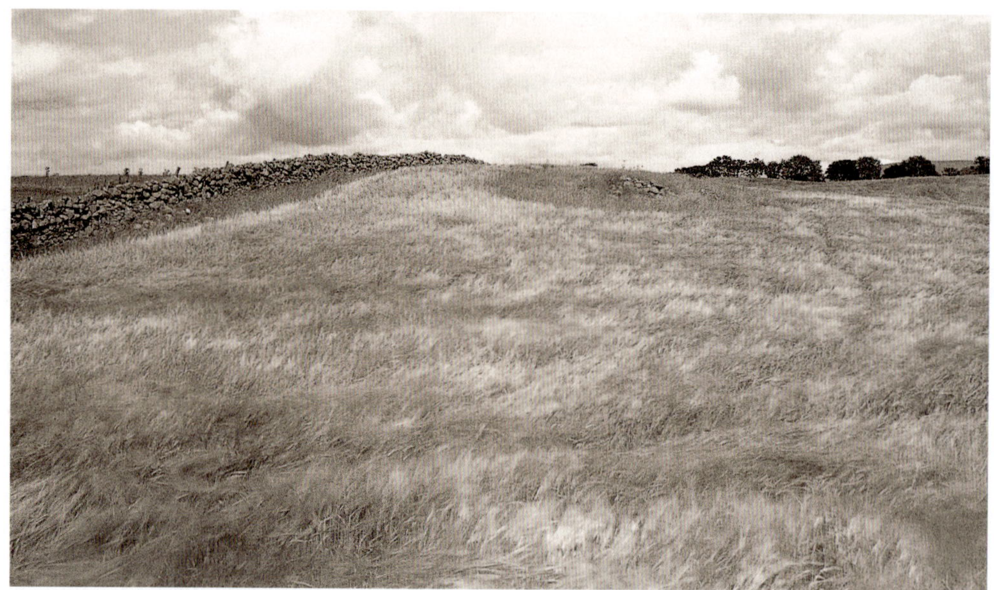

PLATE 5.5 Wheat Field, Torhouse, Scotland. 1985 12 × 20 inch Pd.
The granular effects of Gallery 100 were used to create texture in the sky.

Van Gelder Simili Japon

Mouldmade in Holland of cotton and high alpha cellulose, *Van Gelder Simili Japon* is off-white and is available in 130 gsm in 18 × 25 inch and 25 × 37 inch, and 225 gsm in 25 × 37 inch sizes (Plate 5.1). It has a smooth wove surface with two deckled edges and a neutral pH. *Simili Japon* is one of the few papers that clearly benefits from double coating. Two thin coats, the first with a drop of Tween 20, consistently yield smoother, richer prints, especially on the 225 gsm version. It is also noticeably more contrasty than most papers. The paper has a large fleur-de-lis watermark (a stylization of the initials VG) at the lower right that can be a nuisance if you don't print with wide borders. A new paper offered by Bostick and Sullivan called *Socorro Platinum* is said to be a modified version of *Simili Japon* without the watermark; one side is smoother than the other. It comes in a sheet size of 23 × 29 inch.

Summary of Paper Characteristics

NOTE: A Note on Sources: Unlike chemicals, the cost of papers is fairly consistent between suppliers. Many papers are available from many sources and are indicated with the code (G). Writing and drawing papers are found at stationary stores (SS). For those papers available from specific suppliers, the code is given for reference in the section "Sources."

TABLE 5.1 Fifteen Papers Selected for Platinum and Palladium Printing

Paper Name	*pH*	*Clearing Bath*	*Coating Tool*	*Tone Quality*	*Source*
Arches Platine	N	HCA	brush or rod	9	MA, SK, DS, NYC
Bienfang Graphics 360	A	H_3PO_4/HCA	brush	10	SS
Crane's Kid Finish	N	H_3PO_4	brush or rod	10	SS, BS
Crane's Parchmont	A	H_3PO_4	brush or rod	10	BS, NYC
Crane's Platinotype	A	H_3PO_4/HCA	brush or rod	10	BS, NYC
Fabriano Murillo	A	H_3PO_4/HCA	brush	8	G, DS, NYC
Fabriano Perusia	N	H_3PO_4/HCA	brush	9	NYC
Gampi	A	H_3PO_4/HCA	brush or rod	10	DS, NYC
Lenox (Parsons)	A	H_3PO_4/HCA	brush or rod	10	G, DS, NYC
Masa	A	H_3PO_4/HCA	brush	8	G, DS, NYC
Rising Drawing Bristol	A	H_3PO_4/HCA	brush or rod	10	DS, PT
Rising Gallery 100	B	H_3PO_4/HCA	brush or rod	9	G, DS, NYC
Strathmore Series 500 Bristol	A	H_3PO_4/HCA	brush or rod	10	NYC, PT
Twinrocker Watercolor	N	HCA	brush	9	TR, DS, NYC
Van Gelder Simili Japon	N	H_3PO_4/HCA	brush or rod	9	BS, NYC, PT

TABLE 5.2 Other Papers Exhibiting Coarser Tonal Values

Paper Name	*pH*	*Clearing Bath*	*Coating Tool*	*Tone Quality*	*Source*
Coventry Rag	B	H_3PO_4/HCA	brush	4	DS, NYC
Fabriano Classico CP	B	H_3PO_4/HCA	brush	3	DS
Magnani Italia	B	H_3PO_4/HCA	brush	3	DS
Magnani Pescia	B	H_3PO_4/HCA	brush	4	DS
Moulin Du Gue	N	H_3PO_4/HCA	brush	7	DS, NYC, PT
Saunders Waterford HP	B	H_3PO_4/HCA	brush	5	DS
Somerset Satin	B	H_3PO_4/HCA	brush	5	DS, NYC
Strathmore 400	B	H_3PO_4/HCA	brush	7	SS

The tonal values may improve with double coating.

CHAPTER 6

The First Print

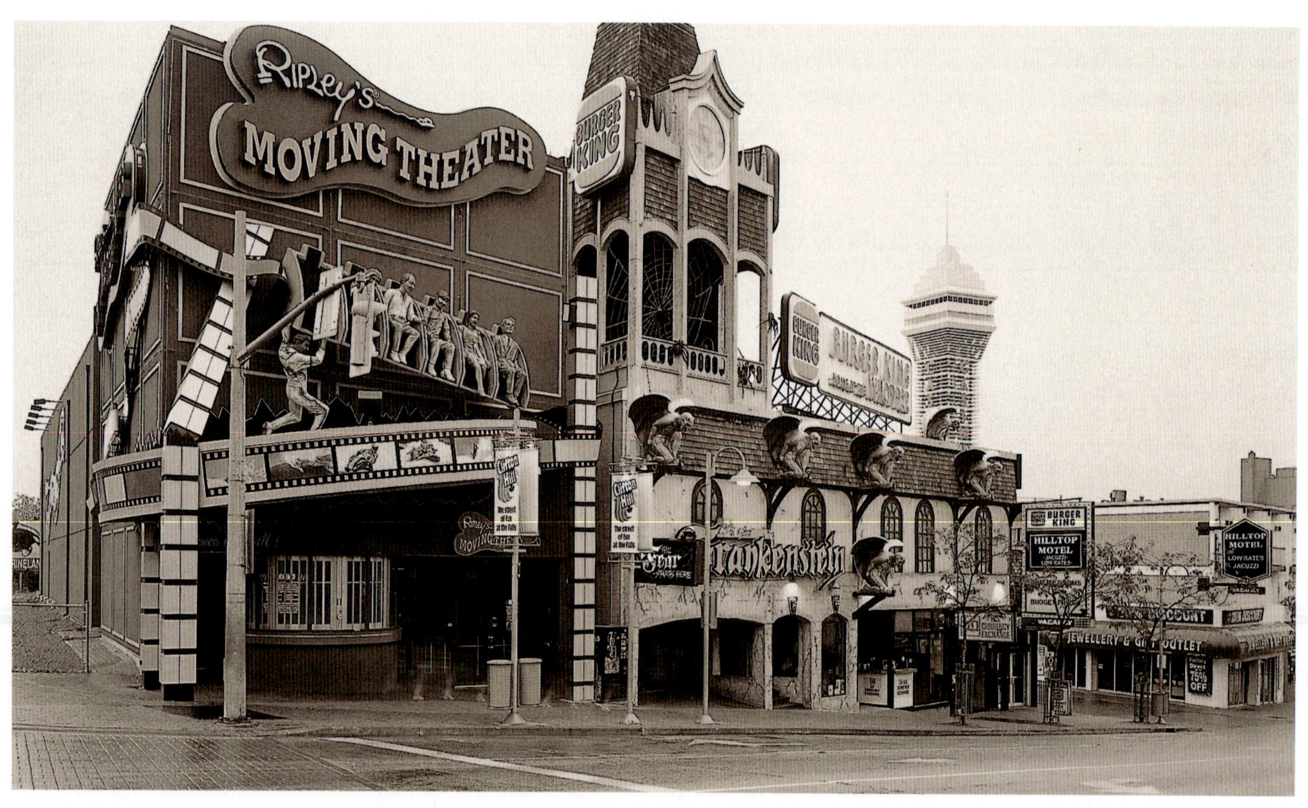

PLATE 6.1 Niagara Falls, Ontario. 1997 12 × 20 inch Pd

If you have made some platinum or palladium prints, you may want to skip this section, and go on to Chapter 7, "Calibration," and Chapter 8, "The Platinum and Palladium Print." If not, now may be the time to cast theory aside for a while and simply enjoy the thrill of seeing—for the first time—a palladium print come immediately to life after contact with the developer. However imperfect it may be, do it! And if you do not have a UV light source, do it in the sun!

The Sun Print

The sun was the first source of light for photographic printmaking. It is still the primary UV light used by many platinum/palladium photographers.

Complete supplies are not needed. Later on, you can supplement as necessary. Review Chapter 2, "Setting Up a Laboratory," regarding work space. Scan Chapters 7 and 8 for a general idea of procedure. See Table 8.1, "Algorithm for Platinum and Palladium Printing," for the basic procedures in the making of a platinum and palladium print. You can read them in more detail later.

The Basics

Chemicals

Purchase a basic *palladium* kit. The Bostick and Sullivan (BS) kit will contain:

The metal salt, 15 or 25 ml
Two sensitizers (with and without restrainer)
Developer (Ammonium citrate)
Clearing agent (EDTA)

Paper

Purchase 25 sheets of 11 × 14 Platinotype from BS, or get a package of Crane's Kid Finish from the stationary store.

Utensils

11 × 14 corrugated cardboard
4 oz. glass beaker containing distilled water and dropper
Blotter or fiberglass drying screen
Blow dryer
Brush (Start with a one-inch camel hair negative dusting brush. The coating rod or *Puddle Pusher*® will be discussed later in Chapter 8, "The Platinum and Palladium Print," under "Coating Instruments.")
Clean blotter
Clock-timer
Cotton gloves
Four trays not previously used for silver
Plastic 1 oz. medicine cups
Plastic pushpins
Print washer
Printing frame with a hinged back
Scissors and drafting tape (not masking tape)
Thermometer

Negative

Go through your stack of negatives to find the one with the most contrast (the shadow density must be almost transparent, but still show detail), or follow the instructions in Chapter 3, "The Negative," to produce one.

Procedure[1]

1. Pick a sunny day; work between 12:00 A.M. and 3:00 P.M. Choose an indoor space with soft incandescent lighting as your "laboratory."

2. For the paper coating, work in proportions of 12 drops of ferric oxalate sensitizer added to 12 drops of metallic salt. Depending on the size of the area to be coated, the total of 24 drops can be divided or multiplied as needed. If your first print is from a 4 × 5 negative (or two 2 1/4 negatives), a total of 24 drops will do.

NOTE: For platinum and palladium printing, contrast control is achieved by varying the proportions of two mixtures of ferric oxalate sensitizers: one (No.1 or A) is ferric oxalate only; the other (No. 2 or B) contains a restrainer, potassium chlorate.

3. Examine your negative. If it appears thin (if you are a silver printer, it most likely will be), use one part ferric oxalate sensitizer No. 1 (A) to five parts ferric oxalate No. 2 (B). (Later on, I will refer to these as A and B.) If the negative has more contrast (grade 1 silver paper),

[1] At this stage, you can rely on the instructions that come with the kit, or you can read ahead to get a better handle on the process. Check the illustrations in Chapters 7 and 8 for more information on coating.

use a 3:3 mixture of sensitizer. If it is really "contrasty," choose a 4:1 mixture.

4. Using the dropper, put the solution in a plastic medicine cup. Add an equal number of drops of palladium salt (BS solution No. 3). Refer to the photo illustrations on coating the paper in Chapter 8, "The Platinum and Palladium Print."

5. Anchor the paper to a smooth surface with drafting tape. Lightly scribe the area to be coated with a hard pencil. Allow at least 1/2 inch beyond the negative size.

6. Holding the brush in your working hand, use the other to pour the mixture on to the center of the area to be coated. Brush *quickly* to cover the image area completely. Make only two or three passes, then stop. Streaks may show; this is not of consequence.

7. Tape the paper to corrugated cardboard. Using a hair dryer set at medium, position it eight to twelve inches from the paper (Figure 8.16). Dry by constantly moving the dryer. Dry the back side. The coating should take on an orange color. Do not burn; burning will show as a deep orange or rust color. *Avoid breathing in the direct vicinity. Turn you head aside, or wear a mask.* (See Chapter 2, "Setting Up a Laboratory," for drying units.)

8. Clean the glass of the printing frame. Position the dull side of the negative on the coated paper, and orient in the center of the glass so the hinge of the back will fall midway across the negative. Lock in position. You may want to include a small step tablet (see the Step Tablet in Chapter 7, "Calibration"). Open one side of the back and peel back the paper to check that the negative does not shift (Figure 6.1). If there is a problem, the pressure can be increased by the addition of portions of felt between the paper and back.

9. Lock the holder, and place in the sun (Figure 6.2). Set a timer. After three minutes, stop the timer, unlock one half of the frame, and peel back the paper (Figure 6.3). Do this in the shade. For assessment, concentrate on the highlight and shadow areas of the print. Most likely, you will see a printing out image in the shadows, but nothing in the highlights. Lock the frame, place in the sun and restart the timer. Repeat this process every minute until a *barely discernible* image appears in the highlight area. Stop and record the time.

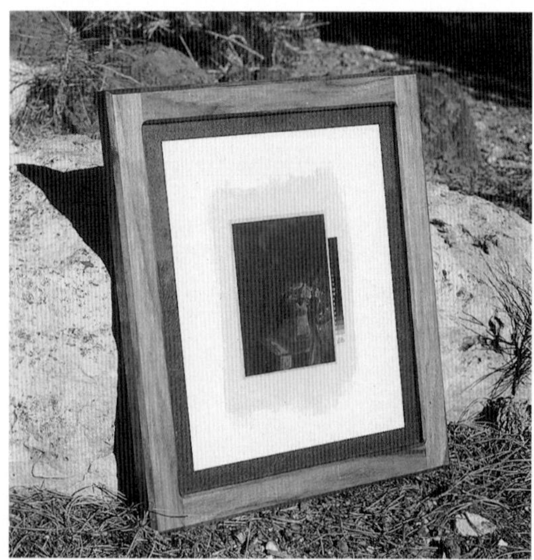

FIGURE 6.2 Exposure in the Sun

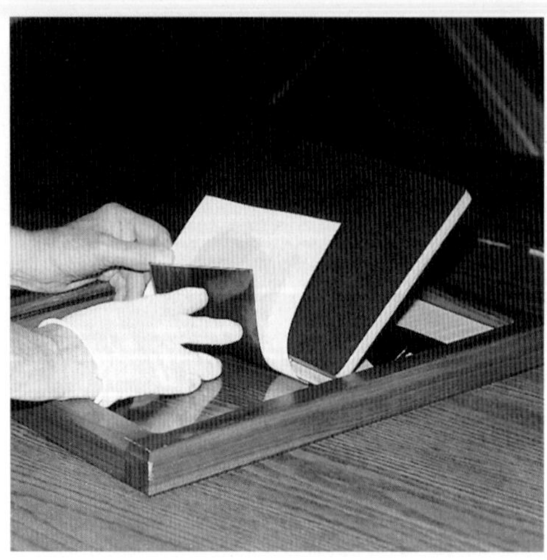

FIGURE 6.1 Checking Registration

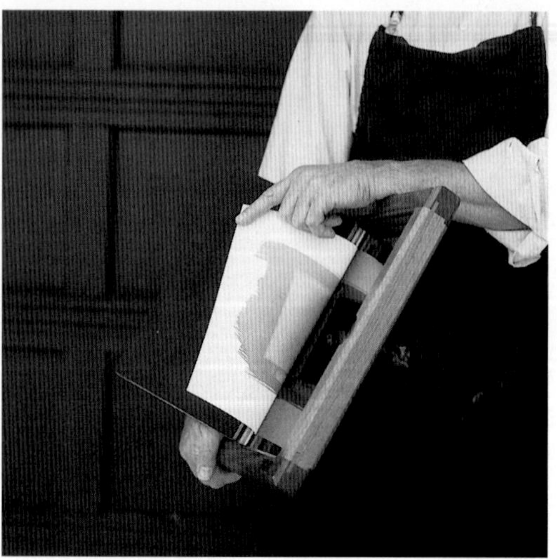

FIGURE 6.3 Checking Exposure

10. In the wet area of your lab, divide the clearing agent into three trays. Position a clean dry tray at one end. Work in soft incandescent light, such as a 40-watt bulb placed four feet from the trays. Pour the developer into a beaker. For now, use it at room temperature. Put the print face up in the dry tray. Prepare yourself (and any companion) for one of the profound joys of photography.

11. Refer to Figures 8.8 to 8.20 in Chapter 8, "The Platinum and Palladium Print." *Quickly* pour the entire amount of developer (at least one liter) onto the print. The full image will appear *immediately.* Set the timer for two minutes. Drain the print, rinse in running water and place into the first of the clearing trays. Agitate for five minutes. Keep the print face up. Repeat five minutes each in the other two trays. The paper will become quite fragile at this time; it is probably wise not to use print tongs. The print will slightly bleach. Don't worry, there will be considerable dry down.

12. Wash fifteen minutes in rapidly changing water. Avoid direct contact with the water stream—it may punch a hole in the print. Place face up to dry on a blotter or drying screen.

Assessment of the Print

If the negative is somewhat within the range of the paper coating, the print may be quite satisfactory. Using the basic controls of contrast control and printing time, the image can be fine-tuned to display many of the unique characteristics of the palladium print. Test strips can be made, printing only a portion of the negative. (For drying with the hair dryer, pin them to the corrugated cardboard.) It is likely that many platinum printers work with this trial and error method, gaining intuitive experience with time.

As appealing as printing by intuition may be, for many the time comes when more controls are needed for this costly process, particularly in the duplication of prints and the management of problematic negatives. As with a myriad of endeavors, mastery is based on the understanding and practice of technique.

CHAPTER 7

Calibration

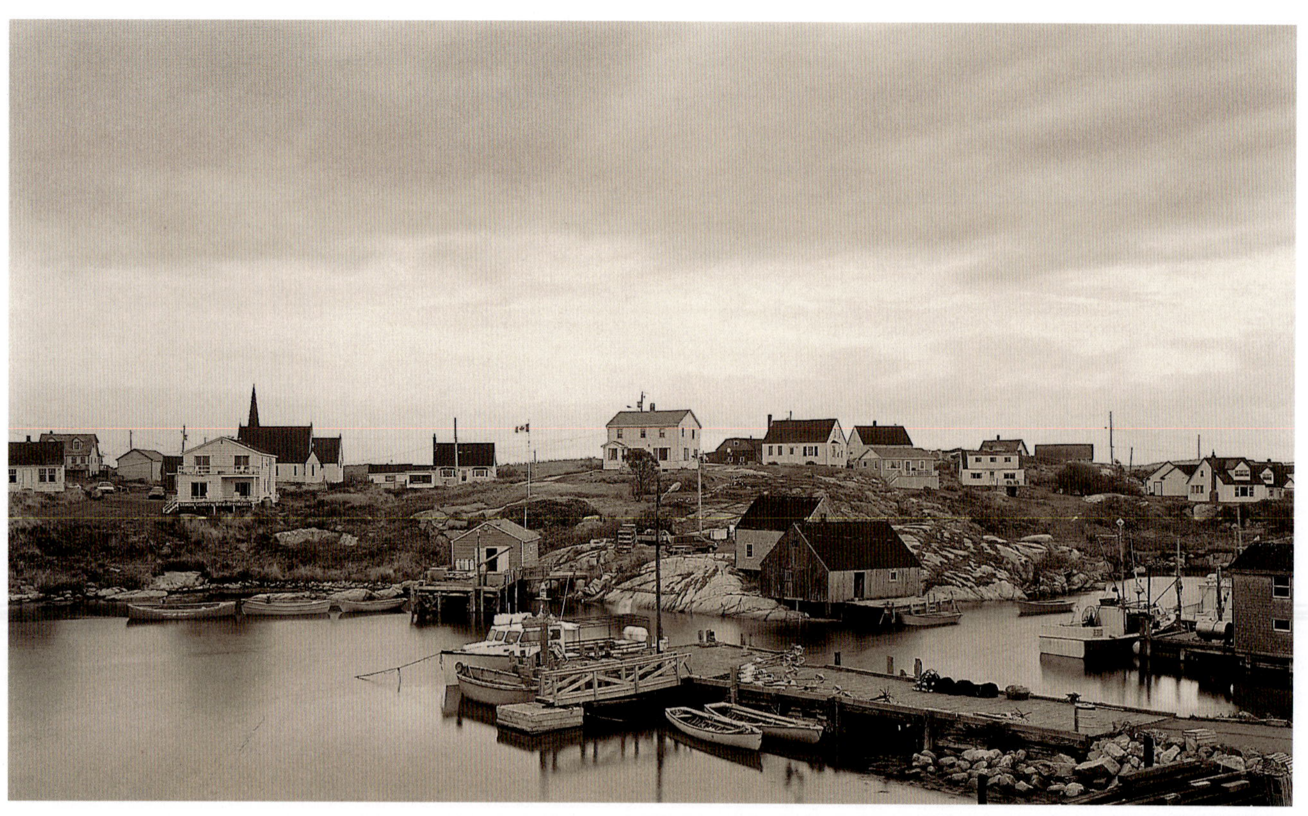

PLATE 7.1 Peggy's Cove, Nova Scotia. 1997 12 × 20 inch Pt/Pd

Calibrating the Light Source

The sun may be appealing as a source of ultraviolet light; however, it is quite inconsistent. For the more committed platinum printer, an indoor artificial light source is a necessity. The various types available are discussed in Chapter 2, "Setting Up a Laboratory."

For reproducible results, an intensity of effective ultraviolet light should be standardized. With an "ideal" platinum or palladium negative and a coating of materials mixed for medium contrast, the printing time should be approximately five minutes. This amount of time, not long enough to be burdensome, still allows for burning and dodging procedures.

Specific types of light sources present other considerations. With a point source, such as a mercury vapor bulb, the print must be placed at a distance far enough to avoid noticeable vignetting at the corners. If a large negative is used, this distance may produce printing times too long to be practical. With a bank of fluorescent tubes, the ideal distance may be three to four inches, causing an uneven spread of light from each bulb and the space between the next. This "scalloping" effect can be solved by moving the printing frame occasionally during printing. This is another reason for designing the light box to radiate down from a horizontal position.

Following the determination of a time/distance factor, the contrast controls available with the combination of light, sensitizers, and paper can be analyzed.

Choosing a Print-to-Light Distance

Adjustment of most light sources will begin by choosing an optimum light-to-print distance. The intensity of light is a function of the square of the distance from the light source. Therefore, a print placed two inches from the light source will receive four times the light as a print placed four inches. The same effect would be achieved between distances of five and ten inches.

$$\frac{(2\times 2)}{(4\times 4)} = \frac{4}{16} = \frac{1}{4} \qquad \frac{(5\times 5)}{(10\times 10)} = \frac{25}{100} = \frac{1}{4}$$

To calculate less convenient proportions, use the same formula. For the differences between six and nine inches, do the following:

$$\frac{(6\times 6)}{(9\times 9)} = \frac{36}{81} = 0.44 \text{ or } \frac{4}{9}$$

Therefore, a print placed at nine inches would receive 4/9 or 44% the amount of light as a print placed at six inches.

In practice, once this general concept is understood, the light source can be optimized by experiments with a negative of known values: the step tablet.

The Step Tablet

A step tablet is a manufactured negative with 21 steps or "wedges" of *transmission densities*. Starting at a transmission density of 0.05, each successive step increases by one half stop (0.15) (Table 7.1). Each step is numbered, so by contact printing the negative, the numbered transmission density can be matched to the *reflective density* produced on the print.

Transmission Densities

Step tablets come calibrated or uncalibrated. The calibrated version is more expensive and not generally necessary. The uncalibrated versions are accurate enough for any use in normal photography. Simply assign the transmission densities listed to each numbered step (see Table 7.1). The range of transmission densities (the *density range*) of the step tablet far exceeds the reproduction capabilities of any photographic print material.

A variety of step tablets are available:

0.5 × 5 inches (Figure 7.1)

Kodak Photographic Step Tablet #2, uncalibrated and calibrated	$25.00–$45.00
Stouffer T2115	$6.00

4 × 5 inches (Figure 7.2)

Stouffer TP 4 × 5	$25.00

(Sources: Photo Supply, DI, GAS)

TABLE 7.1 The Step Tablet Transmission Density Values

Step Nr.[a]	*Transmission Density*	*Step Nr.*	*Transmission Density*
1	.05	11	1.55
2	.20	12	1.70
3	.35	13	1.85
4	.50	14	2.00
5	.65	15	2.15
6	.80	16	2.30
7	.95	17	2.45
8	1.10	18	2.60
9	1.25	19	2.75
10	1.40	20	2.90
		21	3.05

[a] To avoid confusion regarding the mixture and step tablet numbers, I will use *No.* for contrast mixtures and the European abbreviation *Nr.* for the step tablet.

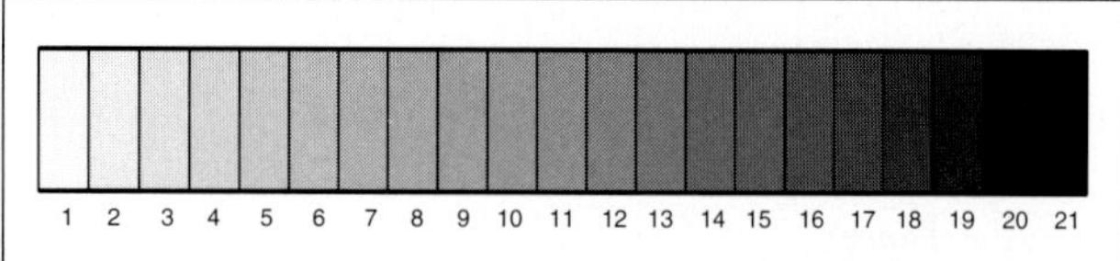

FIGURE 7.1 The 0.5 × 5 Inch Step Tablet as Seen through Transmitted Light

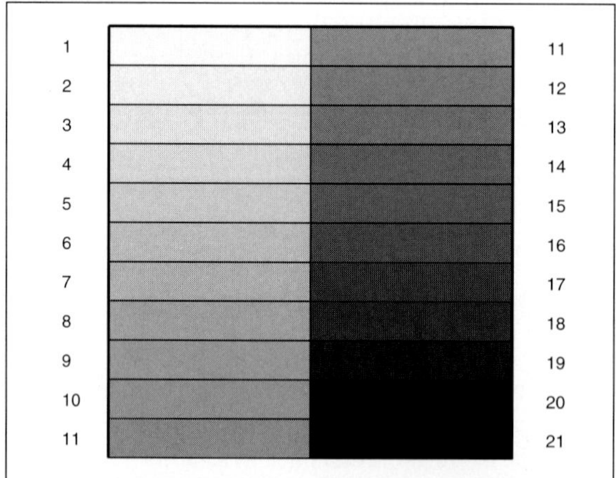

FIGURE 7.2 The Stouffer 4 × 5 Inch Step Tablet Showing Transmission Densities. The step numbers have the same transmission densities as the smaller 0.5 × 5 inch step tablet shown in Figure 7.1.

The smaller step tablets are good for beginning work and for placing alongside of prints for "fine tuning." For more extensive work, such as paper or film testing, the 4 × 5 inch is recommended.

Reflective Densities

The print made from a step tablet can be quantitatively measured with a reflection densitometer (Figure 7.3). When comparing relative densities, however, the eye can be quite sufficient. In fact, the eye is more sensitive than the densitometer when noting barely discernible changes in whites.

Note in Figure 7.3 that only a portion of the step tablet is printed. The number of steps that can be printed represents the latitude or *exposure scale* (ES) of the photographic paper. This can be altered by changing contrast grades and paper development techniques. The portion of the step tablet printed is a function of *printing time* and the *speed* of the photographic paper. Therefore, if in Figure 7.3, for example, more printing time was given or a faster material was used, the darker

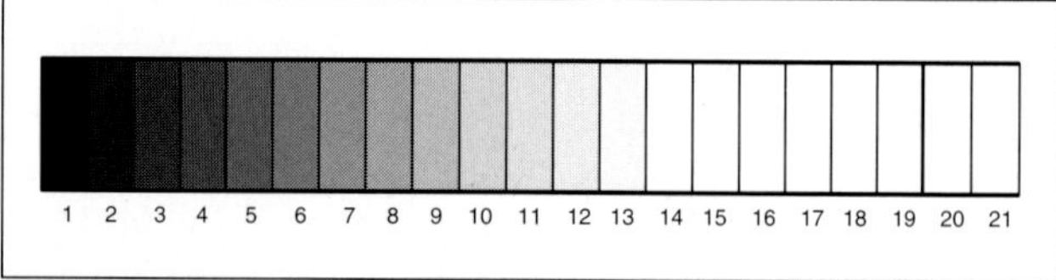

FIGURE 7.3 The Printed Step Tablet Showing Reflected Densities

steps would move from left to right, that is, from lower to higher (more dense) step numbers.

If, when a negative is printed, a step tablet is also included alongside, similar transmission densities of the negative and step tablet can be compared to the printed image. Using the step tablet values as a known entity, adjustments can be made in printing time and contrast to improve the image. At the end of Chapter 8, "The Platinum and Palladium Print," see the section entitled "Using the Combined Step Tablet and Print to Adjust Printing Time and Contrast"; consult Plates 8.2 to 8.8 as well. With practice, printing speed and paper contrast can be determined with this method. A reflective densitometer is not needed, as discussed in the next section.

The "Visual Comparison Densitometer"

If transmission density values are placed for comparison, the human eye is capable of distinguishing subtle relative differences. The "visual comparison densitometer" is simply a dark cardboard through which a small circular hole has been cut. Looking through the aperture, shades of gray can be isolated from others. Comparisons can be made from a known transmission density to match print values. (See Figures 7.4 and 7.5.) If, for example, one wishes to know the shadow trans-

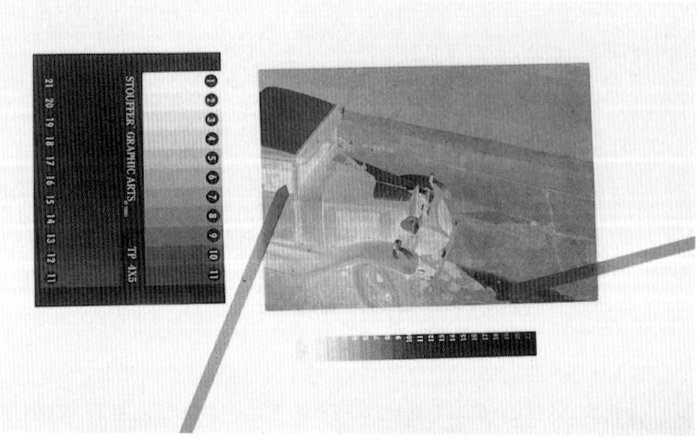

FIGURE 7.4 Examining Transmission Density

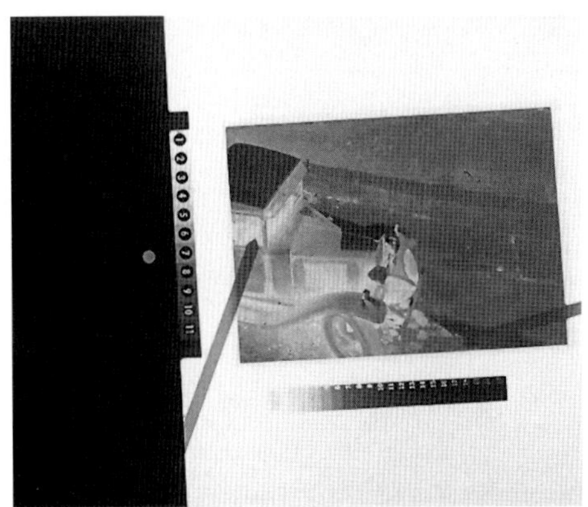

FIGURE 7.5 Examining Transmission Density with the "Visual Comparison Densitometer"

mission density of a negative, isolate it, and then find the matching value in the step tablet. If it is step Nr. 3, that transmission density is 0.35.

Technique: Time/Distance A+B Method

The two most commonly used methods to make platinum/palladium (Pt/Pd) prints will be covered in the chapter:

Restrainer in the sensitizers *(A+B Method)*

Restrainer in the developer *(The Dichromate Method)*

The A+B method is the most popular and versatile, and it will be featured in this text. The Malde/Ware method and the Ziatype are found in Appendix D, "The Ammonium-Based Processes."

The basic supplies used for the *first print,* covered in Chapter 6, are applicable here. However, since standardization is the goal, you must choose a metal (either platinum/palladium or pure palladium), paper, and developer. Using the notes in Chapter 6, "The First Print," you may want to experiment a bit to determine choices, check with other platinum printers, or take a workshop. At this point, it is highly recommended that detailed notes regarding metal and sensitizer combinations, paper, light and distance, developer and temperature, and clearing agent be kept. It is best that they are recorded on the paper next to the printed image.

As a start, I would recommend the following:

Platinum/palladium salts mixed 1:1.

Sensitizers.[1]

Crane's Natural Crest White Wove (Platinotype) paper from BS.

Potassium oxalate developer at 90°F (32°C).[2]

Review the section on clearing agents in Chapter 4, "Chemicals." As well as calibrating the light source, the effectiveness of clearing agents can be checked on the step tablet prints. Too strong a clearing agent will bleach the print. Too little action will not clear the highlights.

The goal in this procedure is to establish a light-to-print distance that will cause at least two of the least dense of the steps of the step tablet to merge with the portions of the print not covered by the step tablet at a printing time of ten minutes (400 units for the nuArc printer).[3] The merging of maximum blacks will show that the printing distance has the capability or "horsepower" to reach a maximum paper black at a reasonable time. If more than three blacks merge, the print to light distance is probably too short.

A standard time of ten minutes will allow easy divisions and multiplication for advanced sensitometry. In actuality, following this standardization, an "ideal" negative with a shadow density of 0.3 and 1:1 proportions of the two sensitizers will print in five minutes.

1. For use with the 0.5 × 5 inch step tablet, cut the paper to 7 × 1.5 inches. With the Stouffer 4 × 5 step tablet, cut the paper to at least 4.5 × 5.5 inches. Also, with the 4 × 5 step tablet, it is helpful to trim the borders on one side until the clear portions are at the edge. Then the blacks produced by the scale can easily be seen as they merge with the maximum paper black. Note that some papers have a preferred printing side.

1. Bostick and Sullivan produces two No. 2 ferric oxalate mixtures containing different amounts of the potassium chlorate restrainer: 0.6% (No. 2 Pt) and 1.2% (No. 2 Pd). The 1.2% produces a shorter paper exposure scale and is made to compensate for the greater scale of Pd over Pt/Pd mixtures. At this time, I recommend the No. 2 Pt 0.6% sensitizer. For reasons to be subsequently discussed, I also prefer this mixture for the pure Pd print.

2. Potassium oxalate, in my opinion, is the most natural and versatile of developers. With Pt/Pd mixtures it produces a slightly warm tone. In the pure Pd print, the warmth of tone is accentuated, particularly at higher developer temperatures. Slightly heating the developer facilitates its action, enhances the print tone, and produces a slight increase in printing speed.

3. Light integrators, which measure light in units, are part of most commercial plate burners. It is best if they are adjusted to allow for exposures from four to ten minutes, allowing enough time for dodging and burning.

2. Coat paper with a mixture[4] of 50% each of sensitizers A and B with an equal amount of 50% each of the platinum and palladium salt solutions (see next section for coating techniques). Mark the back with pencil: *Mixture No. 7 Pt/Pd.*

NOTE: Hereafter, I will use "A" for ferric oxalate with no restrainer and "B" for the one containing potassium chlorate.

3. Pin each end of paper to corrugated cardboard with a plastic pushpin.

4. Dry with a hair dryer. Remove paper from cardboard. (Note: the pins may be hot!)

5. Tape step tablet, shiny side up, to paper with two small pieces of drafting tape. You should be able to read the numbers. It is helpful to place and remove the tape from clothing a few times to remove the excess adhesive.

6. Place the paper in the printing frame and choose a print-to-light distance. Twelve inches is a good start for a mercury vapor lamp; 3 inches is good for a fluorescent light box. Set the nuArc at 400 units.

7. Expose for 10 minutes or 400 units with a nuArc printer.

8. Develop, clear, and dry the strip. You can also dry the strip in a microwave at a 50% setting.

9. Look at printed steps (Figure 7.6). There should be two to three black steps that are maximum black, indistinguishable from each other. If there are too many, increase the distance to light or adjust the light integrator. If you do not have enough, decrease the distance. Having the square of the distance concept in mind, you can make adjustments accordingly. Do not worry about clear steps on print at this time.

10. When print distance is established (try to stay at 10 minutes, particularly if you plan to use advanced sensitometric techniques), go on to contrast control.

Technique: Contrast Control

The step tablet print obtained in the previous test represents the contrast obtained with a 1:1 or "normal" mixture of sensitizers, comparable to a "Grade 2" paper. Now, it will be seen that we have at least twelve more varying contrast grades available in Pt/Pd. Six have less contrast than the 1:1 mixture of sensitizers A and B, and six have more contrast, for a total of thirteen. They will be identified as contrast grades No. 1 through No.

[4] If you are committed to pure palladium (Pd), standardize with only the palladium salt and sensitizers.

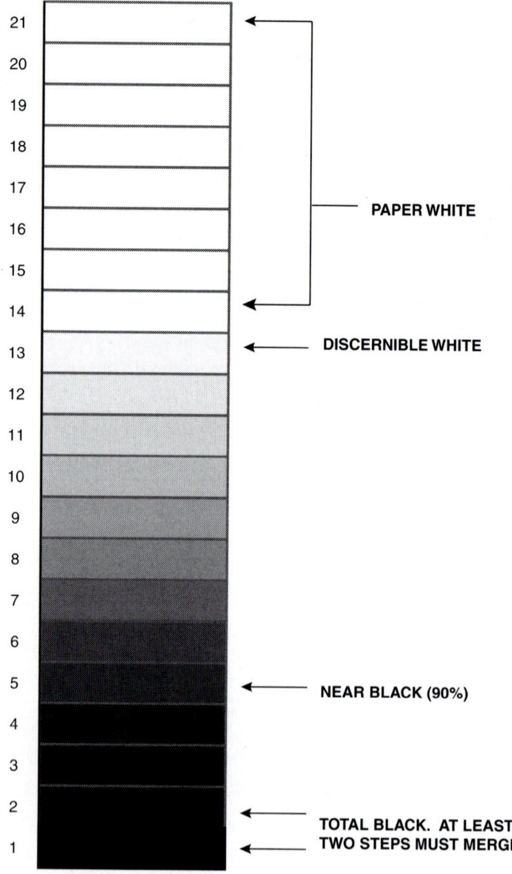

FIGURE 7.6 Reading the Step Tablet to Determine Printing Time

13. The "normal" mixture of 50% each of A and B will be termed contrast mixture No. 7.

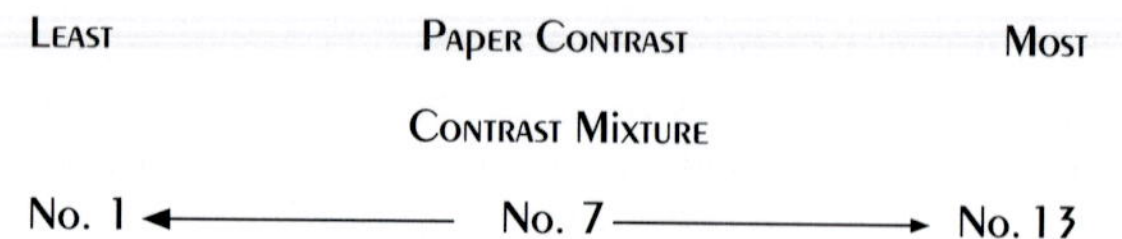

Contrast is determined by mixing proportions of A and B up to a total of twelve drops. (You may want to look ahead to Table 7.2, "Standard Negative Contrast Ranges for Platinum/Palladium Prints," to understand this concept.) Because of the smaller area to be coated, I chose those combinations of twelve that can be divided by two.

1. Cut seven strips of paper each to the appropriate size. Mark them 1, 3, 5, 7, 9, 11, and 13. Here it helps to have a number of step tablets.

2. Refer to A-B contrast mixtures in Table 7.2. Use mixture Nos. 1, 3, 5, 7, 9, 11, and 13. Note that since

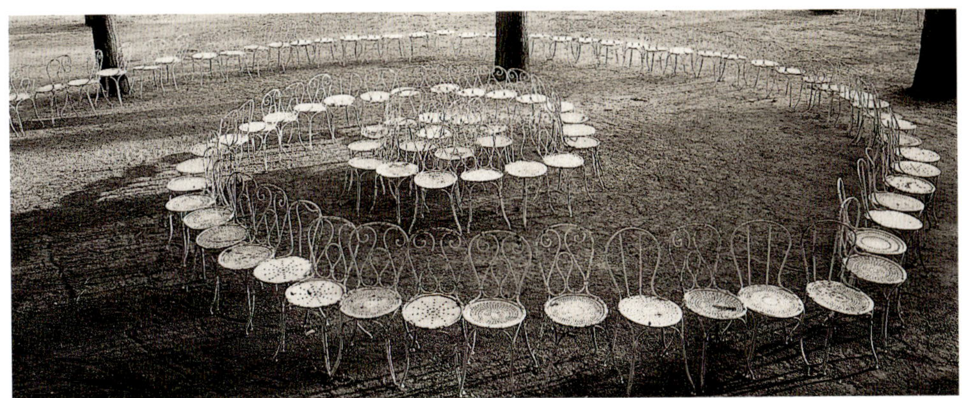

PLATE 7.2 Chairs I, Vichy, France. 1994 7 × 17 inch Pd

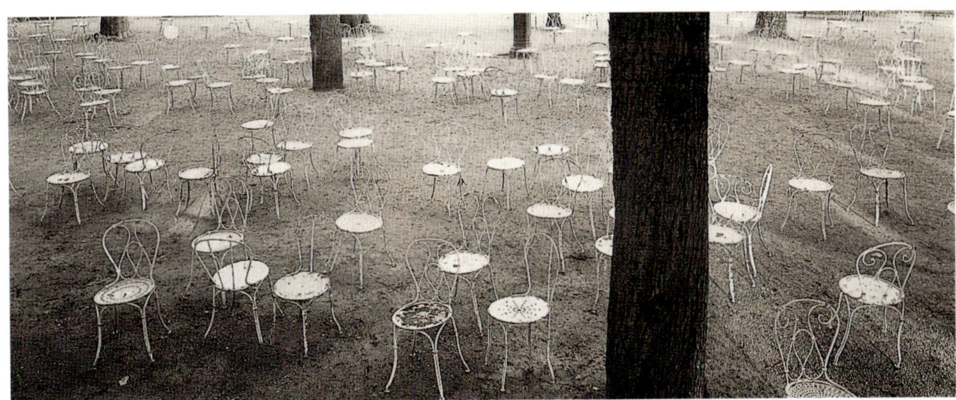

PLATE 7.3 Chairs II, Vichy France. 1994 7 × 17 inch Pd

all drops are even-numbered, you can divide all proportions in half; for example, mixture No. 3 is A–5 drops, B–1 drop, and C–6 drops. Coat each strip as before. Each time, you must start with a clean dry brush or use the coating rod described in the next chapter. With the coating rod, you will need at least one 1 ml hypodermic syringe that can be cleaned and dried with each mixture.

3. Print each strip at the predetermined time/distance. Develop, clear, and dry all strips.

4. Align the strips side by side in good light, black on bottom.

5. Following Figure 7.7, find the blackest step and go up two steps to near black (90%). In the illustration, it is step Nr. 5. This should be at a point where the shadow is easily discernible from maximum black (Dmax). It usually lies two steps from maximum black. The near black is called *IDmax*. Including the near-black step, count steps until you reach the barely discernible white step.

NOTE: The concept of the 90% black will be further discussed in Part Two, "Sensitometry for the Platinum/Palladium Process." Briefly, the blackest portion of the characteristic paper curve does not separate easily, producing shadow areas that are blocked. When viewing a monochromatic print without another tone for comparison, the human eye will translate any reasonable black tone to its designed place in the total scale. The 90% black meets this criterion and utilizes the more vertical portion of the paper curve that is capable of separating tones of black. This phenomenon was defined by Minor White to be a *convincing black*. (See Chapter 3, "The Negative.") Also, see Davis, *Beyond the Zone System* (1998).

NOTE: I have already noted that a reflection densitometer is not necessary for platinum printing. At this time, you may discover the sensitivity of the human eye, particularly in its ability to discern tones of white. In this aspect, it is more accurate than the machine!

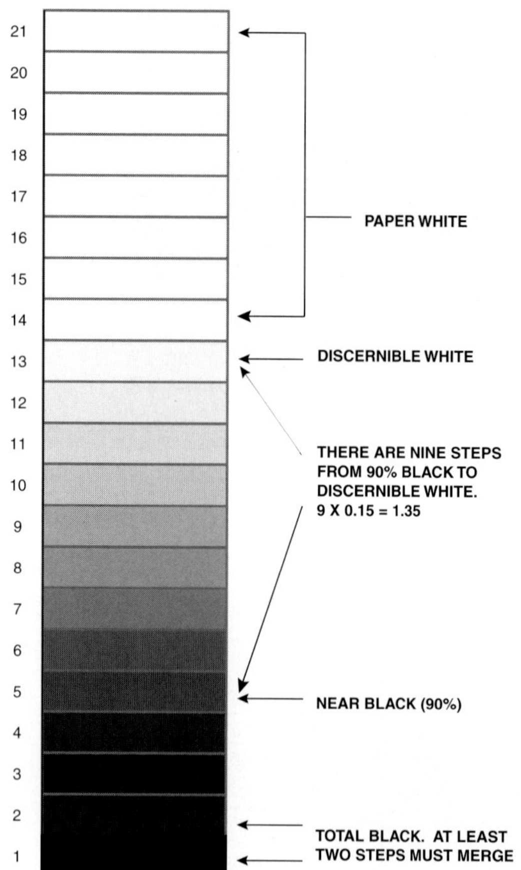

FIGURE 7.7 Reading the Step Tablet to Determine Contrast Mixtures (Mixture No. 7)

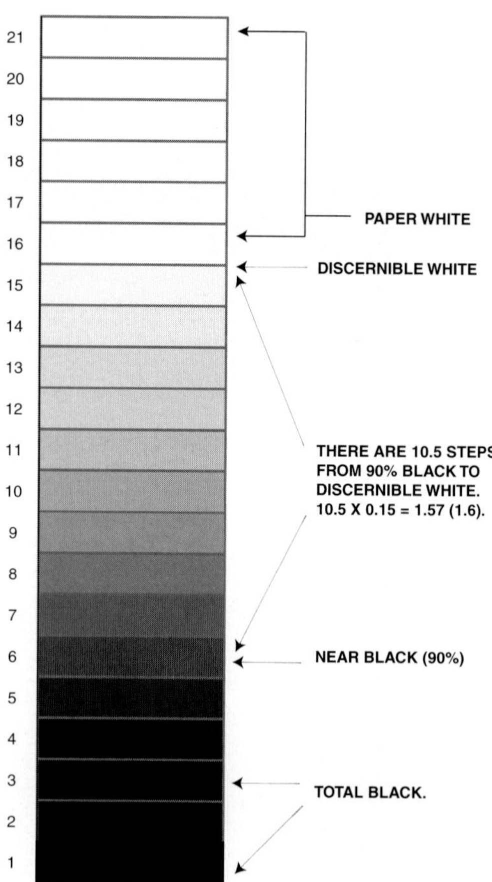

FIGURE 7.8 The Step Tablet from a No. 3 Contrast Mixture

6. Each step of the step tablet represents 1/2 stop of negative transmission density, or a 0.15 density increase or decrease (Figure 7.1). Each two steps represents one stop or a 0.3 density change. If you count nine steps for mixture No. 7, the ideal negative for that contrast mixture is 1.35 (9 × .15 = 1.35) (Figure 7.7).

Under normal conditions, mixture No.1 should produce twelve steps between 90% black and discernible white. This mixture can be used with a negative of 1.8 density range (12 × 0.15 = 1.8). Unfortunately, without any restrainer, it is subject to fog. More practical is a No. 3 mixture that provides nearly as much density range with minimum fog: 1.6[5] (Figure 7.8). Note that the 90% black step has moved from step Nr. 5 to step Nr. 6, indicating that the No. 3 mixture has a faster printing speed (1/2 stop). Step Nr. 6 has 0.15 or 1/2 of a stop more density than Step Nr. 5; *therefore, since the same 90% black is printed though more density with mixture No. 3, it is 1/2 a stop faster than mixture No. 7.*

For a useful test, use the full twelve drops to make a No. 2 step tablet print (11A:1B). There should be no fog and you should yield a contrast of 1.7 (Figure 7.9). If you have fog with this mixture, check your laboratory lights by doing the same coating in the dark. Forty-watt lights at a distance of four feet should produce no fog. If you get fog while coating in complete darkness, the ferric oxalate is probably old, and a significant portion has gone to ferrous. See "Fog versus Stain" in Chapter 10, "Problems."

Mixture No. 13 should produce seven steps from 90% black to discernible white for a 1.05 to 1.10 negative density range (Figure 7.10). Note that in this case the increase amount of restrainer used has slowed the printing speed one full stop. The 90% black is now in step Nr. 3. *Therefore, since the same 90% black is*

[5] It is actually 1.57. In reading densities, we round off to the nearest 0.05.

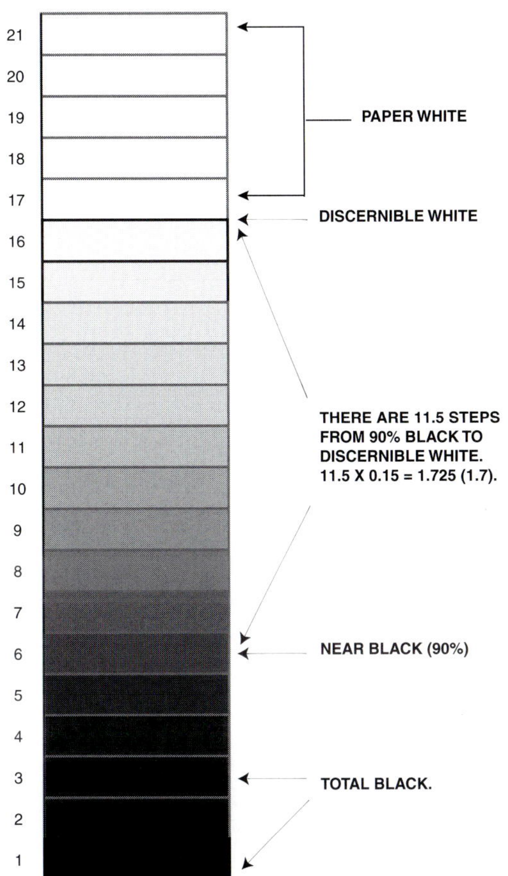

FIGURE 7.9 The Step Tablet from a No. 2 Contrast Mixture

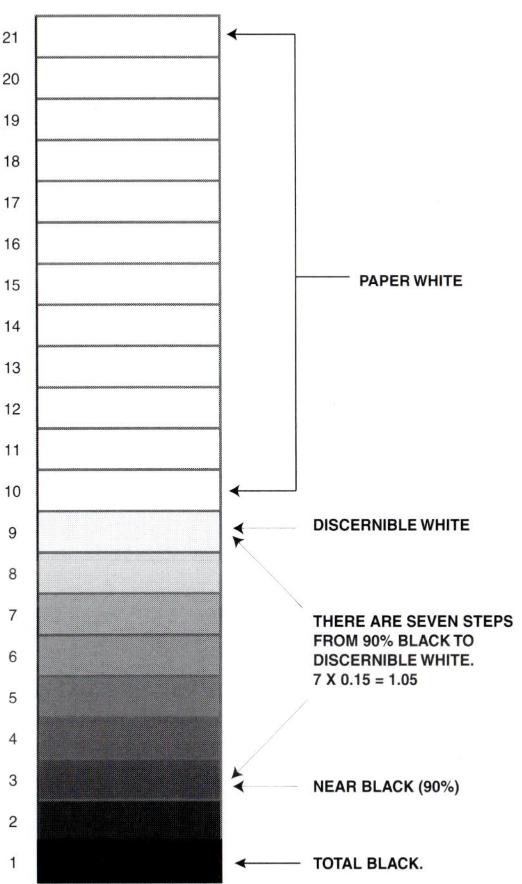

FIGURE 7.10 The Step Tablet Made from a No. 13 Contrast Mixture

printed through less density with mixture No. 13, it is 0.3 or a full stop slower than mixture No. 7. Note that with this mixture, two maximum black steps may not merge. This is not significant; we know that this mixture is capable of producing a maximum black.

NOTE: Compared to the standard No. 7 (normal) contrast mixture, the lower numbered contrast mixtures exhibit faster printing speeds. The higher numbered contrast mixtures have slower printing speeds. These differences will be quantified in Chapter 12, "Using the Print Curves."

Palladium

When using pure palladium, similar tests should be done for printing speed and contrast mixtures. If the same sensitizer BS No. 2 Pt is used (0.6% chlorate), printing speed should be approximately the same as with Pt/Pd. Realize, however, that palladium has an inherently greater latitude (exposure scale). *With a negative at a given density range, palladium will require more restrainer than Pt/Pd to produce a comparable image and will, therefore, exhibit a slower printing speed.* A negative with a 1.4 density range (DR) can print with a No. 7 Pt/Pd mixture. The same negative will require a No. 11 contrast mixture with Pd.

If BS Sensitizer No. 2 Pd is used (1.2% chlorate), pure Pd will approximate the contrast found with Pt/Pd. But the increased concentration of chlorate will significantly slow printing speed. If this is your choice, tests must be done with this concentration.

Standard Negative Contrast Ranges: The A+B Method

If the tests are done correctly, there will be surprisingly little differences found between one laboratory and another. The characteristics are reproducible to the point that *Standard Negative Contrast Ranges* can be listed for each combination of metal and sensitizer (Table 7.2).

NOTE: *Note, however, that the choice of paper and developer may effect printing speed.* Extreme variations of developer temperature may cause perceptible changes in paper contrast.

About the *Standard Negative Contrast Ranges*

- Ferric oxalate with 0.6% restrainer was used with both Pt/Pd and Pd.
- For teaching purposes, the DR of a No. 7 mixture has been set from 1.35 to 1.40.
- The Pt/Pd mixture is 50% of each metallic salt.
- Note that intermediate, even numbered mixtures may be used in printing.
- A No. 13+ mixture can be employed by using all Ferric oxalate B with 1.2% Chlorate (BS No. 2 pd). The DR for Pt/Pd will be 1.0. The DR for Pd will be approximately 1.2.
- Using a brush, a total of 24 drops should be enough for a 5 × 7 print. Use 48 drops for an 8 × 10 print. With a coating rod, following practice, 1/3 less material can be used.

Standard Negative Contrast Ranges: The A+B Method for the Pyro Negative

Utilizing the conversion data described in Chapter 3, "The Negative," a similar Standard Negative Contrast Range table can be constructed for the pyro negative (Table 7.3).

TABLE 7.2 Standard Negative Contrast Ranges for Platinum/Palladium and Palladium Prints. A+B Method

Mixture	*Negative Contrast*	*Solution*	*Drops*
No. 1	[a] Very Contrasty	A	12
	Platinum/Palladium (1.8)	B	0
	Palladium (2.1)	C	12
No. 2	Very Contrasty	A	11
	Platinum/Palladium (1.7)	B	1
	Palladium (1.9)	C	12
No. 3	Contrasty	A	10
	Platinum/Palladium (1.6)	B	2
	Palladium (1.8)	C	12
No. 5	High Medium	A	8
	Platinum/Palladium (1.5)	B	4
	Palladium (1.7)	C	12
No. 7	Medium	A	6
	Platinum/Palladium (1.4)	B	6
	Palladium (1.6)	C	12
No. 9	Low Medium	A	4
	Platinum/Palladium (1.3)	B	8
	Palladium (1.5)	C	12
No. 11	Thin	A	2
	Platinum/Palladium (1.2)	B	10
	Palladium (1.4)	C	12
No. 13	Very Thin	A	0
	Platinum/Palladium (1.1)	B	12
	Palladium (1.35)	C	12

a. Expect fog with the No. 1 mixture. Fogging should not occur with intermediate mixture No. 2.

TABLE 7.3 The Effective DR of D-76 and Pyro Negatives. *The conversion factors presented here will vary with the character of the stain and the nature of the blue filter.*

Developer	*Density Reading*	*Percent*	*Contrast Mixture and Converted DR*						
			No. 2	No. 3	No. 5	No. 7	No. 9	No. 11	No. 13
D-76	Clear Filter	100%	1.7	1.6	1.5	1.4	1.3	1.2	1.1
Pyro	Blue Filter	60%	1.15	0.95	0.9	0.9	0.8	0.7	0.65
Pyro	Clear Filter	50%	0.85	0.8	0.75	0.7	0.65	0.6	0.55

The Dichromate Method: Contrast Control Ingredient in the Developer

(The following information is presented courtesy of Phil Davis.)

Printing with the Dichromate Method

The printing process will be identical to the one just described. Only potassium oxalate developer can be used. It is best used for the Pt/Pd print.

The main advantage of this technique is that all papers and test strips can be coated at the beginning of the printing session. The disadvantages are as follows:

- You will need a separate bottle of developer for each contrast range.
- Only potassium oxalate developer can be used.
- Pure palladium may not work well with this process. (This can be remedied by the addition of platinum 1:5 to the metal salt mixture.)

To calibrate with this method, you should mix the developer/restrainer combination as needed for the tests (Table 7.4). At least 1,000 ml should be mixed for each, with the appropriate sodium dichromate added to each 200 ml quantity. Very shortly, you will have at least six developers.

NOTE: For my 12 × 20 prints, I use three liters of developer. This method is, therefore, impractical for users of ultra large formats—unless you have the space and the checkbook for at least six one-gallon jugs of potassium oxalate.

1. Coat seven test strips as you would with "A+B" Method No. 1. *Use only sensitizer A.*
2. Mark the strips 1, 2, 4, 6, 8, 16, and 32. These numbers refer to the number of drops of 50% sodium dichromate per 200 ml of *potassium oxalate* developer.
3. The rest is the same as the A+B Method. Develop at 90°F. Keep developers in marked bottles. Do not discard the developer; replenish in increments of 200 ml with the proper number of drops of dichromate/200 ml.

Standard Negative Contrast Ranges: The Dichromate Method

A Standard Negative Contrast Range chart for the dichromate method can be similarly constructed. Note that the density ranges for appropriate negatives approximate those used with the A+B method. (Table 7.4).

TABLE 7.4 Standard Negative Contrast Range for the Dichromate Method

Negative Contrast for Pt/Pd 200 ml of potassium oxalate	*Drops of 50% sodium dichromate/ 200 ml of potassium oxalate*
Very Contrasty (1.80)	1
Contrasty (1.60)	2
High medium (1.50)	4
Medium (1.40)	6
Low medium (1.30)	8
Thin (1.20)	16
Very thin (1.10)	32

CHAPTER 8

The Platinum and Palladium Print

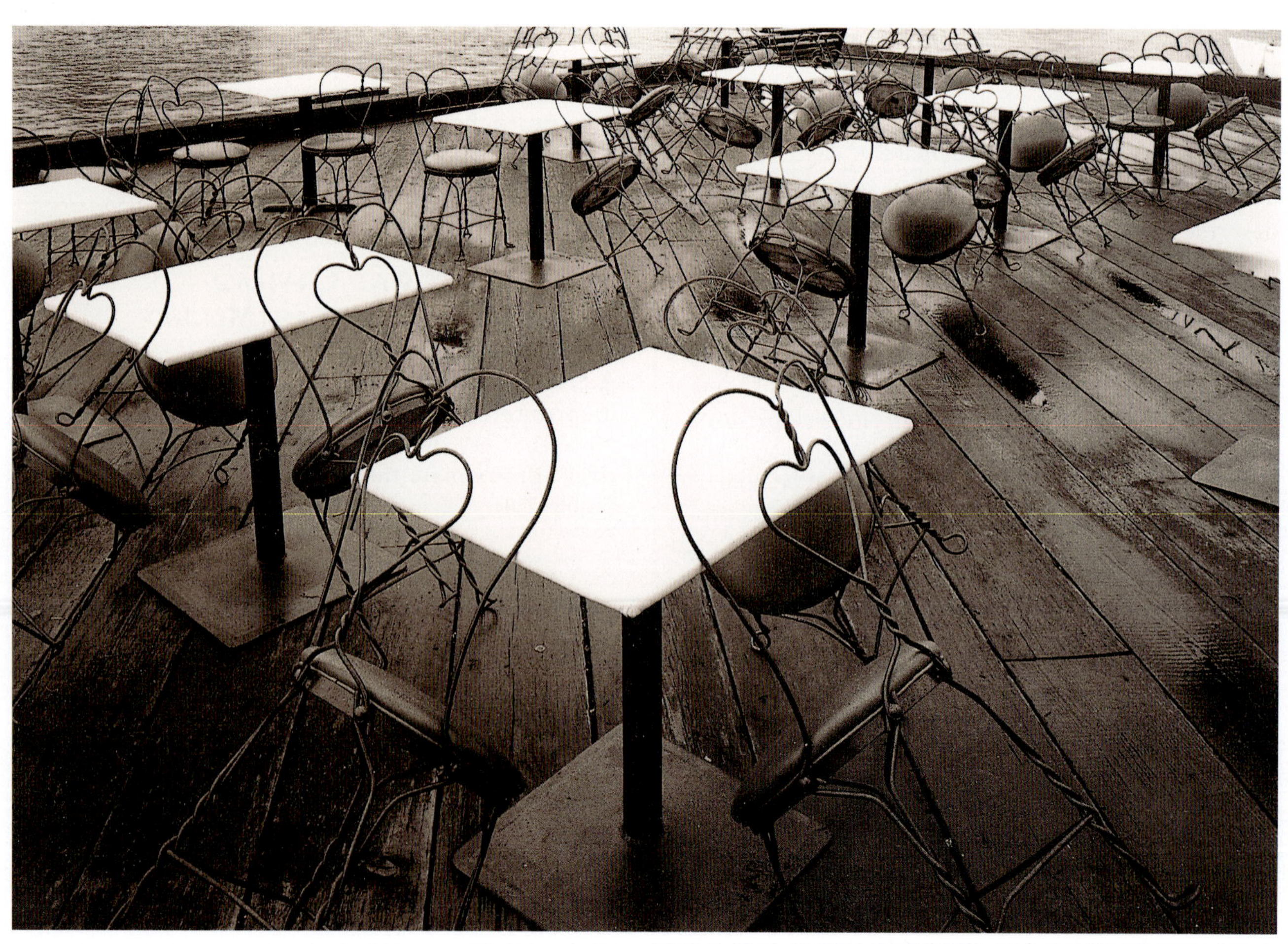

PLATE 8.1 Chairs and Tables, British Columbia. 1981 5 × 7 Pt/Pd

The following is a comprehensive guide to the making of platinum/palladium (Pt/Pd) or palladium (Pd) prints using the A+B method. Additional variations to the basic processes are covered in Chapter 9, "Advanced Technique." The Malde/Ware method and the Ziatype are introduced in Appendix D, "The Ammonium-Based Processes." An algorithm of the basic procedures for making a Pt/Pd and Pd print using the A+B method is provided (Table 8.1). Until you become familiar with the process, I recommend that you copy Table 8.1 below and Table 7.2, "Standard Negative Contrast Ranges," and keep them in your laboratory.

Discussions of "The Test Strip" and "The Final Print" are presented separately, in sequence, in two later sections of this chapter. The making of the test strip does not require the refinement of technique needed to make an acceptable final print. Nevertheless, I recommend that you read both sections and see the illustrations before starting.

Additional equipment will be required over that needed for the "first print." For the sake of completeness, I provide the entire list here.

TABLE 8.1 ALGORITHM FOR PLATINUM AND PALLADIUM PRINTING

	Read Negative	
↓		↓
Visual Assessment	or	Transmission Densities
	Choose Metal Salt (C)	
↓		↓
6 Drops Pt : 6 Drops Pd	or	12 Drops Pd
	Choose Contrast Mixture A : B	
←High Contrast Negative	Medium Contrast Negative	Low Contrast Negative→
	Contrast Mixture No.	
↓ 1 ↓ 2 ↓ 3 ↓ 4	↓ 5 ↓ 6 ↓ 7 ↓ 8 ↓ 9	↓ 10 ↓ 11 ↓ 12 ↓ 13
	See Table 7.2. *Standard Negative Contrast Ranges*	
↓	Choose Printing Time	↓
Minus 1 Stop ←	Normal	→ Plus 2/3 Stop
	Mix Sensitizers A+B 12 Drops and Metal Salts 12 Drops = 24 Drops or Equivalent	
	↓	
	Coat Paper	
↓		↓
Brush	or	Coating Rod
	Heat Dry Coating	
	↓	
	Expose to UV Light	
↓		↓
Light Box 3-12 Minutes Normal	or	nuArc 200-500 Units Normal
	Develop 2 Minutes	
↓		↓
Potassium Oxalate	or	Ammonium Citrate
	Clear Three Baths of 5 Minutes Each	
↓	↓	↓
Dilute Acid or	Hypo Clearing Agent	or EDTA
	Wash 15-20 Minutes	
	↓	
	Screen Dry Print	

Utensils

- 11 × 14 Corrugated cardboard
- Black felt tip marker
- Blow dryer
- Brush or coating rod (Puddle Pusher®)
- Canned air[1] or air syringe
- Clean blotter
- Clean kraft paper or newsprint
- Clean towels
- Clock-timer
- Corrugated cardboard
- Cotton applicators (Q-tips®)
- Cotton gloves
- Distilled water, 1 gal
- Drafting tape
- Glass beaker containing distilled water and dropper, 4 oz.
- Glass beakers or graduates
- Hypodermic syringe needed for the coating rod: 1 to 10 ml based on print size
- Kodak or Stouffer's photographic step tablets (for calibration)
- Paper
- Pencil
- Plastic 1 oz. medicine cup or shot glass
- Plastic pushpins
- Plateglass working surface (for coating rods)
- Printing frame, plateglass sandwich or vacuum easel
- Printers' Rubylith, either paper or acetate
- Scissors
- Thermometer

With all but the smallest negatives, it is desirable to make a preliminary test strip. It is also valuable to concurrently print the smaller 0.5 × 5 inch step tablet along with the test strip. Each step represents a 0.15 or 1/2 stop density difference. If the test strip is not satisfactory, make adjustments in contrast and printing time by referring to the step tablet image. See "Using the Combined Step Tablet and Print to Adjust Printing Time and Contrast" at the end of this chapter.

[1] Due to environmental concerns, many photographers prefer not to use canned air. If your laboratory has the space, or if you are adjacent to a storage area, you can rent a "C" tank of nitrogen gas. You *must* use a reducing valve to control gas pressure.

The Test Strip

Coating the Test Strip

1. Cut a 1 × 3 inch section of the paper you will use. If you plan to also print the step tablet, cut two pieces. Note the data in pencil on the back of the strips.

2. Choose a contrast mixture and printing time. Refer to Chapter 3, "The Negative," and Table 7.2, "Standard Negative Contrast Ranges for Platinum/Palladium Prints." If you are reasonably certain of the contrast mixture, you can mix enough material, or even coat the paper for the final print at this time. With larger negatives, I would resist this temptation.

3. Each extreme of mixture has disadvantages. Mixture No. 1 has a tendency to fog (no restrainer). Mixture No. 13 tends to be grainy (too much restrainer).

4. Work on a clean blotter over kraft paper or newsprint. When coating the test strip, place it over scrap paper that can be discarded. A 9.5 × 14 inch legal pad works well. After each test strip is coated, the top page can be torn off. The sensitizer (ferric oxalate) will go to ferrous oxalate with time or exposure to light. The ferrous oxalate causes the platinum or palladium to convert to the metallic state (which makes the print). See Appendix C, "Principles of the Developing and Clearing Process."

5. Place proportions from droppers in a 1 oz. plastic cup or shot glass. *Do not agitate the metal solutions.* They are in a supersaturated state. Shaking causes the particulate metal salts at the bottom of the bottle to rise to the surface and on to your paper—on the sky, naturally.

6. Place all droppers back in the bottles. *Never leave an open bottle on the table.*

7. Wet the brush with 1 or 2 drops of distilled water. Work it into the brush or follow the directions for the coating rod.

8. Using a separate dropper stored in distilled water, place 6 to 8 drops of coating material on strip(s) and immediately coat the paper.

9. Pin the strips to the cardboard and blow dry. Use the dryer 8 to 12 inches away from paper, constantly moving. Do not burn the paper coating. (See the next section, "The Final Print.") It is at this point that the most hazardous exposure to the metal and sensitizer salts may occur. To prevent the particulate matter from

entering the respiratory system, do this in a well-ventilated area. Keep the dryer at arm's length.

10. Place one strip with its emulsion side against the dull side of the negative, choosing an area that has a representation of shadows and highlights. At the side, place the other strip in contact with the step tablet.

11. Print at a predetermined time. For printing in the horizontal position, printers' Rubylith can be used to add or subtract different times.

Materials used for Developing and Clearing Test Strip

- Clock timer
- Developer in stainless steel or Pyrex beaker (1 qt. for 11 × 14 paper)
- Hot plate or heated stir plate
- Thermometer
- Tongs or (if you prefer) rubber gloves
- Tray (empty) for developer
- Trays (4) in sink, the first attached to running water, the others containing 2 quarts each of clearing agent

Developing and Clearing

1. Heat the developer to 90°F and pour into first tray. With ammonium citrate, you may wish to use it at room temperate for cooler tones. More printing time will be required than with heated potassium oxalate. The last three trays will have equal amounts of clearing agent (2 qts. each).

2. Immerse strip(s) in developer quickly. Development will be instantaneous. Develop for 1 1/2 to 2 minutes. Drain the strip, rinse in running water, and place it in first clearing bath. Gauge the contrast and printing time. The final print will be slightly darker than the strip. This part takes time and practice. The print will continue to lighten in clearing agents; don't worry, it will darken when dry. A microwave can be used to dry the test strip. Try 50% power at 10 minutes.

3. Examine the dry strip. Make sure that the highlight areas of the image and the step tablet have completely cleared. If not, change the concentration or type of clearing agent. Check the shadow values. Compare to the print of the adjacent test strip. Refer to "Using the Combined Step Tablet and Print to Adjust Printing Time and Contrast" at the end of this chapter.

4. When strip is satisfactory, coat the paper for the final print.

The Final Print

The Coating Instruments

One of the secrets for good coating is to use the right amount of material (approximately 8 to 10 drops for each 10 square inches). *Many printers err by not using enough coating material.*

The method used to measure the coating solution varies with the size of the negative. Remember, the relationships are proportional; while single drops may be significant for a 4 × 5 image, they are of less consequence for 11 × 14 or 12 × 20 sizes. Use droppers of the same manufacture, particularly when measuring the ferric oxalate. For absolute measurements of minute amounts, a pipette or 1-ml syringe can be used.

Generally, images 8 × 10 and smaller are measured in drops. For 7 × 17 and larger, it is easier to measure in milliliters (ml), using calibrated graduates of 5 to 10 ml size. Normally, 1 ml equals 12 to 18 drops. This is easily tested using your droppers. The following are suggested volumes for each print size using a brush (Table 8.2). These volumes must be adjusted for paper type, humidity, and your technique. *If you err, use too much, rather than too little solution.* For a coating rod, reduce the amount by approximately 1/3.

Brushes or coating rods may be used. Consult Chapter 5, "Paper," to find the best method for particular papers. The use of foam brushes is *not* recommended; they abrade the paper surface.

Brushes

Camel hair or Japanese Hake brushes are best for smaller prints (Figure 8.1). Purchase those of good quality with ferules made of plastic or good stainless steel. During coating, loose bristles are a nuisance. For larger (11 × 14 on up) prints, the flexible bristles of these brushes may leave areas uncoated, necessitating more

TABLE 8.2 Recommended Volume of Coating Solution for Image Size. Reduce 1/3 when Using the Coating Rod.

Image Size in Inches	*Total Volume of Solution*
4 × 5	< 24 drops
5 × 7	24-36 drops (1.5-2 ml)
8 × 10	45-60 drops (2.5-3 ml)
7 × 17	6 ml
11 × 14	8-10 ml
12 × 20	12-14 ml

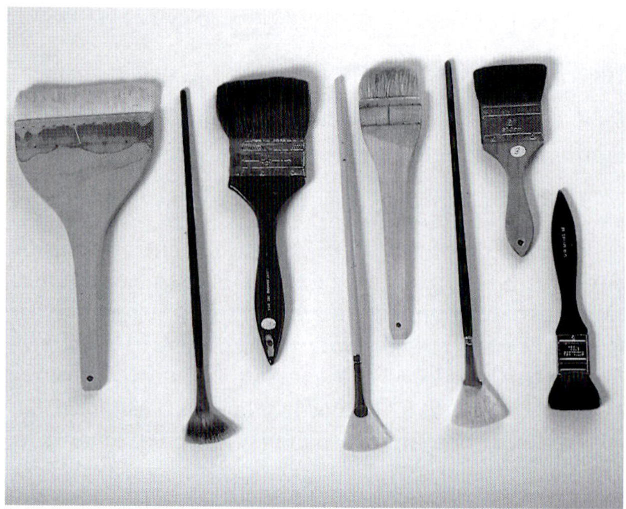

FIGURE 8.1 Brushes

passes to cover the paper. I use a high-quality China bristle three-inch house brush[2] (hog bristle) for more body. Overly expensive watercolor brushes are not necessary.

The brush should not be wet or bone dry. Each extreme causes the material to be drawn into the bristles instead of reaching the paper. For normal darkroom humidity, I place one or two drops of distilled water on the brush and work it in by rubbing it in a dry palm. (In this manipulation, take care not to splash on the paper; one drop of water on the surface will produce a permanent mark.)

Brushes are cleaned and recycled by first rinsing them in water, followed by a soak in the clearing agent. After a thorough rinse, they can be hung to dry. *Do not reuse a brush until it is dry.* Some larger natural bristle brushes come in a cardboard cover. Do not discard it, but replace it over the bristles before they are completely dry. This "former" will assure a tight grouping of the bristle tips for the next coating.

NOTE: A number of methods have been used to indicate the area to be coated on the paper. Some platinum printers scribe and outline with a hard pencil. Once a pencil mark has gone through processing, it cannot be erased. Others outline the area with masking tape. A method I have found useful with thinner papers is to place a template of black construction paper, or a rectangle drawn with a felt marker, directly under the paper to be coated. Its outline can be seen through the paper to determine the coating area.

Coating Technique: Brush

With most papers, regardless of how well sized, a water spot will form around the stagnant solution a few seconds after the solution contacts the paper. Therefore, it is essential that the solution be dispersed, however imperfectly, as quickly as possible. After the borders have been reached, the coating can be refined.

Put the liquid in a beaker or plastic cup (Figures 8.2 and 8.4). Inspect the brush for any particles or loose bristles. Examine the paper surface, blowing off any dust. If there is a defect, discard the paper. Holding the brush in your working hand, pour the entire solution, forming a bead in the center of the coating area (Figure 8.5 and 8.6).

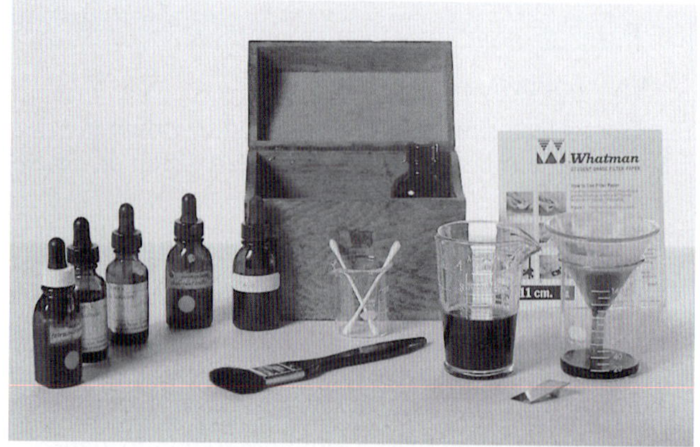

FIGURE 8.2 The Coating Solutions

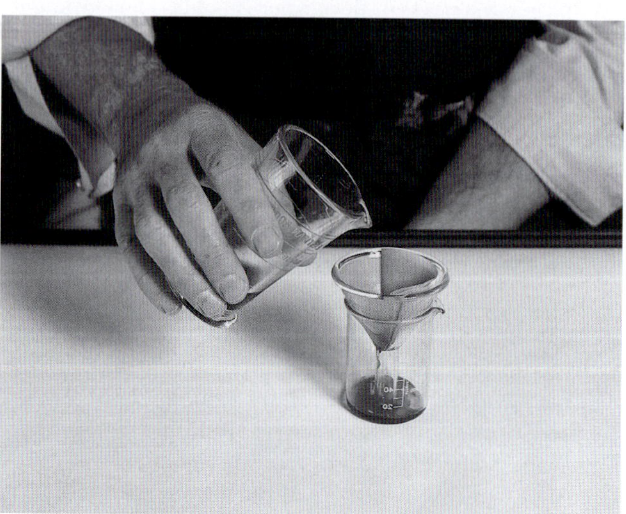

FIGURE 8.3 The Filtering of Metal Salts

2. Note that some China bristle brushes available in paint stores have been pre-oiled by the manufacturer for ease with oil based paints. Avoid these, or remove the oils with solvents before use with Pt/Pd.

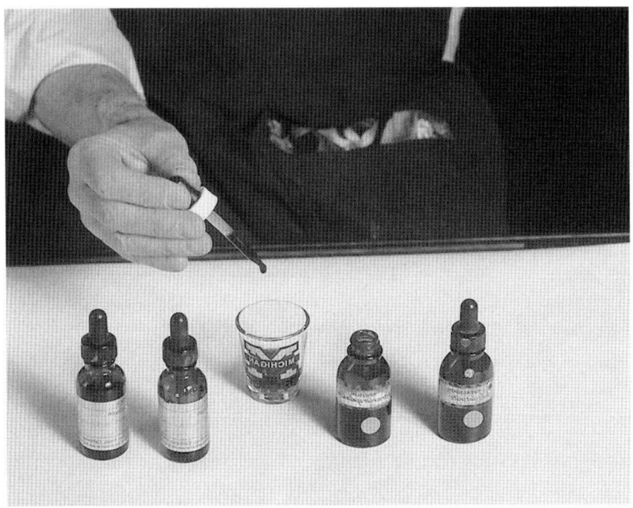

FIGURE 8.4 Measuring the Coating Solutions

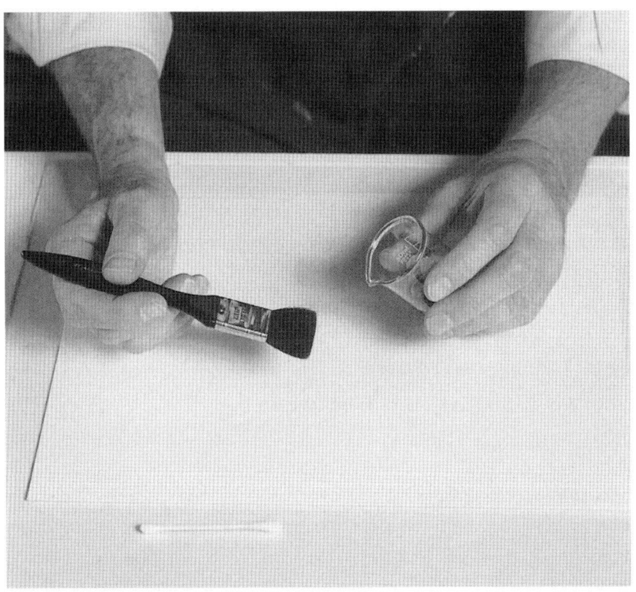

FIGURE 8.5 Ready to Coat

Immediately, sweep the material in all directions with the brush until a film covers the entire coating area (Figure 8.7).

Take a cotton applicator in the other hand. Now, using only the weight of the brush, slowly pass it across the image area. If a particle or free bristle appears, lightly take a swipe at it with the cotton applicator (Figure 8.8). *If unsuccessful after two tries, quit.* Otherwise, the cotton applicator will readily mark the softening paper nap. The particle can be dealt with later, after drying, by flicking it off with a razor blade. An undissolved metal salt (precipitant) may present problems. It may not be possible to remove it with a razor blade. Don't dig a hole in the paper; it can likely be covered during spotting. To decrease the chances of this occurring, take care not to shake or stir up the bottle of metal salt.

Keep in mind that this should not be the artistic part of platinum printing. Trying to perfect the coating

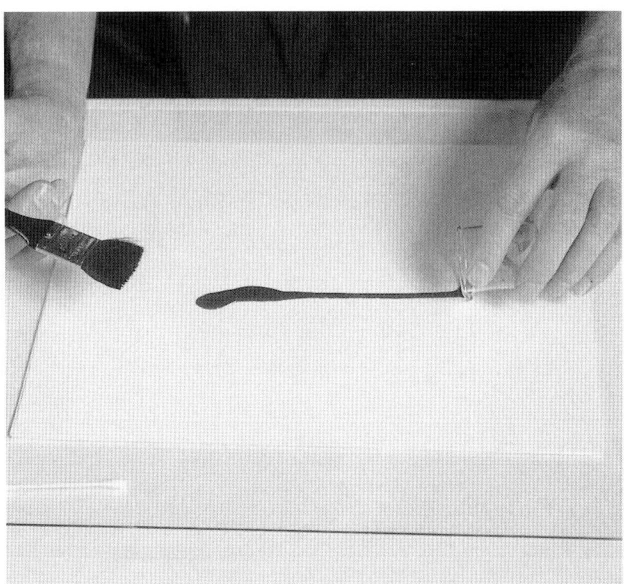

FIGURE 8.6 Pouring the Solution on the Paper

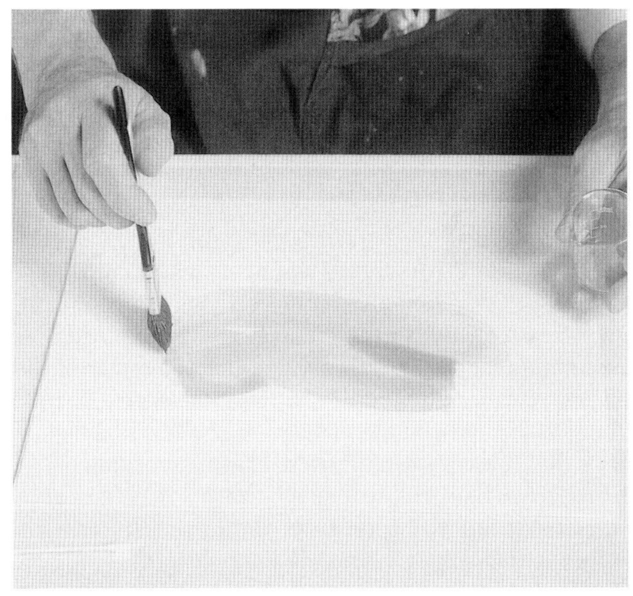

FIGURE 8.7 Beginning to Spread the Solution

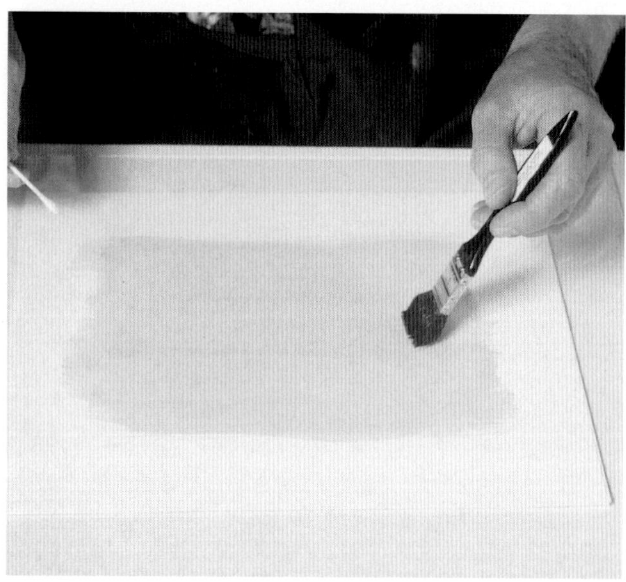

FIGURE 8.8 The Finished Coating Showing the Cotton Applicator in Position

after the paper nap has softened can ruin an image. (Softening begins five seconds following the introduction of liquid.) If the paper is well sized and suitable for platinum, what appear to be streaks of uneven coating will disappear at development.

NOTE: Skies: If you have a landscape with a difficult "Zone VI" sky, a number of precautions can be taken to increase the odds for a satisfactory coating. After examining the paper, rather than using the center of the paper, pour the liquid onto the foreground area below the sky. Then sweep the material to the sky, making sure that it is completely covered before working in other areas. This will reduce the chance of a water spot affecting the more diffuse areas of the print. If a particle appears that cannot be immediately removed with the cotton applicator, make sure it will be positioned in the foreground. Rotate the paper if necessary. Note the area at the corner of the paper with a light pencil mark, for once the emulsion is dry, you may not be able to find the defect. If you do not want the pencil mark on the final print, erase it before development.

Coating Rods

Various forms of glass rods were available in the past; now, some have been produced with a handle, facilitating ease of coating. A number are available, including the Puddle Pusher®, which comes in sizes from 4.5 to 12 inches (Figure 8.9). *(Sources: BS, EE)*

The length of rod should be slightly more than the width of your coating area. The coating rod requires practice. It is not applicable for all papers (see Chapter 5, "Paper"), so do some tests using only sensitizer. The thinner papers may wrinkle too soon to allow sufficient passes with the rod. A sheet of plate glass that is completely level is required as a coating surface. The emulsion is best "injected" under the rod with a hypodermic syringe.

Coating Technique: Rod

Determine how much solution is necessary. Generally the rod will require only two-thirds the amount needed for a brush. Draw it into a syringe of appropriate size. Do not use the needle. Have a cotton applicator handy. If you are right-handed, balance the rod on the left side just outside of the coating area (Figure 8.10). Stabilize the rod with your left hand while you inject a bead of liquid along the contact area between the rod and paper (Figure 8.11). It should be thoroughly drawn in to create a continuous film between the rod and paper along the width of the coating area. Now, using the right hand, manipulate the rod so the volume of material (which should be a continuous bead) is still in contact with the rod but adjacent to the coating area. With slight pressure, draw the bead *slowly* across the coating area (Figure 8.12). If done properly, the paper should be completely coated. There should now be a bead on the other side (Figure 8.13). "Capture" it by repositioning the rod, and slowly draw to the other side (Figure 8.14). If bare areas remain, it may be necessary to draw the material vertically across the image area. This is best avoided.

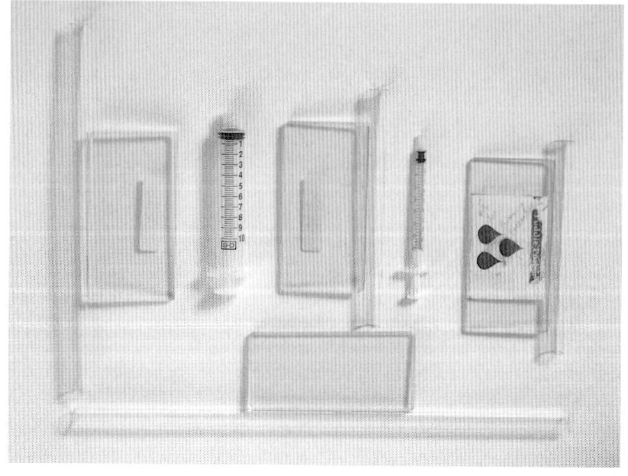

FIGURE 8.9 The Coating Rods

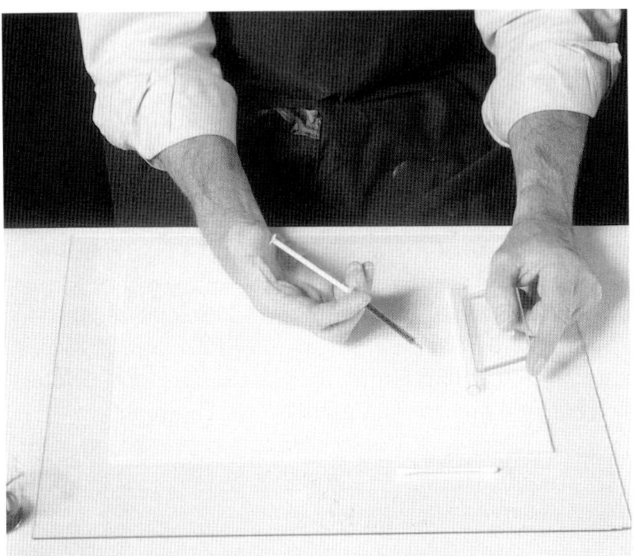

FIGURE 8.10 The Coating Rod and Syringe in Position

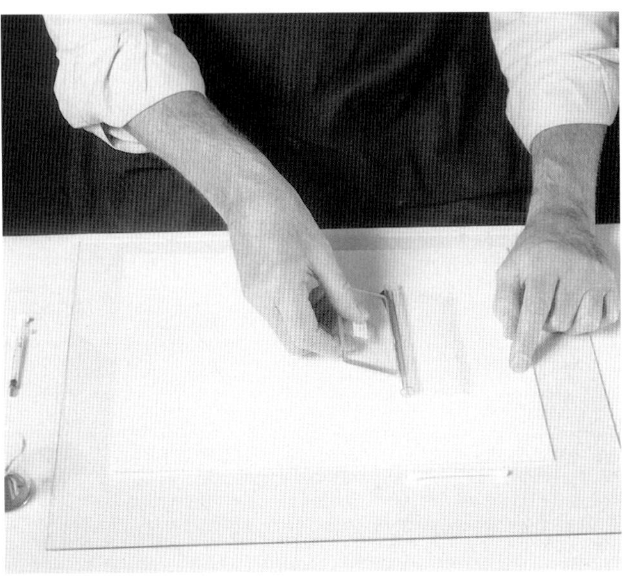

FIGURE 8.12 Beginning to Draw the Rod across the Paper

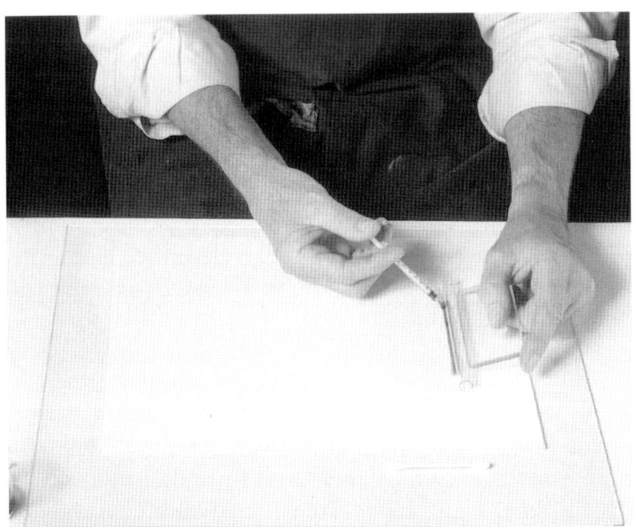

FIGURE 8.11 Laying Down a Bead of Coating Material

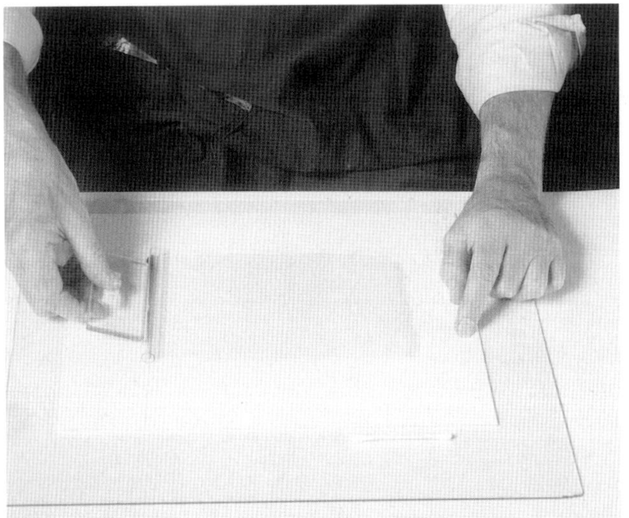

FIGURE 8.13 After the First Pass with the Rod

You will note that the paper soon begins to wrinkle. This is the time to stop. Sop up the excess solution at the edges with a cotton applicator (Figure 8.15). Do not attempt to introduce it into the image.

The Brush versus the Coating Rod

Work with both a brush and a coating rod before you make a decision. There have been some questions regarding too light a coating produced by the rod. Our testing (Keith Schreiber and the author), which involves the reading of Dmax produced by the brush or rod, does not confirm this. With good technique, equal results can be obtained in most cases. It is important, however, to use adequate solution with the rod. While the rod may be more economical, *do not skimp to save costs.* Move the rod slowly and steadily to allow for maximum penetration of the coating material into the paper.

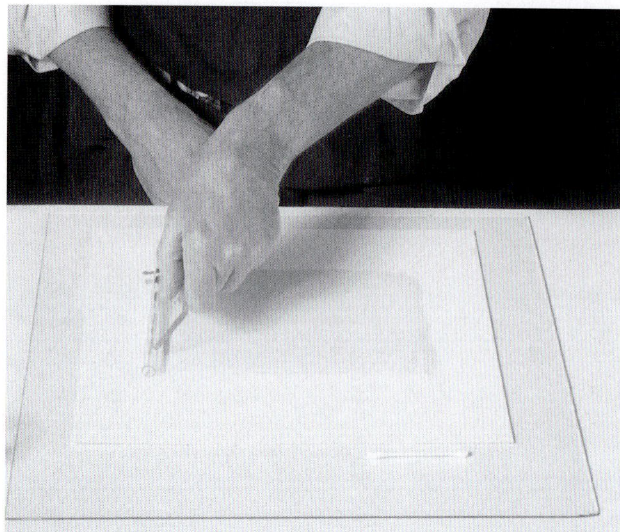

FIGURE 8.14 "Capturing" the Bead for Another Pass

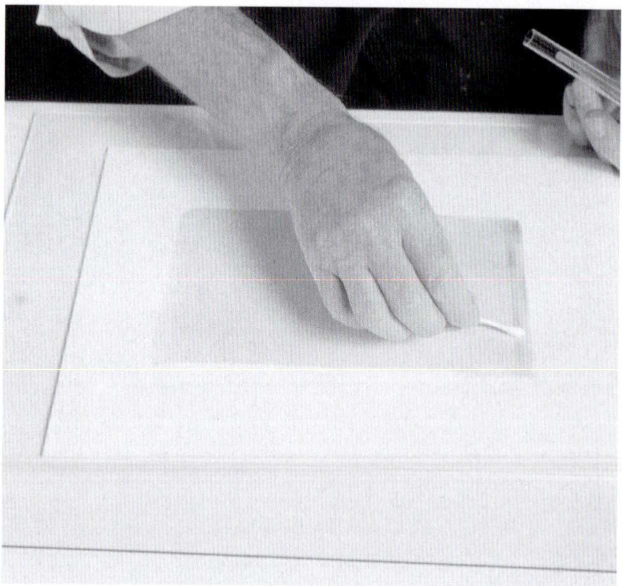

FIGURE 8.15 Using the Cotton Applicator to Take Up Excess Solution

Making the Final Print

Coating

1. Measure the coating solutions in a beaker or plastic medicine cup (Figure 8.4). Until a level of competence is reached, or unless the print had been made previously, it is best to include a step tablet adjacent to the print in case minor adjustments are to be made. See "Using the Combined Step Tablet and Print to Adjust Printing Time and Contrast" at the end of this chapter.

NOTE: Filtering Coating Solutions: Precipitated metal salts in the image are an annoyance that seems to vary with the phase of the moon. It is best to take precautions to avoid them at all times, as some may be impossible to remove from the final print. (See the section on "Spotting" in Chapter 9, "Advanced Technique.") Use student-grade filter paper in a glass funnel (coffee filters are not of a fine enough grade). (See Figure 8.3.)

2. Mix in Tween 20 if desired (a little goes a long way). *(Sources: BS, FR)*

NOTE: Tween 20® is a polysorbate surfactin. It has the effect of decreasing the surface tension of the coating emulsion, causing more adequate wetting of the surface fibers of the paper. With some papers (but not all), it facilitates a smoother gradation of tones. Too much will defeat the effect of the surface sizing of the paper and cause water spots. Use sparingly. It comes in a 10% solution. *At the most, use one drop of 10% for 60 drops of coating.* A safer way is to dilute to a 1% solution. Shake the beaker immediately before pouring the coating material on the paper.

3. Use a brush or a coating rod as described earlier in this chapter. Allow the coating to air dry 2 to 5 minutes before drying with heat.

NOTE: The effects of air drying before applying heat: Keith Schreiber and I have done studies as to the benefits of air drying prior to heat drying. Universally, platinum printers each have their own formula for air drying time. Times range from 1 to 30 minutes, and in some cases, even allowing them to dry overnight. For most papers, waiting 2 to 5 minutes allows the material to saturate the surface tubules of cellulose fibers, resulting in smoother tones and less granularity. Air drying causes some side effects. As the coating soaks in, there may be a drop in Dmax. This may not be enough to be significant. (Consult the discussion of *convincing black* in Chapter 7, "Calibration.") There may be a minimal speed increase and shortening of the exposure scale of the paper (less contrast). It is best to experiment using the 4 × 5 inch step tablet. See Chapter 9, "Advanced Technique," for additives and double-coating techniques.

Drying

1. Using a hair dryer at medium settings, or a drying apparatus, blow dry both sides (Figures 8.16 or 9.2). (See Chapter 9, "Advanced Technique," for how to construct a drying apparatus.) Use in a well-ventilated area. Use the blow dryer at 8 to 12 inches. The coating should become light orange (Pt/Pd) to orange (Pd). Be careful not to burn the paper. Burning, particularly with palladium, causes a severe increase in printing speed. The immediate effect is seen as areas darkened beyond the normal light orange tone of a dried emulsion to a rust color. After developing, these areas will appear as dark blotches in and out of the image area. Inadequately drying the paper is the surest way I know of ruining your negative, short of stepping on it. Once the wet ferric oxalate/platinum salt attaches to the emulsion side of the negative, it creates a permanent stain for which I have never found a remedy.

2. Examine the dry coating with a dim light. Any spots or bristles can be scratched away using a single-edged razor blade. (It is much easier to deal with the problem now, than to try to etch or spot the developed print.) Metal precipitant generally cannot be removed. Save it for spotting.

Exposure

1. Sandwich the paper and the negative in the printing frame. (See the discussion of printing frames in Chapter 6, "The First Print," as well as Figures 6.1 and 6.3.)

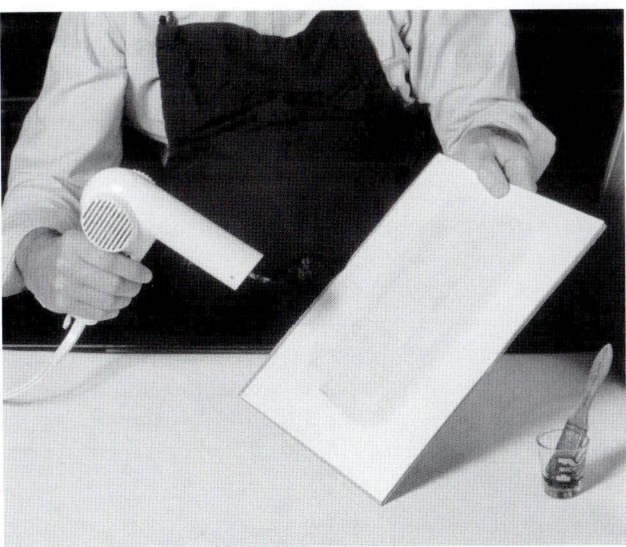

FIGURE 8.16 Using the Hair Dryer

Handle the negative with cotton gloves. Use compressed air or an air syringe to clean the glass of the printing frame and to dust off the negative. If dust is continuously attracted by static charges, use an anti-static solution (see "Sources"). Check the contact of negative and paper in the printing frame before placing under UV light. While looking through the glass, squeeze the center of the back. If you see movement, the contact is bad. Add layers of felt between the paper and the back.

NOTE: Mylar: There may be a tendency for bits of paper coating to come off on the negative. If found immediately, many can be removed by using the tip of the finger covered by a cotton glove. If this is a concern, particularly with multiple printings, place a one-mil piece of Mylar between the negative and the paper before printing. With larger negatives, however, the Mylar can difficult to handle.

2. Set the timer for determined time and expose the print[3] (Figure 8.17). While this is occurring, you can begin to heat the developer and clean up. Discard the plastic cup and wash the brush, soaking it in clearing agent for one minute and washing again. Now squeeze it dry with a clean towel. Hang it up to dry.

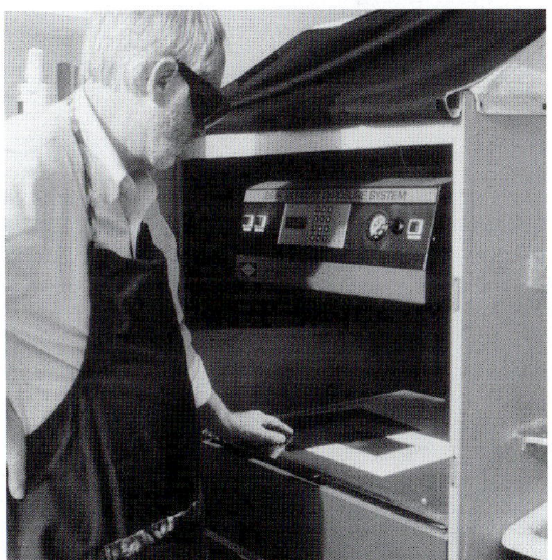

FIGURE 8.17 Exposure in the Plate Burner Using Rubylith to Dodge and Burn

[3] If a fluorescent bank of lights is used as a UV light source, it is best to leave it on during the entire printing session. The intensity of UV light is quite inconsistent for a period after lighting the bulbs. Simply shield it when not in use.

Dodging and Burning

The platinum printer will find that routine dodging and burning is not generally needed. Unlike the making of a silver gelatin print, the extreme latitude and long toe (explained in Chapter 11) of the platinum or palladium print carries tonal values throughout the scale of the image. Nevertheless, some areas, such as a disproportionately light sky, may improve with a simple increase in exposure. It is here that a horizontal printing surface facing upward is appreciated. Sheets of Rubylith® material can be placed upon the glass (Figure 8.17). If you followed the recommendations for standardizing a ten-minute printing time (usually five minutes for a good negative), the Rubylith can be allowed to remain in position from five to ten seconds, lessening the exposure to your hands and eyes. *Use anti-actinic glasses* (see "Sources"). When the print is removed from the frame, you will see a printing-out image (Figure 8.18).

Developing and Clearing

1. *Quickly* slide the print into preheated potassium oxalate developer at 90°F. Another method is to place the print face up in the dry tray and rapidly pour the developer over it. Development will be instantaneous (Figure 8.19). Any portion of the print not receiving immediate development will permanently streak. Never develop a print face down. Ammonium citrate developer can be used at room temperature for cooler tones. Printing time is decreased approximately 1/2 of a stop, requiring about 30 to 50% more exposure.

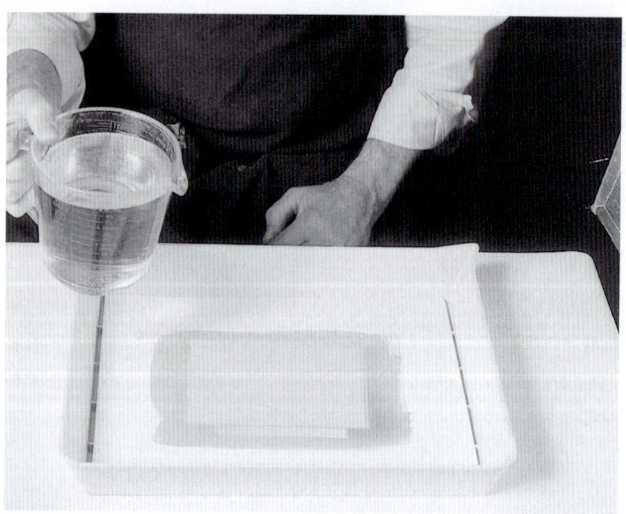

FIGURE 8.18 The Printing Out Image

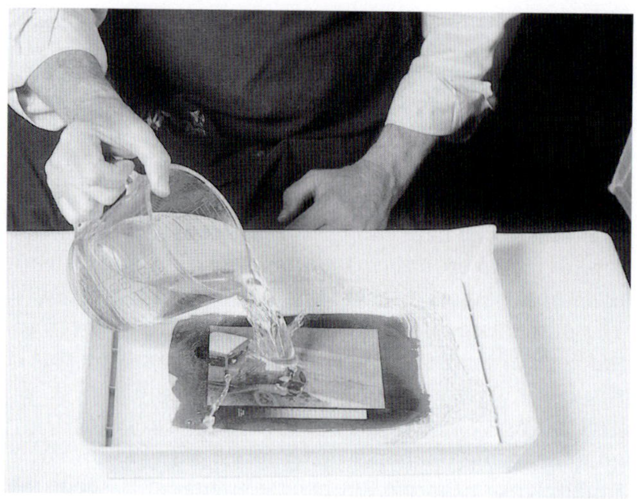

FIGURE 8.19 Pouring the Developer Showing the Developed Image

NOTE: Although we generally can work safely under a 40-watt bulb, the metal salts are extremely sensitive to light at the instant of reduction. This may cause black streaking from areas of intense black to extreme white. Following the suggestion of Jim Enyeart, I turn off all lights except for a distant reference light before applying the developer. The room can be fully lighted after the first few seconds.

2. Develop, with constant agitation, for 1 1/2 to 2 minutes.
3. Lift print by grasping generous parts of two corners and allow it to drain into the developer tray. (Take care with tongs; you may tear off a corner.)
4. Place the print directly into the first clearing bath. If a sulfite or EDTA clearing bath in used, rinse in running water before the first bath. Clear five minutes with constant agitation (Figure 8.20).
5. Clearing in the second and third baths will also be 5 minutes each. As paper becomes soaked, more care is needed in transferring it to avoid tearing. The final two baths require only intermittent agitation. When the first bath becomes cloudy, empty it and move the second and third baths over. Replace the first clearing tray with new solution, now making it the third bath. For an exhibition quality print, the last bath should always be completely clear.
6. If residual print acidity is a concern, a final soak for five minutes in sodium carbonate or sodium acetate can be done before washing. See Chapter 4, "Chemicals."

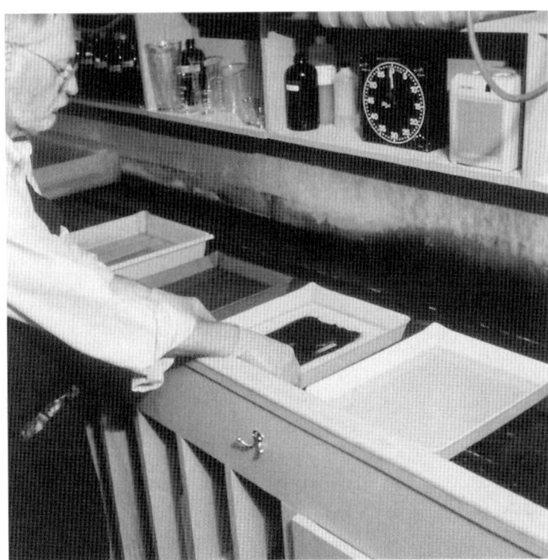

FIGURE 8.20 In the Clearing Baths

7. The final step is a 15 to 30 minute wash in running water. Either a hose or siphon can be used. Avoid having water strike the print directly from the top (you will punch a hole in the print). Generally, platinum prints do not require as much washing as silver prints, but intermittent complete changing of water is recommended.

8. After washing, place the print, face up, on a clean blotter or drying screen (Figure 2.5). See Chapter 9, "Advanced Technique," for print finishing.

Using the Combined Step Tablet and Print to Adjust Printing Time and Contrast

I have recommended that a small 0.5 × 5 inch step tablet be included adjacent to the print. The following sections represent examples of how printing time and contrast can be modified using the step tablet as a reference. A transmission or reflection densitometer is not required to use this technique.

The "Visual Comparison Densitometer"

As shown in Chapter 7, "Calibration," if transmission density values are in place for comparison, the human eye is capable of distinguishing subtle relative differences (Figures 7.4 and 7.5). The same principles can be applied to reflective densities. Looking at a value through the small aperture in the "visual comparison densitometer," the values can be isolated from others. Comparisons can be made to match print and step tablet shades of gray.

Use the following principles:

Shadow values are changed by printing time.

Highlight values are changed by contrast mixture.

- When both shadows and highlights are too dark, reduce printing time.
- When both shadows and highlights are too light, increase printing time.
- When shadows are good and highlights are too dark, shorten the scale by going to a higher contrast mixture. Use approximately[4] the same printing time.
- When shadows are good and highlights are too light, lengthen the scale by going to a lower contrast mixture. Use approximately the same printing time.
- When shadows are dark and highlights are good, shorten the scale by going to a higher contrast mixture. Use less printing time.
- When shadows are light and highlights are good, lengthen the scale by going to a lower contrast mixture. Use more printing time.
- When both shadows and highlights need correction, alter the scale by going to a different contrast mixture. Change the shadows by altering printing time.

For the purposes of illustration, I have placed seven printing combinations together (Table 8.3). A "good" print has been located in the center for reference (Plate 8.2). While the limitations in reproduction (Plates 8.2 to 8.8) may not convey the nuances found in the actual prints, using the following graphic examples will allow you to visualize the differences between the reproductions. When doing these corrections on actual prints, the "visual comparison densitometer" is helpful to isolate print tones.

Both Shadows and Highlights Are Too Dark

1. Find the textured shadow area. In this case, it is too dark (Figure 8.21).
2. Find the print shadow value in the step tablet. It is step Nr. 3.

[4] We know that changing the contrast mixture will have a small effect on printing time. Therefore, printing is slightly altered by contrast mixture. It may be not enough to notice, but use a test strip. As we shall see in Chapter 12, "Using the Print Curves," we can accurately calculate both variables.

TABLE 8.3 Seven Printing Combinations to Show Corrections for Shadow and Highlight Values. Bisbee, Az. 1979 5 × 7 inch Pt/Pd

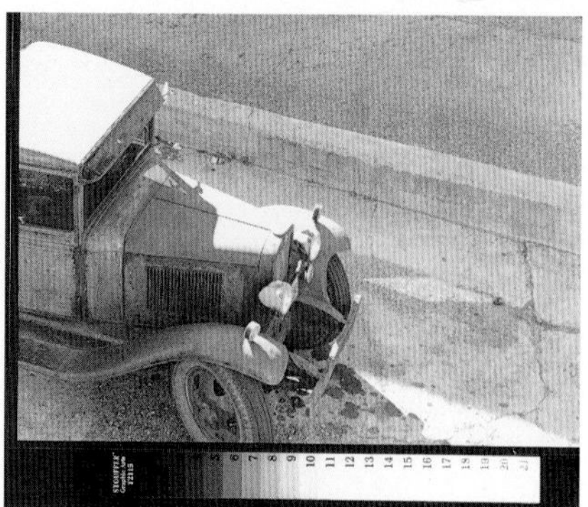

Plate 8.5. Shadows are good. Highlights are too dark.

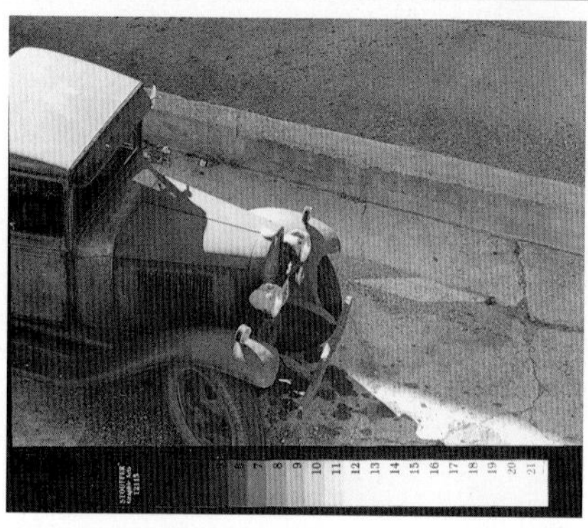

Plate 8.3. Both shadows and highlights are too dark.

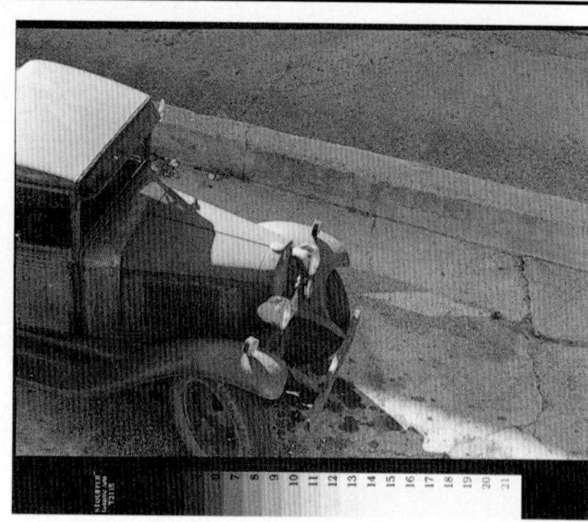

Plate 8.6. Shadows are good. Highlights are too light.

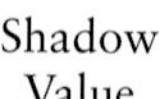

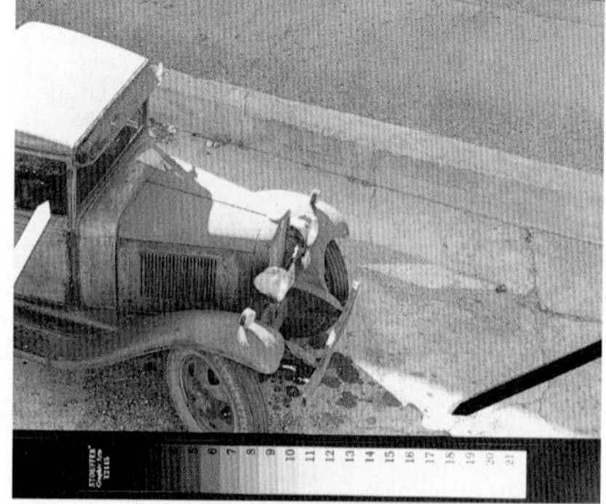

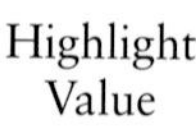

Plate 8.2. Good.

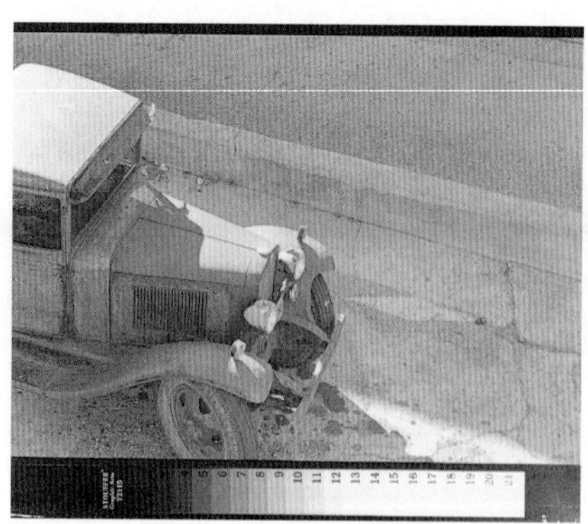

Plate 8.7. Shadows are too dark. Highlights are good.

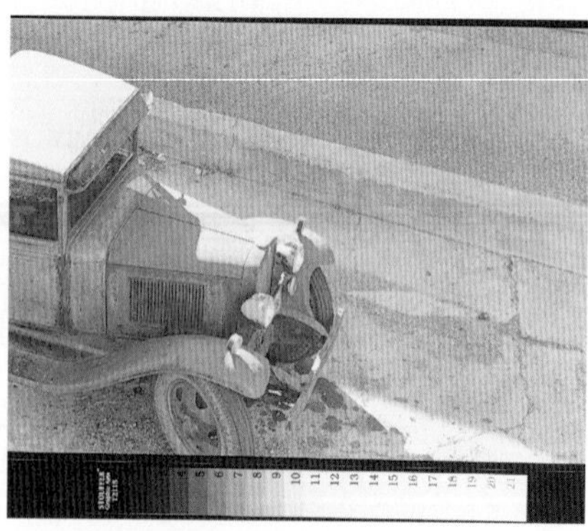

Plate 8.4. Both shadows and highlights are too light.

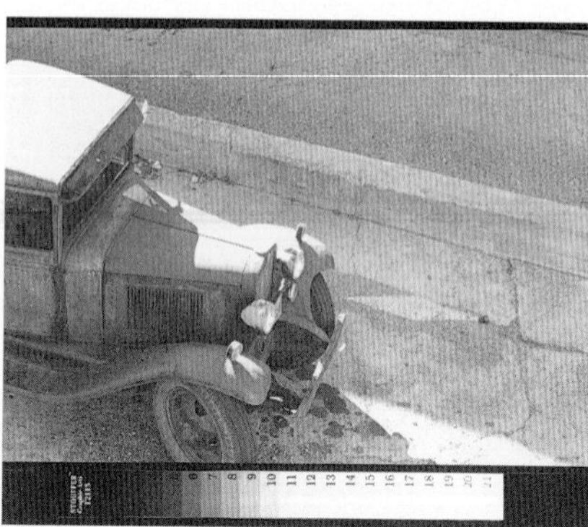

Plate 8.8. Shadows are too light. Highlights are good.

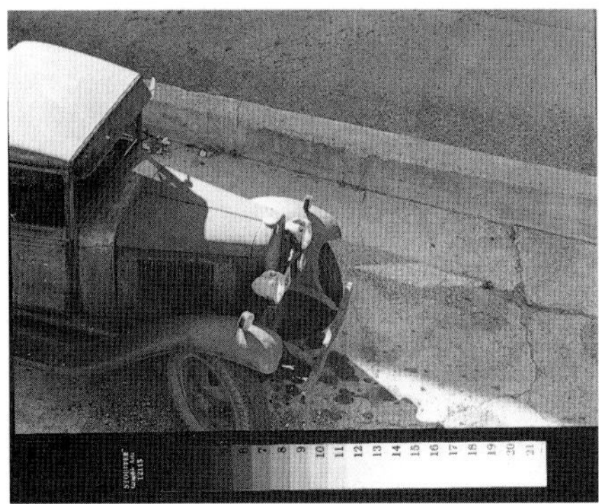

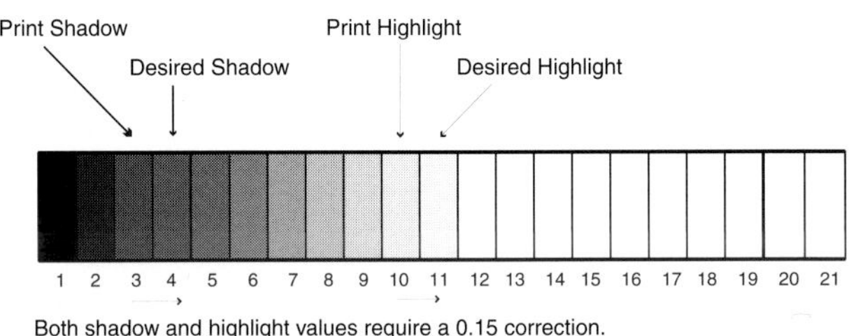

FIGURE 8.21 Both shadows and highlights are too dark.

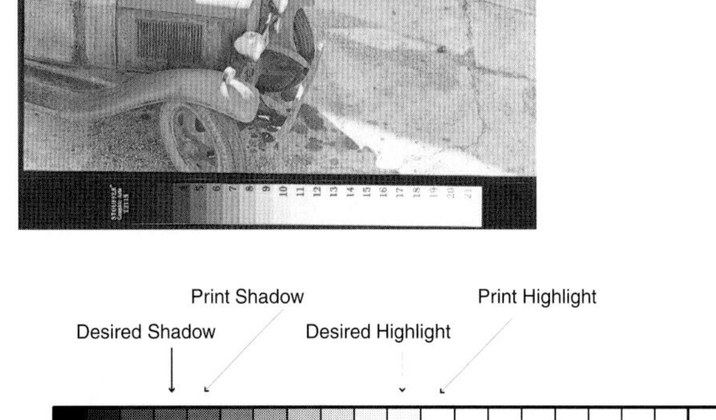

FIGURE 8.22 Both shadows and highlights are too light.

3. Find the step tablet value where you want your print shadow value to fall. In this case, it is Step Nr. 4, 0.15 lighter.
4. Find the print highlight area. In this print, it is too dark.
5. Find that highlight area in the step tablet. In this case, it is step Nr. 10.
6. Find the step tablet value that you want for textured highlight. In this case, it is Nr. 11, 0.15 lighter than Nr. 10.
7. To make a print with both shadow and highlight values 0.15 lighter,[5] reduce printing time 1/2 stop or 33%.

Both Shadows and Highlights Are Too Light

1. Find the textured shadow area. In this case, it is too light (Figure 8.22).
2. Find the print shadow value in the step tablet. It is step Nr. 5.
3. Find the step tablet value where you want your print shadow value to fall. In this case, it is Step Nr. 4, 0.15 darker.
4. Find the print highlight area. In this print, it is too light.
5. Find that highlight area in the step tablet. In this case, it is step Nr. 12.
6. Find the step tablet value that you want for textured highlight. In this case, it is Nr. 11, 0.15 darker than Nr. 12.
7. To make a print with both shadow and highlight values 0.15 darker, increase printing time 50% (1/2 stop).

Shadows Are Good, Highlights Are Too Dark

1. Find the textured shadow area. It is good (Figure 8.23).
2. Find the print shadow value in the step tablet. It is step Nr. 4.
3. Find the step tablet value where you want your print shadow value to fall. In this case, it is step Nr. 4, the same value. No change in printing time is indicated.

[5] For changing contrast, refer to Table 7.2, "Standard Negative Contrast Ranges." Note that changes in the .05 or .15 range can be achieved by using the even No. mixtures.

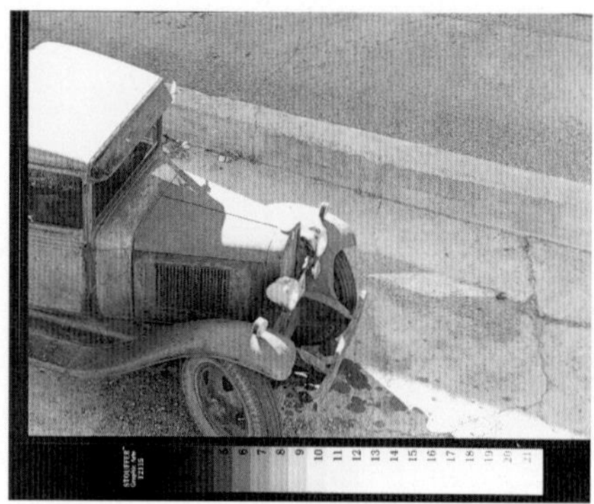

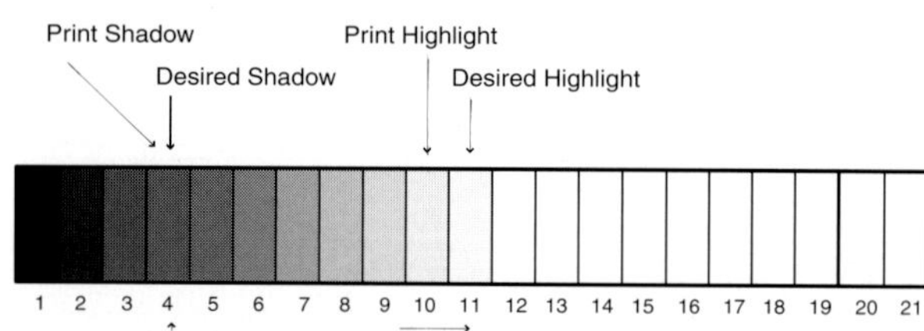

Shadow values require no correction. To lighten highlights, shorten the contrast scale by 0.15. Use essentiallt the same printing time.

FIGURE 8.23 Shadows are good. Highlights are too dark.

4. Find the print highlight area. In this print, it is too dark.
5. Find that highlight area in the step tablet. In this case, it is step Nr. 10.
6. Find the step tablet value that you want for textured highlight. In this case, it is Nr. 11, 0.15 lighter than Nr. 10.
7. To make a print with shadow the same, and highlight values 0.15 lighter, shorten contrast scale by 0.15. (Use a *higher* No. contrast mixture.) Use essentially the same printing time, or increase ±10%. (See the section "Standard Negative Contrast Ranges" in Chapter 7, "Calibration.")

Shadows Are Good, Highlights Are Too Light

1. Find the textured shadow area. It is good (Figure 8.24).
2. Find the print shadow value in the step tablet. It is step Nr. 4.
3. Find the step tablet value where you want your print shadow value to fall. In this case, it is step Nr. 4, the same value. No change in printing time is indicated.

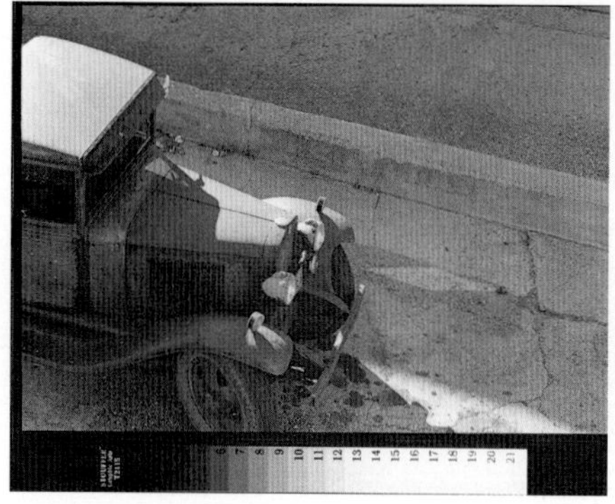

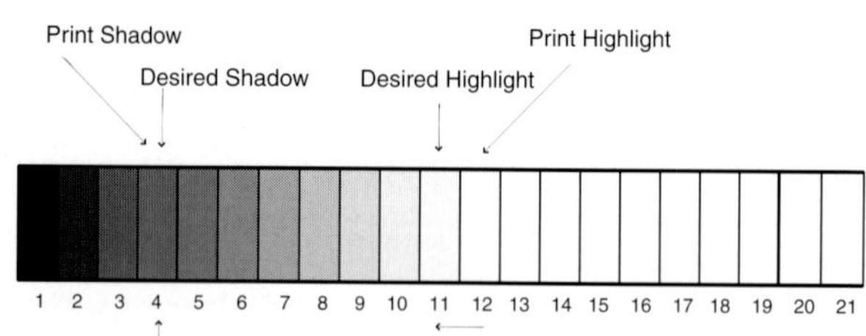

Shadow values require no correction. To darken highlights, lengthen the contrast scale by 0.15. Use essentially the same printing time.

FIGURE 8.24 Shadows are good. Highlights are too light.

4. Find the print highlight area. In this print, it is too light.
5. Find that highlight area in the step tablet. In this case, it is step Nr. 12.
6. Find the step tablet value that you want for textured highlight. In this case, it is Nr. 11, 0.15 darker than Nr. 12.
7. To make a print with shadow the same, and highlight values 0.15 darker, lengthen the contrast scale by 0.15. (Use a *lower* No. contrast mixture.) Use essentially the same printing time, or decrease ±10%.

Shadows Are Too Dark, Highlights Are Good

1. Find the textured shadow area. It is too dark (Figure 8.25).
2. Find the print shadow value in the step tablet. It is step Nr. 3.
3. Find the step tablet value where you want your print shadow value to fall. In this case, it is step Nr. 4. Printing time must be decreased 33%.
4. Find the print highlight area. In this print, it is good.

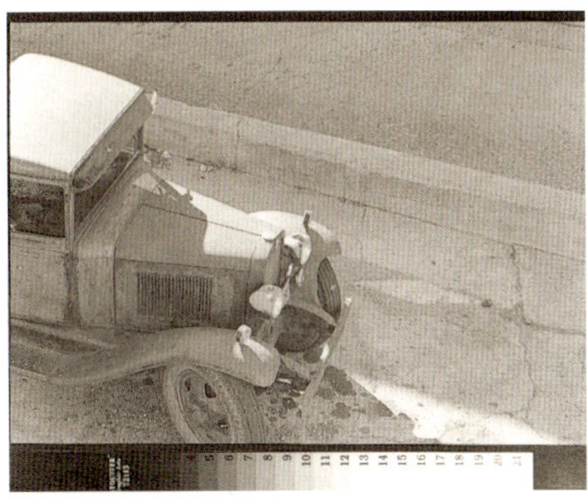

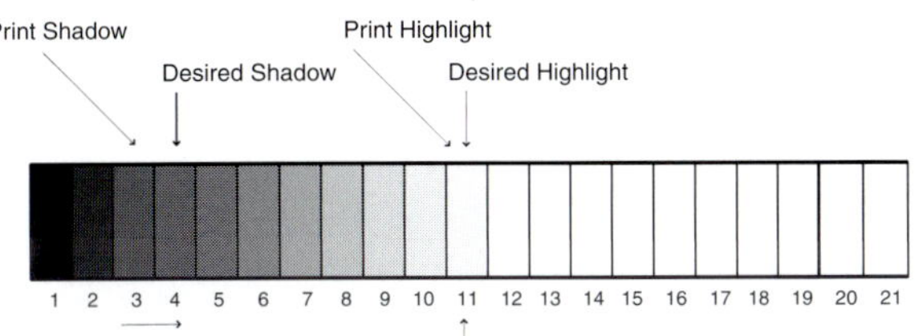

Shadow values require a 0.15 correction. To keep highlights the same, shorten the contrast scale by 0.15. Use less printing time.

FIGURE 8.25 Shadows are too dark. Highlights are good.

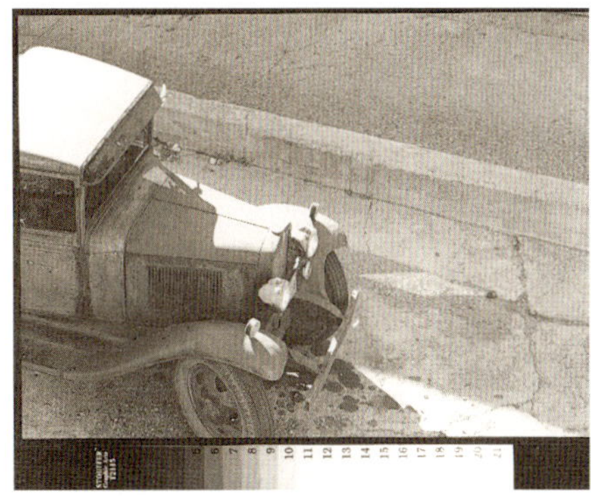

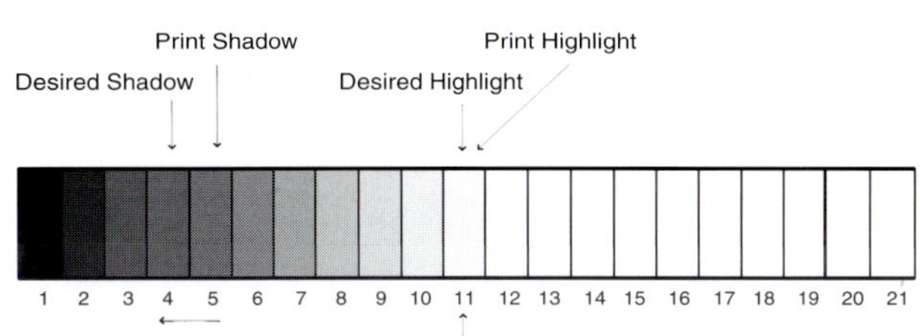

Shadow values require a 0.15 correction. To keep highlights the same, lengthen the contrast scale by 0.15. Use more printing time.

FIGURE 8.26 Shadows are too light. Highlights are good.

5. Find that highlight area in the step tablet. In this case, it is step Nr. 11.
6. To keep the highlights at step Nr. 11, while raising shadow values, the contrast scale must be shortened by 0.15.
7. Printing time must be decreased 33% and contrast shortened by 0.15.

Shadows Are Too Light, Highlights Are Good

1. Find the textured shadow area. It is too light (Figure 8.26).
2. Find the print shadow value in the step tablet. It is step Nr. 5.
3. Find the step tablet value where you want your print shadow value to fall. In this case, it is step Nr. 4. Printing time must be increased 50%.
4. Find the print highlight area. In this print, it is good.
5. Find that highlight area in the step tablet. In this case, it is step Nr. 11.
6. To keep the highlights at step Nr. 11, while lowering shadow values, the contrast scale must be lengthened by 0.15.
7. Printing time must be increased 50% and contrast lengthened by 0.15.

More Combinations

We have been working in half-stop increments. For each two-step correction, one full stop is needed, either halving or doubling printing times or contrast mixtures, and so on. When there are more extensive discrepancies between desired shadow and print values, the principles discussed must be brought together to make the final print. As corrections get more complicated, more test strips are needed before the final print is made. When the principles discussed in Chapter 12, "Using the Print Curves," are utilized, the initial test prints can be made with more accuracy.

CHAPTER 9

ADVANCED TECHNIQUE

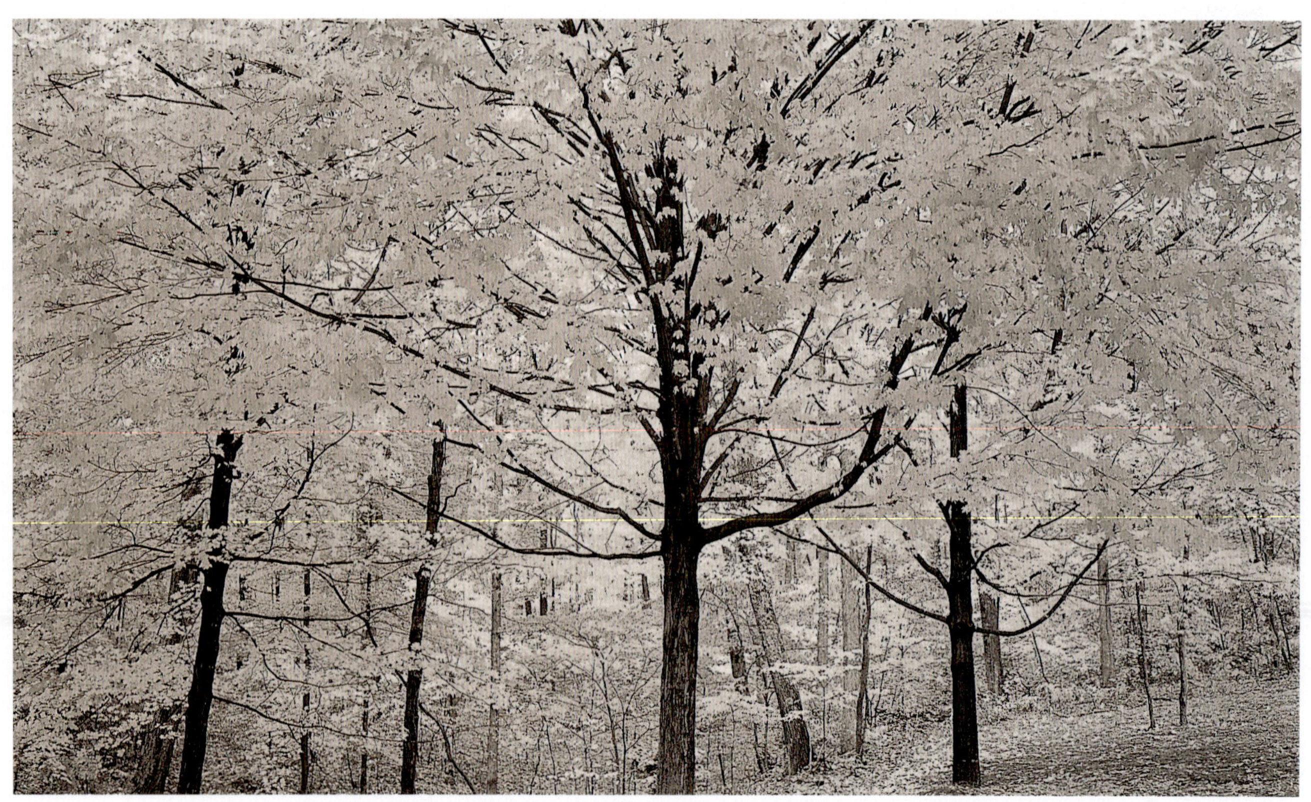

PLATE 9.1 Yellow Maples, Bernheim, KY. 1988 12 × 20 inch Pd. The yellow-orange tone of the leaves have been accentuated by using palladium developed in potassium oxalate at 120°F.

Masking of Negatives

(The material presented here is courtesy of Tom Millea.)

The methods previously described will show the black brush strokes around the print. If you prefer a white border, you must mask the negative before printing.

Materials

Metal straight edge
Printer's red masking paper (Rubylith®)
Ruby tape, 1/4 inch (available from any print shop)
Self-healing cutting base
X-ACTO No. 16 blade *(Sources: GA, LI)*

Process

1. Scribe on the red masking paper the borders you wish to create for the final image. Usually, this is done to just eliminate the base + fog portion of the negative, however, the image can be cropped if desired. This is a delicate operation. For the first time, you may want to ask to watch a printer to do it.
2. Working over the cutting base, carefully cut along the lines. Take great care at the corners, as any defects will show at the corners of the final print.
3. In coating the paper, you may not want to show pencil marks. (They will not erase after development.) It is best to use the black construction paper or felt marker template (discussed in Chapter 8, "The Platinum and Palladium Print") to demarcate the coating borders.
4. Place the negative, dull side up over the opening and tack down two sides (the base + fog area) with two or more pieces of ruby tape.
5. Place the negative with the dull side against the coated paper. See Table 9.1 for the order of materials in the printing frame.
6. Print accordingly. If a border is visible around the image, you have fogging problems (see Chapter 10, "Problems").

TABLE 9.1 Order of Materials in the Masking of a Negative

	Masking of the Negative
⇓	Glass
	Printer's Mask
	Negative
	Paper
⇓	Back or Base

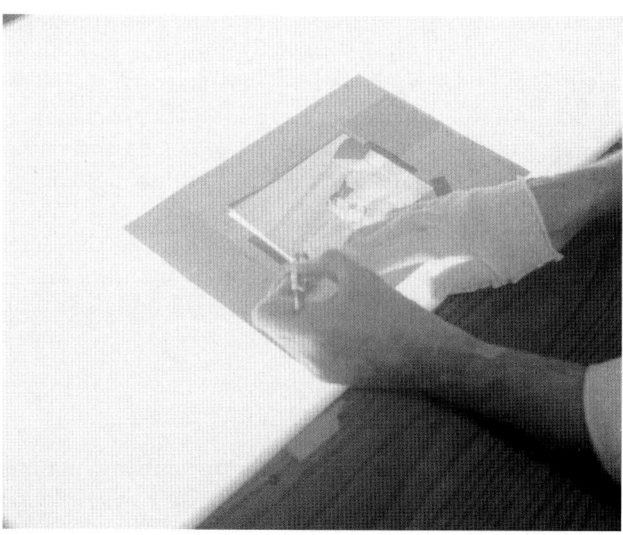

FIGURE 9.1 Masking of the Negative

Working Light

Some platinum printers have recommended the use of a yellow safelight during coating. My tests have shown no difference between a safelight, a low incandescent light, and complete darkness. Avoid fluorescent, bright light, or daylight. Have enough light to see well for coating. Dry under a dim incandescent light (two 40-watt bulbs at least four feet away). During the first instant of development, turn off the lights (Chapter 8, "The Platinum and Palladium Print").

The efficacy of the safelight is easily tested (Chapter 10, "Problems").

Humidity and Temperature

Relative humidity that is too high or low may affect the absorbency of the paper to be coated. My laboratory maintains a humidity of 40 to 60%, which gives consistent results. Other printers work well in the high or low extremes. Paul Caffel of Bath, England makes exquisite prints while working in a relative humidity of 85%!

For reproducible results, once a satisfactory humidity has been found, it is recommended that you maintain it. It is also recommend that you use this environment to store the paper at least eight hours before coating. Coating should be done in the wet area of your lab (Chapter 2, "Setting Up a Laboratory"). Providing that you do not have forced air heating, the dampness from the sinks tends to stabilize a moderate amount of moisture in the environment. Also, as 40-watt safelights must be in the developing area, it is the most convenient space to work. If you find unusual absorbency or graininess in your paper, you can correct the situation by exposing the paper overnight to a humidifier or dehumidifier, depending on conditions.

For contrast control by humidity, see the brief description of the Malde/Ware process and the Ziatype in Appendix D, "The Ammonium-Based Processes."

Hydrogen Peroxide

The use of hydrogen peroxide to prevent fogging has been suggested. Some workers also use it as an oxidizer for contrast control. *Expect some fogging when no restrainer has been used.*

If you are using only ferric oxalate solution A, one drop of 3% hydrogen peroxide per ml of coating material will prevent some fogging by temporarily kicking it into the next contrast ratio and slightly decreasing the exposure scale (the same as adding one drop of solution B). (See Appendix C, "Principles of the Developing and Clearing Process.") With one drop of sensitizer B per 11 drops sensitizer A, no fogging should occur. If you routinely need hydrogen peroxide to prevent fogging, you may have problems. (See Chapter 10, "Problems.")

Brushes

Early in my tests, I tried dozens of different brushes hoping to solve coating problems. Eventually, I found that most problems were related to papers. Today, many papers have inadequate surface and internal sizing or pH to make them suitable for platinum printing (see Chapter 5, "Paper"). With suitable paper, many brushes will work. I believe that some unusual coating methods are used because of inappropriate paper. *Don't waste time and chemicals on bad paper.* (See "Brushes" in Chapter 8, "The Platinum and Palladium Print.")

The Use of Sizing Medium in the Sensitizer

Technically, the coating material is not an emulsion unless it contains an emulsifying ingredient. An emulsifier will theoretically add body to the coating, keeping more of it on the surface of the paper. The best product, Liquitex acrylic sizing medium (made by Binny Smith), is, unfortunately, no longer applicable as they have changed the formula.

A sizing medium will provide a body to the coating material. My tests show that it makes coating easier because it holds the emulsion more on the surface and prevents wash off during development. Dmax is increased (+0.1 reflective density).

While many sizing agents will go into solution with distilled water, at this time, I have found no medium other than polyvinyl alcohol that will go into complete solution when added to the acid-coating material. If you plan to test any ingredients, add it to only the ferric oxalate and examine before adding the metal salt. (While some ingredients will go into solution at a neutral pH, most will congeal in the acidic ferric oxalate.)

Polyvinyl alcohol 5% is available as a sizing agent. Used at 1 to 2 drops/ml of coating material, it will provide some body to the coating. Its effectiveness is dependent on the paper, so it is necessary to do visual tests. *(Source: BS)*

Image Color

Image color can be controlled by the sizing, choice of developer, temperature, and toning. Paper base color will also affect the image.

Sizing

Gelatin sizing produces blue-black tones, particularly with platinum. Starch sizing (used by most paper manufacturers) produces warmer, brownish tones. (See Appendix E, "Sizing of Paper.")

Developer and Temperature Controls

Considerable variation is possible with this method. Note that with developer choice, Pt/Pd tones can be similar to those of platinum (Table 9.2).

Combinations of Platinum and Palladium

By combining proportions of metal salts with developer and temperature variations, image hues from neutral gray to warm sepia can be obtained (Table 9.2). With the Ziatype (Appendix D, "The Ammonium-Based Processes"), even cooler slate-colored tones can be created.

TABLE 9.2 Print Tone Related to Metal Salt, Developer, and Developer Temperature

Tone	*Metal*	*Developer*
Cool ⇑	Platinum	Ammonium citrate 68°F
	50% Platinum/Palladium	Ammonium citrate 68°F
	Platinum	Ammonium citrate 90°F
	50% Platinum/Palladium	Ammonium citrate 90°F
	Palladium	Ammonium citrate 100°F
	Platinum	Potassium oxalate 68°F
	Platinum	Potassium oxalate 90°F
	50% Platinum/Palladium	Potassium oxalate 90°F
	Palladium	Potassium oxalate 90°F
Warm ⇓	Palladium	Potassium oxalate 100-110°F

For combinations of platinum and palladium, other than the standard 50% ratios, a number of effects on tone have been reported. Variations between workers are probably explained by differences in technique, paper, and developer. For our tests, we used the Crane's *Crest Natural White Wove* developed in potassium oxalate at 90°F. Ratios of platinum:palladium at 5:1, 3:2, 3:3, 2:3, and 1:5 were used.

Contrary to some findings that the same tone of a 50% mixture can be reached by using a 1:5 platinum:palladium blend, we observed that the 1:5 tone was considerably warmer and more closely approximated a pure palladium print. There were visible color changes from the various mixtures, providing tonal increments between the pure platinum, 50% Pt/Pd, and the pure palladium print. Perhaps others have produced different results and have found a way to economize in the Pt/Pd ratios.

Metal Ions in the Developer

Richard Sullivan has raised a number of questions about the reuse of developer. If one uses the same developer for both Pt/Pd and pure palladium prints, the developer becomes loaded with both platinum and palladium molecules. When using this developer, therefore, you cannot produce either a "pure" platinum or "pure" palladium print; each has a minuscule amount of the other metal. For palladium, if there is any question of permanence as compared to platinum, the platinum introduced by the developer will help. In the case of pure platinum prints, if toning, redevelopment, or intensification is anticipated, it may be wise to do some tests with prints processed in new developer.

Toning

Gold chloride, mercuric chloride, potassium phosphate, uranium nitrate, lead oxalate, and other substances can be used to alter image tone, either in the sensitizer or as a toning bath. Of these, I will be discussing only gold chloride. (Also, see Toners in Chapter 4, "Chemicals.")

Gold chloride 5% may be used in the sensitizer or as a direct toner to cool the image color of a platinum or Pt/Pd print. In the sensitizer, place one drop of gold chloride per ml of coating material. This may also reduce granularity. As a toner, brush gold chloride directly onto the wetted print, usually with glycerin to control application (Crawford, 1979; Nadeau, 1994; Sullivan and Weese, 1998 [gold toning formula]). When the desired tone is reached, rinse the print and place for one minute in Dektol; then wash.

Glycerin

At the turn of the century, many pictorialists used glycerin to selectively develop the platinum print. Much of the historic literature, including the writings of Alfred Steiglitz, contains references to this technique. While the most grievous practices of romantic expression might not fit in with our time, the practice can be a valuable tool for those who wish another method of image manipulation.

Glycerin can be obtained from a pharmacy or any chemical supplier. It is mixed with developer, either in a single bath or in various concentrations. Because proficiency requires some practice, it is best to start with only one concentration of 50% glycerin/developer, which will be used in conjunction with 100% developer. After beginning with this concentration, other ratios can be tried.

Materials

Brushes to apply glycerin/developer

Developer

Glass sheet, slightly larger than the paper

Glycerin

Jars, to contain the various concentrations of glycerin and developer

Running water

1. The print is exposed to UV light in the usual way. Some recommend overexposure.
2. Arrange three jars: 100% glycerin, 50% each glycerin/developer, and 100% developer.
3. Wet the glass with pure glycerin and "stick" on the print, face up. Immediately cover the print with pure glycerin. You will see the printing out image.
4. Using the two solutions containing developer, paint the image to enhance selected areas. The process can be arrested at any time by flooding the area with pure glycerin or using blotting paper.
5. When satisfied, thoroughly flush the print with running water and clear.

Richard Sullivan and Carl Weese describe a *brush development* that utilizes ammonium ferric oxalate and potassium chloroplatinite. The technique is similar to the one just described, but use only a cold bath or potassium oxalate developer and glycerin (Sullivan and Weese, 1998).

Double Coating

Our (the author and Keith Schreiber) studies have shown that the efficacy of double coating is dependent upon the paper used. With many papers, if well coated, a single coating is equal, and frequently superior to, a double coat. Some papers, usually the heavier ones (see Chapter 5, "Paper"), may benefit from double coating with a smoother tone and a deeper Dmax. With most, the double coat mucks up what could have been a good coating, creating blotches and a diminished Dmax.

You must test the paper using your own technique. Here, the Stouffer 4 × 5 step tablet is valuable. The steps are large enough to gauge the smoothness of tone and Dmax. You do not need sensitometric machinery to visually assess the differences.

For double coating, some dilute each application of coating agent with 30 to 50% distilled water. Allow the first coating to air dry for 3 to 5 minutes, heat dry, and recoat. If you decide to double coat your final print, you must anticipate a change in printing speed, and do the appropriate test.

Simili Japon and Platine papers both can benefit from double coating. With these papers, Keith Schreiber uses the standard concentrations of ferric oxalate and metal salts. With the Simili paper, add one drop of 10% Tween 20 per 2ml of coating material. (See Tween 20 in Chapter 8, "The Platinum and Palladium Print.") The first coating is allowed to air dry only for one hour. Following the second coating, the paper is head dried in the normal manner. The Dmax of both papers is increased significantly, as well as smoothness of tone. Because of the increased intensity of black, the ES of the paper is somewhat shortened.

Platinum printers throughout the world have developed many other unique variations for double coating. For more information, the reader is encouraged to explore the many Web sites and e-mail addresses available on this subject.

Drying of the Coating

Natural drying in room air can be precarious; times are dependent on temperature and humidity. It could take long enough to cause some of the ferric oxalate in the coating to go to ferrous and result in fogging. Most platinum printers, therefore, use a method of speed drying with hot air to dry the emulsion. The common method is to use a hair dryer or a drying cabinet. With a hair dryer, there is always the tendency for uneven drying and the possibility of burning the coating. Also, the close proximity needed to operate the hair dryer may expose the respiratory system to the bits of coating material that can enter the air when in the dry state. The drying cabinet is superior for even drying, but few people have access to one of sufficient size. A commercial dryer is available from Edwards Engineering. *(Source: EE)*

To help solve these problems, I have devised a method utilizing two commercial hair dryers and diffusing cones, both available at a beauty supply store.

Materials

Fiberglass window screen, 2 × 3 feet

Lumber, 1 × 4 inches and 8 one-inch round-headed wood screws

Particle board, 5/8 × 12 × 24 inches

Two high-quality commercial hair dryers (1200 to 1400 watts) and diffusing cones[1]

Two swag hooks and cord

Method

1. Tape the handles of the hair dryers together, overlapping them so that the nozzles are at opposite ends and both are pointing in the same direction (Figure 9.2).

2. With the diffusers installed on the dryers, place them on the board, open end down. Measure the distance between the center of the cones (it should be about 10 inches).

3. Cut two holes one inch smaller than the outer diameter of the diffuser cones along the center of the long axis of the particle board. Place the centers of the holes at the measured distance between the centers of the cones. The dryers should sit over the board with the cones pointing downward over the holes.

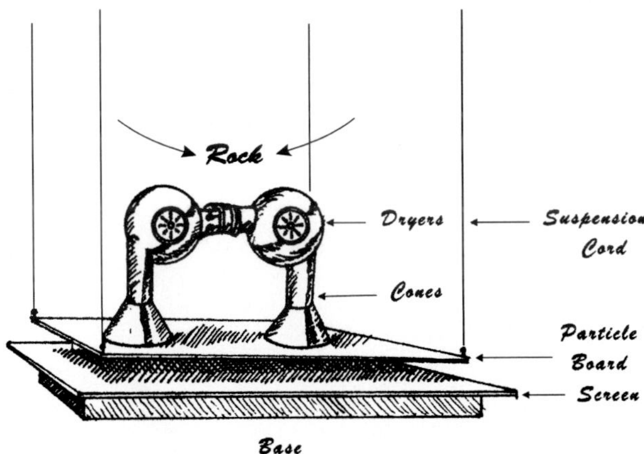

FIGURE 9.2 The Drying Apparatus

[1] High-quality dryers, usually special-ordered from beauty shops are in the $60.00 range. Unlike the less expensive variety, they can be quite efficient at medium power, which extends the life of the diffuser and minimizes the chance of burning the print.

4. Attach the dryers and diffusing cones with the wood screws. You may want to catch the lip of the cones with the heads of the screws rather than puncture the plastic.

5. Make a rectangular base with the lumber to support the window screen. Cut away some wood to allow for ventilation. Place the support and the screen on your counter.

6. Place the swag hooks on the ceiling directly over the screen about 20 inches apart. Center their position with the axis between the dryers. Making loops with the cord, pass each one around one end of the board. Notch the board two inches from the ends to prevent slippage. Suspend the entire apparatus from the ceiling so that the board rests 3 to 4 inches over the screen.

7. With the freshly coated paper lying face up on the screen, the board with the attached dryers is gently rocked back a forth over the paper. By periodically maintaining that motion and rotating the print, even drying should occur in 3 to 5 minutes. The combined current draw of 2400 to 2800 watts will strain the circuit breakers, so you will probably want to choose a circuit with no other load.

Preparation of the Final Print

Drying

If you are in low humidity, remove the print from the drying screen before it is bone dry and press under a heavy object. (An old chemistry book will do.) After a few hours, flatten the print under a mounting press set at 200°F. Protect both sides of the print with archival board.

Principles of Etching and Spotting Platinum/Palladium Prints

Materials *(Source: Art Supply)*

#000 Spotter brushes

Burnishing tool (plastic)

Etching blade

Grumbacher Academy or Windsor Newton Burnt Umber Watercolor (tube)

Grumbacher Academy or Windsor Newton Ivory Black Watercolor (tube)

Spotting lamp (a circular fluorescent tube/magnifying glass combination is best)

Watercolor dish

Windsor Newton Dry Ground Titanium White (powder)

It is very difficult to etch or spot black defects, caused by negative pinholes or scratches, from a platinum print. The coating of a platinum print extends deeply into the paper. It is best to cover pinholes and scratches with negative retouching material, such as Crocein Scarlet (Kodak 1463751) before printing (Chapter 3, "The Negative"). Use the shiny side of the negative so that the material will be slightly out of register with the image. It is equally difficult to cover traces of precipitated metal. If this is a problem, strain the metal salt before coating (see Figure 8.3).

Spotting with watercolors, in an undiluted form, will match only the whitest and blackest tones of the print. If it is placed on the midtones, a disagreeable black or white spot will form, many times ruining the print. Therefore, one must work from both extremes, black and white, to the midtone areas, diluting with distilled water as needed, until very little pigment is applied. Work from three wells in the watercolor dish in which watercolors have been blended: white, Pt/Pd blend, and Pd blends. During the time between spotting sessions, the liquid colors will have returned to a dry, caked form (Figure 9.3). Simply add water before spotting.

Generally, a brush size larger than one might anticipate is best. It holds more pigment, allowing more control. A good practice is to use the brush almost dry, with more pigment than appears necessary. The danger in having pigment too thin and wet is that it will not completely cover the spot but bleed a halo over the satisfactory print tones. Dip the brush and mark scratch paper until hardly any pigment remains. Practice on scrap prints. (Platinum printers have lots of those.)

Black Defects

First examine the print under a magnifying glass that allows for binocular vision (Figure 9.4). If the defect is superficial, it may be possible to flick it off with an etching blade. If, during this process, the paper nap has been penetrated, it becomes highly absorbent to pigment. *Dilute* mixtures must be used to restore image tone.

For deeper defects, use Titanium White powder mixed with a small amount of distilled water in the watercolor tray. A thicker mixture will be used against a white background. As the underlying tone approaches light, and then mid-gray, add water drop by drop to make the pigment more translucent. You will note that if properly mixed, it may appear to be too strong, but rapidly seeps into the now unsized paper. A heavier coating of Titanium White may cause an annoying bulge on the surface of the print. After it has thoroughly dried, place a piece of glassine over it and lightly rub with a plastic burnishing tool.

If the etching or white spotting has been overdone, showing a now white defect, save the print for spotting of white defects. The deeper levels of unsized paper surface or Titanium White will both be extremely absorbent. *Use only the most dilute mixture of the dark watercolor.*

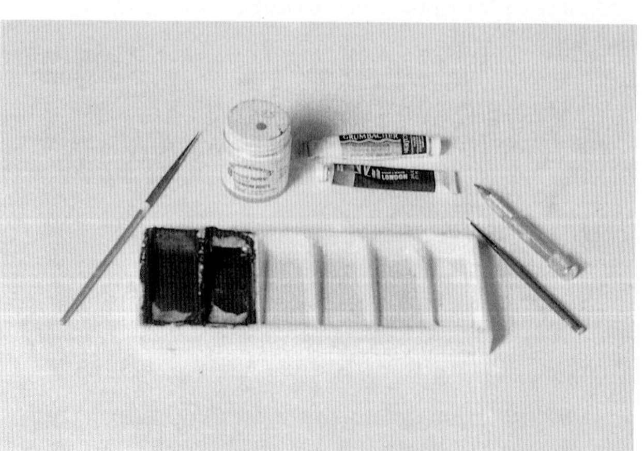

FIGURE 9.3 The Watercolor Dish and Brushes

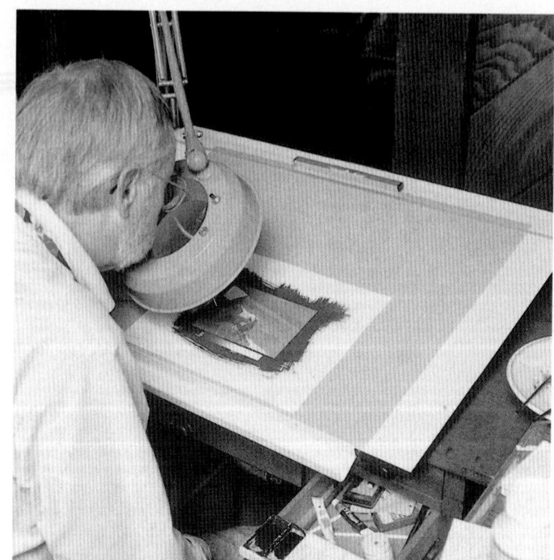

FIGURE 9.4 Spotting the Print Using the Spotting Table and Lamp

White Defects

Usually, these are easier to handle. First one must blend the colors of Burnt Umber and Ivory Black in the watercolor tray with a bit of water to match the print tone. For Pt/Pd, start with a 50% portion of each. With palladium, use two parts Burnt Umber to one part Ivory Black. Try the mixtures on old prints until the ratio is reached, then record it.

Arrange the prints in an order so that those with the defects in the blackest portions are first. Continue to sort in an order of tones until the defects are in the lightest gray areas. Start at the blackest areas with a barely diluted mixture. If, after these are finished, defects remain in lighter areas, place the prints in the stack so that they may be done later with the more dilute solutions. Now, choose the defects in a near black (Zone III). Dilute the mixture in the tray with distilled water until the proper concentration is reached. Paint the scratch pad until the brush is almost dry. Then, holding the pad under the light next to the print defect, spot the pad. Check the match through the magnifying glass. Continue through the tonal scales, diluting, until the lightest areas (Zones VII to VIII) are reached. Lastly, spot the defects created by etching or Titanium White.

Presentation

Lighting

The delicate hues of the platinum and palladium prints change with the color temperature of the lighting. The light in the finishing room should approximate the lighting given the framed and displayed print. Most frequently, some daylight quartz or fluorescent tubes are desirable. For a little more cost, full spectrum color-corrected daylight fluorescent tubes can be used in place of the standard ugly green hardware bulbs.

If one prints for exhibition, the galleries must be visited with attention to the intensity of the lighting given to the artwork. For most, the ceiling spots are more intense than standard room light. Anticipate that the serious collector will have similar lighting, and print accordingly. In most cases, the prints will be made darker than what looks good under normal room light. Otherwise, they will appear anemic under gallery lighting. Unfortunately, in the interests of conserving more precarious forms of art, many museums provide inadequate lighting for photographs.

Matting

Most conservators now discourage dry mounting of all art work. I do not recommend mounting of platinum prints. (Gelatin-sized prints will not stick.) Instead, use corners available from Light Impressions with archival tape. I also do not recommend waxing, lacquering, or coating the final print with any substance.

With all methods of presentation, if glass is to be used, a mat should be inserted to keep the print from touching the glass. The mat should also be composed of archival material; either of rag, or one of the alpha-cellulose-treated wood pulp materials. I prefer that the tone of the mat approximates that of the paper used for printing, as not to detract from the image.

As with many printing processes, the portions of the image to be shown are determined by the artist and, at times, the client (Table 9.3). The more traditional form of matting has been to stop the mat at the borders of the image. The brush stokes are then covered from view.

With an image made from an unmasked negative, a decision can be made to show the entire effects of the brush strokes (Plate 9.2). In this case, the mat would only cover the edges of the print paper. If the negative has been masked during printing, the borders will be that of the printing paper and the edge of the mat (Plate 9.3). An effective variation is to allow only a portion of the black border to show (Plate 9.4). Many platinum printers allow the margins made by the coating material to determine the borders of the print (Plate 9.5). Small Twinrocker Feather Deckle paper can be combined with visible brush strokes to present a contiguous image (Plate 9.6).

As with any art form, there are no rules. If it feels good, do it.

Framing

The choice of frames is a personal matter, generally decided by the owner of the print. However, if a framing shop becomes involved, they can be encouraged to avoid the more decorative varieties of frame that may overpower the image.

The are a number of choices for glass. The best is the rather expensive neutral glass made for artwork (Image Perfect®, Den Glass®, and PerfectGlass®). It does not have the greenish tint of ordinary window glass. For most installations, however, the difference between the two is hardly noticeable. Avoid plastic or nonglare glass as the tones of the print are veiled.

Numbering of Editions

Platinum/palladium is essentially a printmaking process. If Pt/Pd printing represents a new endeavor for the

TABLE 9.3 Five Methods of Displaying Platinum/Palladium Prints

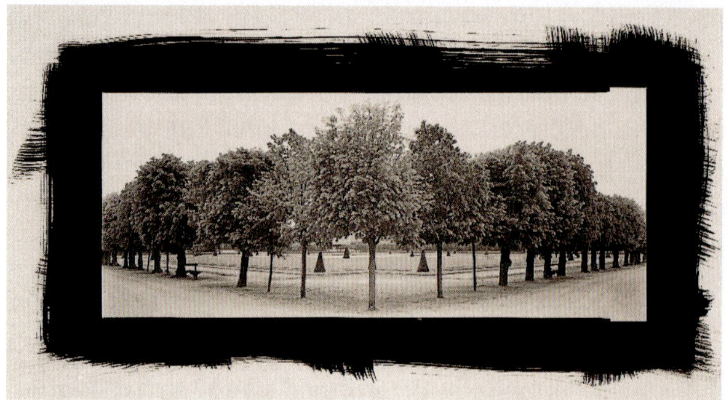

PLATE 9.2 Fountainebleau, France. 1994 7 × 17 Pt/Pd
The unmasked print shows the brush strokes.
Here all were allowed to show.

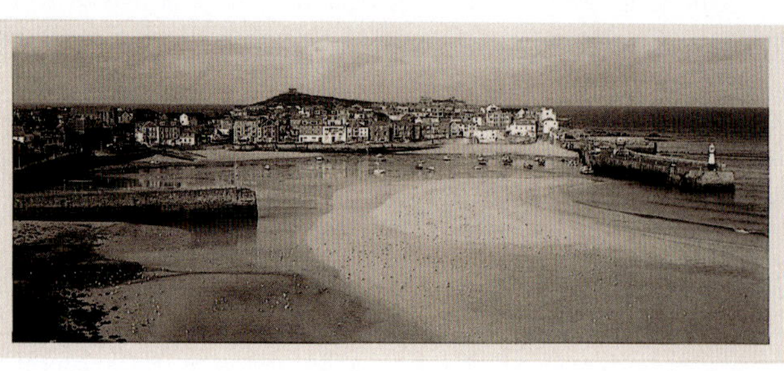

PLATE 9.3 St. Ives England. 1992 7 × 17 inch Pt/Pd. The negative was masked before printing. As the unexposed coating was washed away at processing, the image shows with no brush strokes.

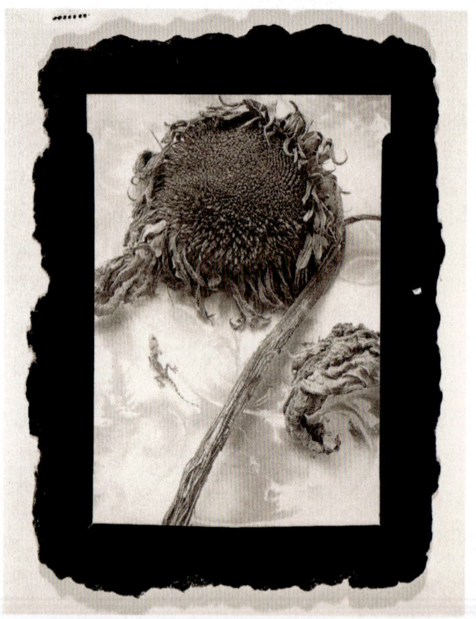

PLATE 9.6 Natura Morta. 1992 7 × 5 inch Pd (© Keith Schreiber)
The 6 × 8 inch Twinrocker White Feather was coated to the edge.

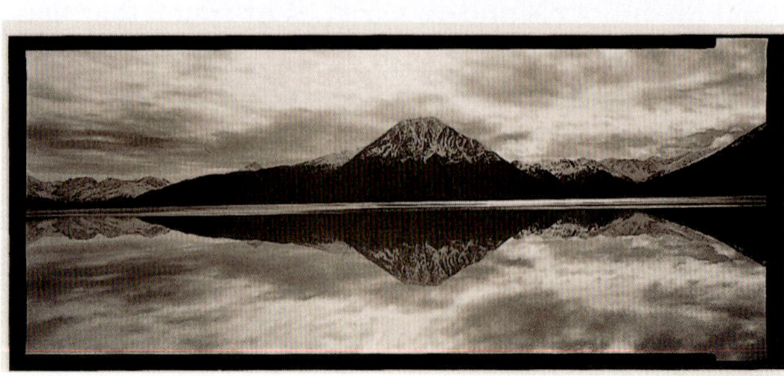

PLATE 9.4 Turnagain Arm, Alaska. 1996 7 × 17 inch Pt/Pd
The brush strokes are only partly covered by the mat.

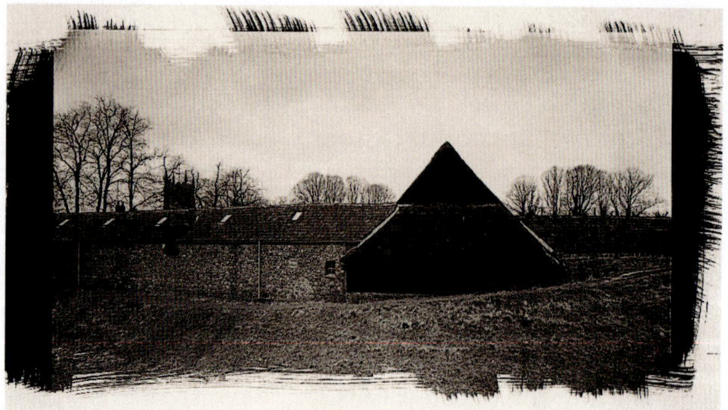

PLATE 9.5 Avebury, England. 1998 8 × 20 inch Pt/Pd
The borders of the image have been outlined by the coating.

photographer, this may be the time to begin numbering and limiting editions. (When I began Pt/Pd, and editioning, it was too late for me to go back and number my silver gelatin prints; there were simply too many in circulation.) The advantages of numbered (and limited) editions far outweigh any reasons for objection.

- An accurate database can identify the location of any print can be kept. In the event of theft, fraud, or loss, the print can be quickly accounted for.
- Most collectors of art would like to know how many copies have been and will be produced before they invest in your print. (Just exactly how many copies of *Moonrise* are out there?)
- Many artists, the author included, use an escalated price structure based on edition numbers. As the number goes up and fewer copies are available, so does the price. A collector owning an early edition number can be comforted by the raising market value.

Handling and Storage of Negatives

Every photographer has their own system for negative storage. For the beginner, however, some suggestions may be in order.

- Use cotton gloves when handling negatives. Never leave an uncovered negative in the lab. Due to electromagnetic forces that are not fully understood, a single drop of water will find its way over twenty feet to land on the sky of your negative.
- Take care in the selection of negative sleeves. Do not use glassine. Light Impressions has a complete collection of archival negative sleeves.
- Keep the complete data with the negative so that reprinting is possible. Record date, portions of metal and Nos. A and B ferric oxalate, amount, light source (distance), exposure time, paper, and type of developer and temperature. I have some preprinted forms that I use. Never keep these forms in contact with the negative. I tape them to the outside of the sleeve.
- Devise some cataloging system that records format, date and/or chronology, and other pertinent information. This number can be entered into a database system.
- Store in a dry, cool place, away from environmental hazards. (A garage is not a good place.) Consider a fireproof safe or file. Keep duplicates at another location.

CHAPTER 10

Problems

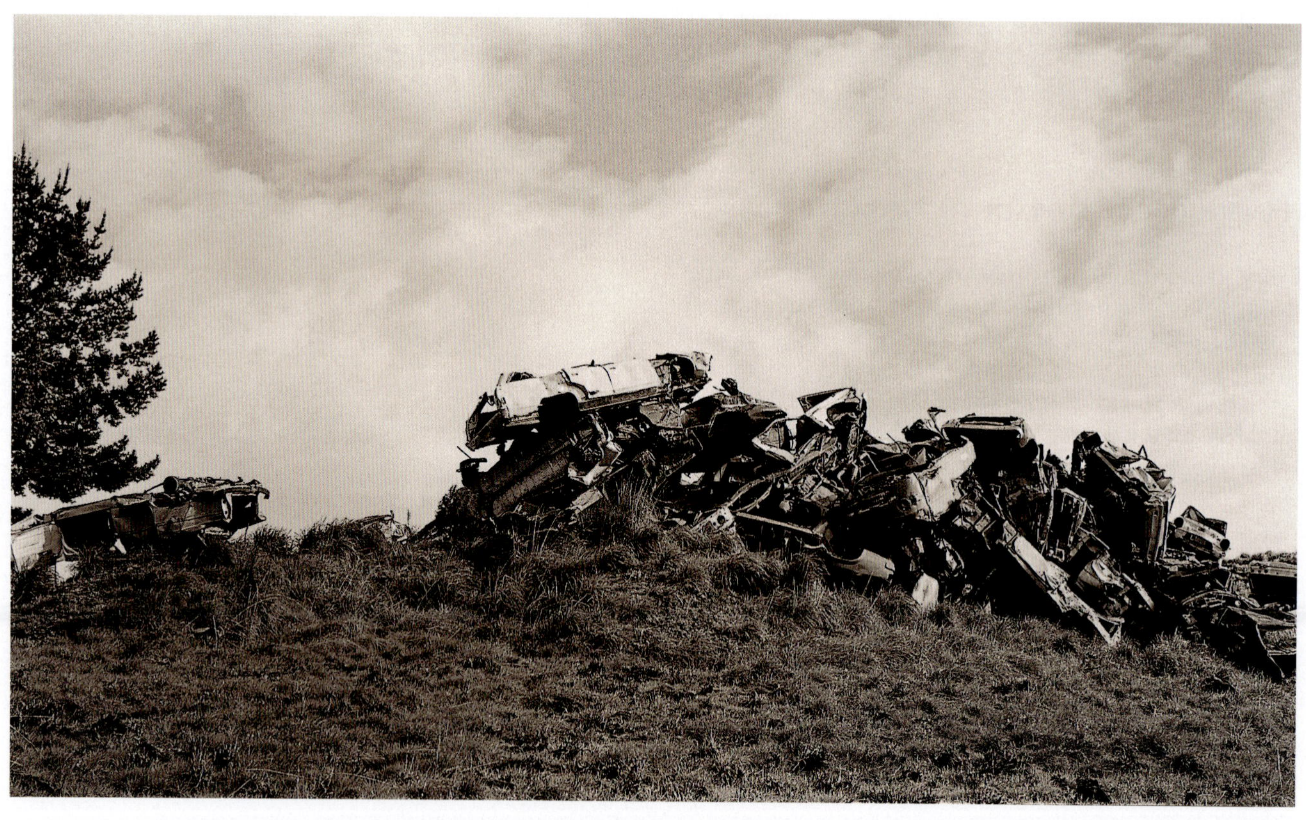

PLATE 10.1 Junkyard. Owaka, N.Z. 1995 12 × 20 inch Pd

Pride goeth before destruction, and an haughty spirit before a fall.
Proverbs 16:18

Platinum printing is an art wherein a historical process is practiced with materials in purposes for which they were not intended. The platinum printer must be prepared to deal with failure, and when a solution is apparently at hand, the Gods will see that you are put into your proper place. The process is, above all, a character builder.

Every platinum printer I know has a shelf loaded with imperfect prints that are not good enough to show, but too valuable to throw away. As the years go on, the stack becomes higher and the problems continue.

> ***Platinum Printer's Prayer***
> *Oh Lord, when a product changes,*
> *in the matter of course,*
> *I pray, that only once, it be better,*
> *instead of worse.*

Chalky or Light Prints

1. Inadequate Sizing: The coating sinks from the surface into the paper fibers. Of the papers listed in any art supply catalogue, the vast majority, particularly those for printmaking, are not suitable for platinum or palladium. Concentrate your experimentation on high-quality, hot-pressed watercolor or drawing papers.

2. Not Enough Coating Material: This is the most common cause for anemic or chalky prints. Take particular care when using the coating rod. It is capable of spreading a quite thin (and inadequate) layer of material.

3. Inadequate Printing Time: This is a most common finding when the light source has not been calibrated, and the print is simply too far from the source to achieve an optimum Dmax for the paper.

4. Too Much Moisture in the Brush: The coating material is drawn into the bristles by capillary action.

5. The Paper Is Too Damp: The coating material is drawn into the deeper paper fibers by the same capillary action.

6. The Paper Surface Is Too Rough: Unless you plan to use a lot of solution or double coat, avoid the matte surface or cold pressed papers.

Uneven Coating

1. Inadequate Sizing or Too Little Coating Material: See above.

2. Wrong Coating Instrument: As with papers, some of the most elegant (and expensive) brushes are meant for other processes and fail miserably with platinum. (See "The Coating Instruments" in Chapter 8, "The Platinum and Palladium Print.")

3. Unsuitable Paper: Too alkaline, too much carbonate in sizing. (See Chapter 5, "Paper.")

4. Paper Surface Is Too Slick: Platinum printers generally prefer a medium vellum surface. Many "plate" finishes repel the coating, forming a useless pool at the side of the image area. The same phenomena would be observed with papers that have been over-sized with gelatin. In that case, many times, portions of the image float off in the developer.

Graininess

1. Materials at Too Low a Temperature

2. Too Much Restrainer: (chlorate or dichromate)

3. Too Much Work with the Brush: This causes the paper nap to rise. Use high-quality brushes. The cheap ones are too abrasive. Do not use foam brushes. Remember, most papers are simply unsuitable. Don't waste time and money trying to make them work.

4. Unsuitable Paper: too alkaline, too much carbonate in sizing. (See Chapter 5, "Paper.")

5. Phil Davis has found that too much ferric oxalate in the sensitizer may increase grain. Decreasing the proportion of sensitizer to metal may also improve granularity as well as warm the tones.

Black Spots on the Print

1. Particulate Matter from Bristles or Coating Material. To prevent this:
    - Inspect the paper under bright light before coating.
    - Vigorously manipulate the bristles to remove any foreign matter.
    - Inspect the coating material while in beaker. Particles usually float to the surface and are easily removed with a cotton applicator.
    - Metal Salt Precipitant: Unquestionably this is the most difficult to remove, as it frequently penetrates deeply into paper fibers. *Do not agitate the bottles of metal salts.* Filter if necessary. (See the discussions of coating techniques in Chapter 8, "The Platinum and Palladium Print.")

Many of these defects can be removed by etching the dried coated paper before exposure with a single edged razor blade, or during spotting. (See "Principles of Etching and Spotting Platinum/Palladium Prints" in Chapter 9 "Advanced Technique.")

2. Negative Pinholes: Pinholes are caused by dust in the camera on the film holder during exposure. This is particularly annoying in low humidity. Dust or vacuum frequently the insides of film holders and camera. Store holders and camera in plastic or Nylon bags. Thoroughly examine the negative on a light table. Cover the pinholes with Crocein Scarlet. (See Chapter 9, "Advanced Technique.")

Fog versus Stain

Fog (a light coating of metal where it should not be) should be distinguished from *stain* (unremoved iron salts). Generally, fogging is uniform and staining is spotty. Remember that some fogging will most likely occur when no restrainer is used. This is due to minute amounts of reduced ferric oxalate (ferrous) found in the freshest of sensitizers. A drop of hydrogen peroxide may help (see Appendix C, "Principles of the Developing and Clearing Process"), but don't use it to mask bad sensitizer or poor working conditions.

Fog can be due to too much UV light in the coating area or too high a concentration of ferrous oxalate in your sensitizer. Test this by coating some strips in the dark and compare fogging areas to strips done in your normal coating light. If you get fog in both strips, the sensitizer is probably bad. If fog occurs only when coated under your lighting conditions, there is too much UV light.

Ferric oxalate is not expensive. Only use analytical grade from platinum suppliers. Store Ferric oxalate in the refrigerator. When in doubt, discard it. If fog persists, try a new brush.

Some workers, who must have consistent, reproducible results, mix the sensitizer from powder the night before printing. The potassium chlorate restrainer in solution B is also somewhat unstable, causing a reduction in paper contrast and, eventually, fogging.

Stain is due to uncleared iron salts. Agitate constantly in the first clearing bath. Make sure fingers or tongs are clean before touching print. (See "Clearing Agents" in Chapter 4.) If a problem exists with a particular paper, the paper fibers could be softened first in a solution of EDTA before clearing. In this case, subsequent baths of hypo clearing agent may be more effective. (See Chapter 5, "Paper," for the recommended clearing agents for each paper.)

Residual iron salts may not be visible to the eye. Examine the dried print under a blue light to detect stain.

If a stain occurs that is resistant to any clearing agents, it may be insoluble iron hydroxide formed either in an alkaline developer or clearing bath. (See Appendix C, "Principles of the Developing and Clearing Process.") Check with pH paper. Add citric or oxalic acid to bring the developer to an acid state, or use an EDTA presoak, or add sodium bisulfite to the clearing bath.

Remember: Fog is archival; stain is most likely, not.

Solarization with Palladium

Solarization differs from the Sabattier effect. The Sabattier effect involves the reversal of the silver image upon introduction of light during the development process. True solarization is based on the concept that, given a layer of metal salts, reduction may occur first on the surface, blocking the deeper layers from receiving as much light as adjacent areas.

Pure palladium has a tendency to solarize under supermaximum exposure. The areas that receive the most light, usually the brush strokes around the image, may actually end up lighter than the shadow areas of the image. If the print is to be matted, this should be of little consequence. If it occurs in the image, coat the palladium heavily, possibly with polyvinyl alcohol in the sensitizer, and plan the shadows as 90% black (the brush strokes will probably solarize). Increasing the proportion of metal to sensitizer may help.

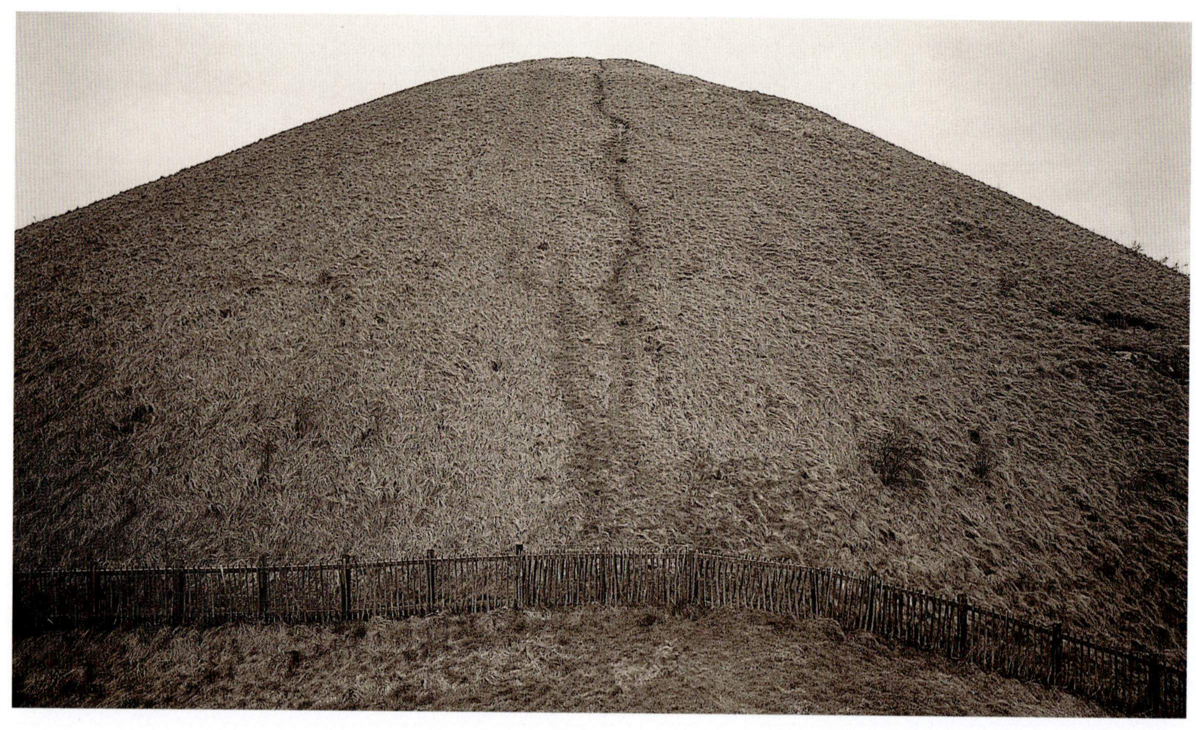

Silbury Hill, England. 1998 12 × 20 Pd

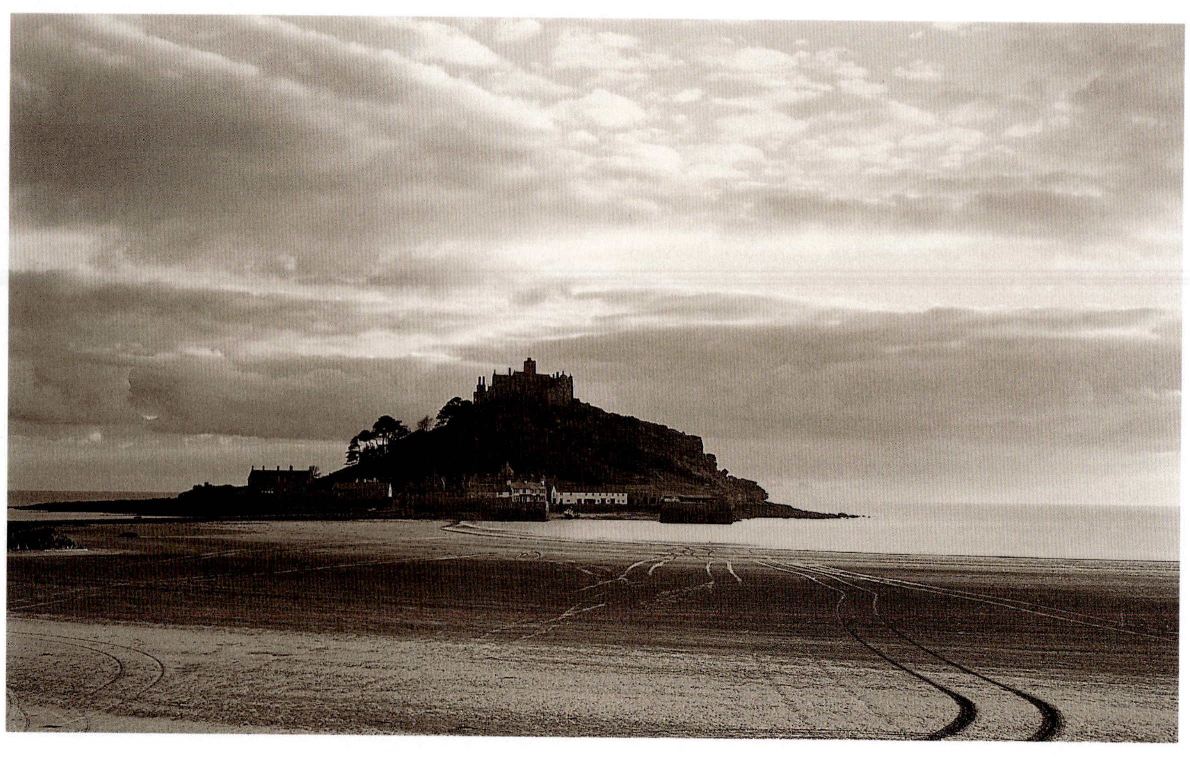

St. Michael's Mount, England. 1998 12 × 20 Pt/Pd

PART TWO

Sensitometry for the Platinum/Palladium Process

CHAPTER 11

The Film and Paper Curves

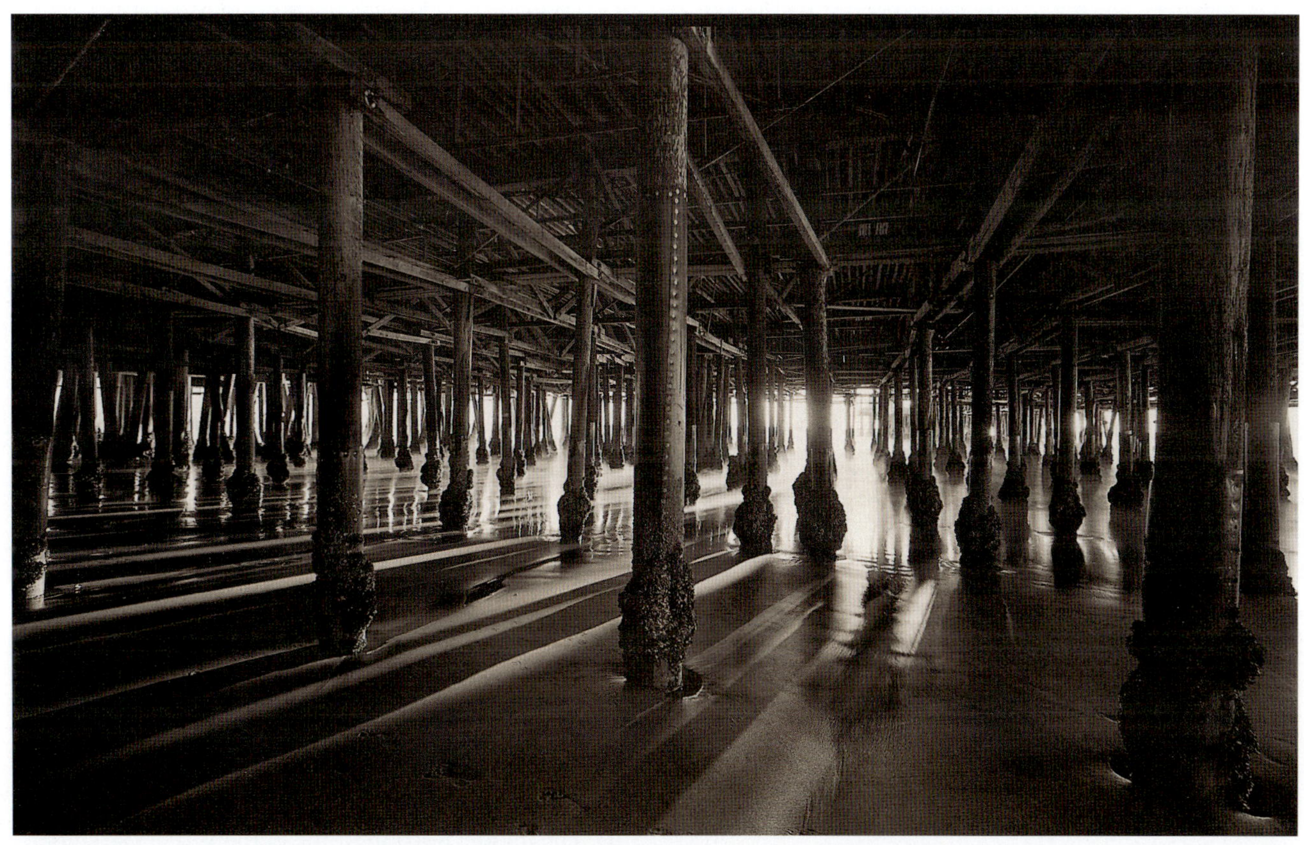

PLATE 11.1 Santa Monica Pier. 1996 12 × 20 inch Pd
For an SBR of 14, TXT was given an ISO of 25 and developed at 7 minutes with D-76 1:1.

It is not within the scope of this text to provide the background necessary to achieve a mastery of the sensitometric techniques applicable to the platinum/palladium (Pt/Pd) processes. Therefore, it is necessary that you read the sections on film and paper in the books recommended in the bibliography, particularly Phil Davis' *Beyond the Zone System* (1998). *Better yet, take a BTZS (Beyond the Zone System) workshop.* They are scheduled through Darkroom Innovations. (See "Sources.")

Before we can add information to the concepts discussed in Chapter 3, "The Negative," we must understand the concepts of plotting, on a graph, the characteristics of how film and paper react to light. For the study of film, transmission densities are read following exposure to a step tablet. With paper, reflective densities are read from an exposure to the same step tablet. By these methods, the properties of both materials can be analyzed. In each case, the amounts of light directed to the material are plotted, from left to right in increasing increments, on the horizontal or "x" axis. The increases in density of either film or paper are plotted on the vertical, or "y" axis. (Look ahead to Figure 12.1.)

If the density of materials increased in direct proportion to the light, the registration of data would form a straight line. That is not the case. The uneven behavior of metal salts do not produce a line but a *characteristic curve,* one that elevates from left to right in response to the increase in light.

Since the vast majority of readers have some experience with silver printing, I provide the essentials of that process, so that they may be compared later to platinum and palladium.

Silver and Platinum/Palladium Curves Compared

(The curves presented are courtesy of Phil Davis Plotter Program®.)

All sources on the subject of sensitometry may not use the same designations in describing reference points on the paper and film graphs. Since the graphics for this text were derived from the Plotter Program, I will present the terminology programmed into that software (Table 11.1). Note that both paper and negatives have extremes of densities that are not normally used in the planning of an image. These are referred to as *Dmin* and *Dmax*. More important are the limits for textured values. These are called the *image densities IDmin* and *IDmax*.

TABLE 11.1 Terminology for Maximum and Minimum Density Values for Paper and the Negative

Paper Reflective Density		*Negative Transmission Density*	
Paper White	Dmin	Base + Fog	Dmin
Threshold of Textured White	IDmin	Threshold of Textured Shadow	IDmin
Threshold of Textured Black (90%)	IDmax	Threshold of Textured Highlight	IDmax
Maximum Paper Black	Dmax		

Dmin	Minimum Density of Materials
IDmin	Image Density Minimum
IDmax	Image Density Maximum
Dmax	Maximum Density of Materials

The Individual Silver Curve

Paper is measured by reading *reflective densities.* In analyzing an individual silver curve (Figure 11.1), one will see that it is indeed not a straight bar, but shows disproportionate response to light, particularly in the shadow and highlight areas.

1. The highlight areas are represented closest to the x axis. The 0.0 marker on the y axis represents paper white (*Dmin*). A horizontal line drawn just above the base indicates *minimum image density*[1] (*IDmin*), the level at which paper begins to respond to light. In this case, it is 0.04. Note that initially, there is little movement when the paper reaches its "threshold." However, once activated, this *toe* portion at the lower left of the graph elevates very abruptly, indicating a rapid change from blank white to texture, leaving little latitude for representation of whites. In Figure 11.1, note the beginning of texture in the white areas of the "Paper Range and Densities" bar.

2. The middle portion of the graph is quite straight, indicating an even response to increases in light, and good separation in the midtones of a silver print.

[1] The 0.0 setting here is based on the paper white. This representation will vary according to the white of the paper stock. Many silver gelatin papers contain a whitening agent that further lightens this value. Papers used for platinum do not. *The important point is to understand that IDmin is the beginning of textured white for a particular paper.* (Table 11.1)

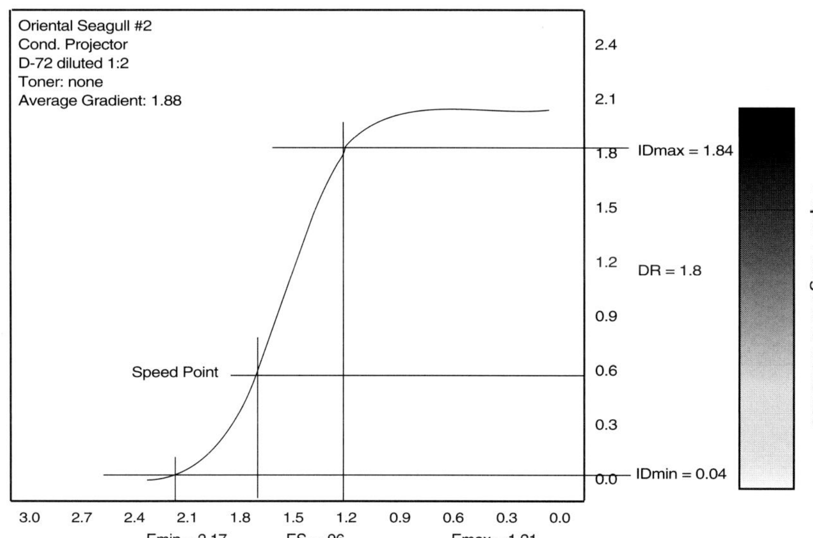

FIGURE 11.1 A Typical Silver Paper Curve. Note the graphic representation of negative densities.

3. The upper portion, or *shoulder,* also shows a sluggish response to light increase. This poor separation in the area of maximum blacks, is seen with monochromatic photographic papers, platinum or palladium included. Note the blockage of black tones represented in the "Paper Range and Densities" bar in Figure 11.1. This characteristic has prompted the American National Standard Institute (ANSI), to eliminate the maximum 10% of black in the standardization of photographic paper. This leaves an approximately 90% range between perceptible white (*IDmin*) and 90% black (*IDmax*). This is obviously not a hard and fast rule; it is simply a tool for paper calibration. The photographer can use this knowledge to deviate from the norm, if so desired. (See the discussion of *convincing black* in Chapter 3, "The Negative" and Chapter 7, "Calibration.")

4. Note that even with the elimination of the 10% blackest portion, the 90% black is at a reflective density (or *IDmax*) of 1.84, showing that silver gelatin paper is capable of reaching the deepest blacks seen in any medium.

5. Observe that the entire silver curve is steep. There is considerable increase in paper density in response to very little change in light. The negative, therefore, must be of low contrast. One can see, at the base, the range of light responsible for the full-range silver print, the exposure scale (ES). Since the light was provided to the film by way of a step tablet, the numbers along the x axis represent step tablet transmission densities. This particular ES indicates the need for a photographic negative with a density range of 0.96, corrected to 0.95.[2]

The Negative for Silver Paper

As I indicated in Chapter 3, "The Negative," the transfer of information from the subject to photographic paper necessitates considerable compression of the density range (DR) of the negative. Note in Figure 11.2 that although the subject brightness range (SBR) of the object photographed is 6.5, the DR of the negative is considerably less. This is represented in the "Negative Range and Densities" bar. To calculate the useful values of a negative, the effective shadow density is obtained by adding the base + fog and lens flare (*Dmin*) to the density at which the curve begins an effective rise. The point at which effective shadow density begins is *IDmin* (Table 11.1).

For highlights, modern film has essentially no limit of *Dmax*, since most films will continue the projection upward off to beyond the confines of the graph. The point, however, where effective highlights end is termed *IDmax*. In Figure 11.2, this is the dark edge of the "Negative Range and Densities" bar.

To further interpret Figure 11.2, The film B+F of 0.06 is added to the density (0.16) at which the curve begins an effective rise. The total is 0.22. This number, which can be easily read by a transmission densitometer, is the *threshold* of shadow detail, or the *IDmin* for this film/developer combination. This is seen as the beginning of texture at the lower end of the "Negative Range and Densities" bar. *IDmin* is subtracted from the

2. With the understanding that the photographic process need not be practiced to impractical tolerances, we round off all densities reading to the nearest 0.05.

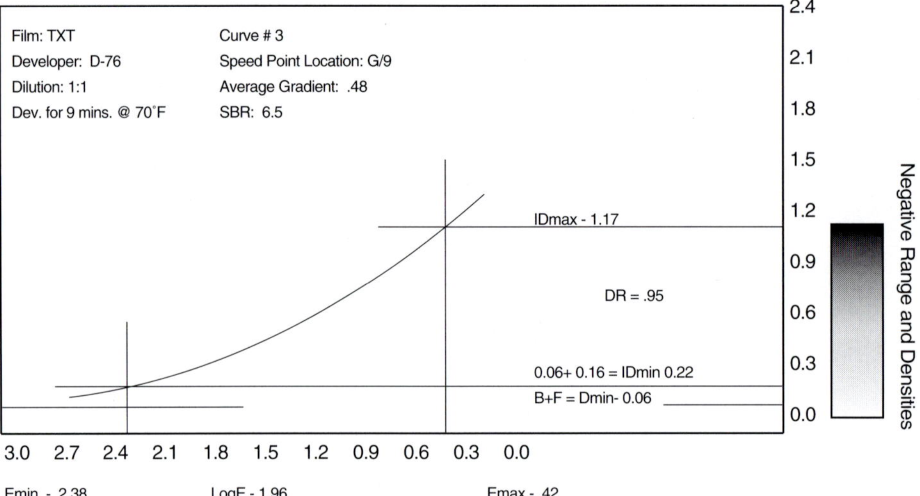

FIGURE 11.2 An Individual Film Curve for Grade 2 Silver Paper Exposed under an Approximately Normal SBR. Note the average gradient of .48. This film was developed in D-76 diluted 1:1.

IDmax of 1.17 (the threshold of textured highlight) to give a density range (DR) of 0.95. This negative has, therefore, been constructed to print on a paper with an ES of 0.95, a little over three stops. In this case, D-76 was used at a 1:1 dilution.

Steepness of the Curve

The steepness of the film curve determines the amount of transmission density the negative will acquire in response to increases in light. As the steepness of the film curve increases, more density range (DR) is formed for a given subject brightness range (SBR) of light. This, in practical terms, is translated to negative *contrast.* A number of methods are used to measure the steepness of the curve. Here, it is the *average gradient.* Note that in Figure 11.2 it is .48 (Kodak, 1998).

The Individual Platinum/Palladium Curve

In examining a Pt/Pd paper curve, note that the terminology is the same. Variations in the numbers and

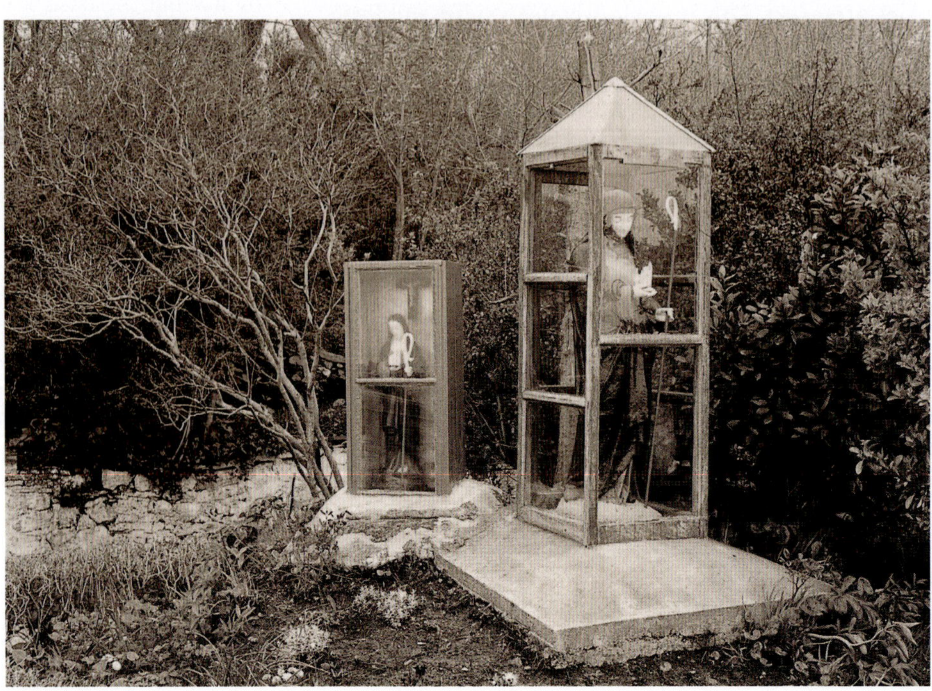

PLATE 11.2 St. Bridget's Well, Ireland. 1986 5 × 7 inch Pt/Pd

graphic representations, however, can be used to note the characteristics of Pt/Pd paper.

A mixture of six drops of A (27% ferric oxalate) and six drops of B (27% ferric oxalate and 0.6% potassium chlorate) will produce the "normal" Pt/Pd curve (Figure 11.3). In examining a Pt/Pd curve (Figure 11.3), note the following:

- In the toe portion of the graph, the transition through the values of textured white is gradual, allowing for great subtlety in the rendition of whites.
- The gradation of midtones is uniform. These last two characteristics help produce the typical platinum print appearance.
- As with silver paper, the leveling at the shoulder indicates that black separation is poor when close to maximum, thus the need for ANSI specifications of 90% black.
- The blacks are not nearly as intense: a 1.50 maximum black reflective density (*Dmax*) compared to a 2.0 silver *Dmax*. The *IDmax* is 1.35 compared to an *IDmax* of 1.84 for silver. (Remember, *convincing black*.)
- There is a wider spread of exposure scale (ES), indicating that a negative of a density range of 1.4 is needed for a print exhibiting a full tonal scale.

The Negative for a Platinum/Palladium Print

The Pt/Pd negative must be processed with considerable more energy than one for silver. In Figure 11.4, D-76 was used undiluted. Note that the average gradient is .72. With an SBR of 6.5, the steepness of the curve now shows an *IDmax* of 1.66. When the *IDmin* of 0.25 is subtracted from the *IDmax*, a density range (DR) of 1.41 (1.40) is obtained. Note the comparative range of densities between the "Negative Range and Densities" bars for silver and Pt/Pd (Figures 11.2 and 11.4).

Contrast Control

Not all negatives will fall into the "ideal" 1.4 DR. Also, a desired interpretation may call for a negative of less or more than that which would produce a full range print. Paper contrast control is possible by adjusting the amount of potassium chlorate restrainer with various mixtures or with ferric oxalate A and B.

A Platinum/Palladium Curve for a High-Contrast Negative

If one uses a No. 2 mixture (11 parts A and 1 part B) to approximate maximum Pt/Pd paper latitude, a negative with a DR of 1.7 can now be used to match the paper ES of 1.7 (Figure 11.5). Remember, a straight "A" mixture will likely fog. Note the accentuated toe at this contrast mixture.

Effect of Fog

When ferric oxalate solution A is used alone with the metal salts, no restrainer is incorporated in the mixture

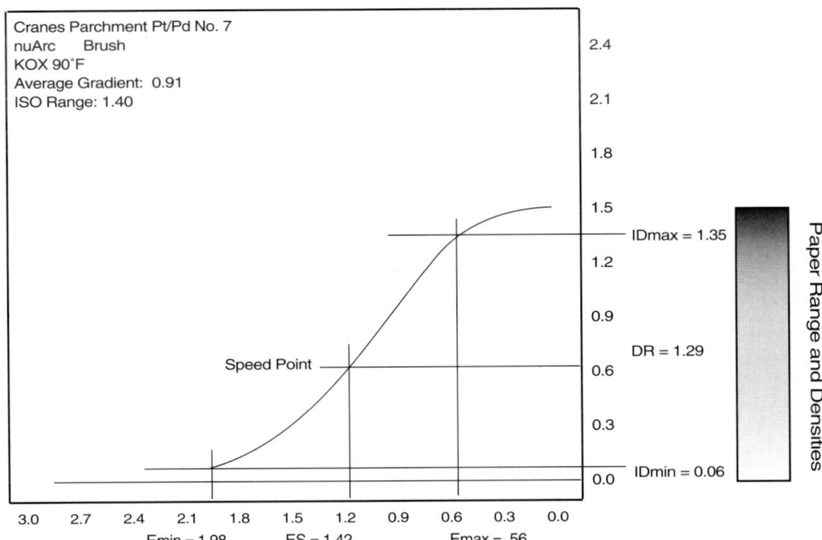

FIGURE 11.3 A Curve for a Medium Contrast Platinum/Palladium Mixture. When compared to the silver paper curve, note the lower *IDmax* on the "Paper Range and Densities" bar and the greater exposure scale on the horizontal axis.

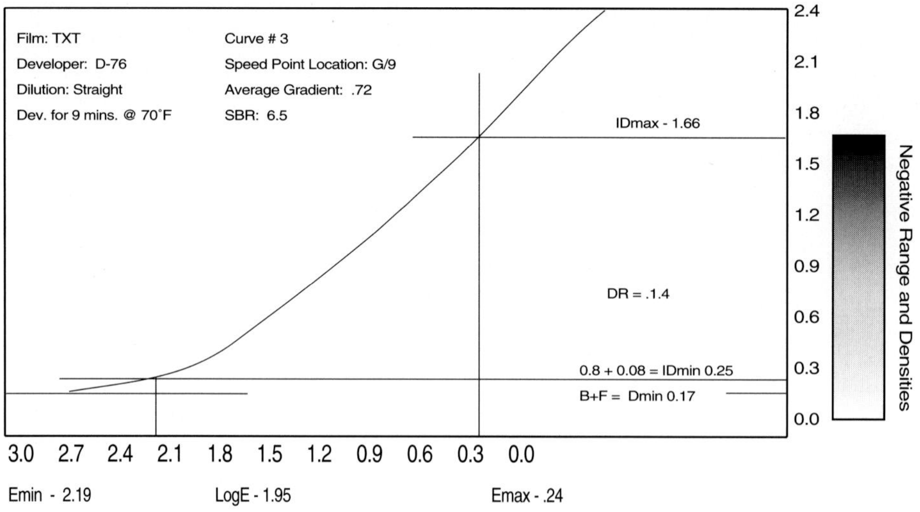

Film: TXT
Developer: D-76
Dilution: Straight
Dev. for 9 mins. @ 70°F
Curve # 3
Speed Point Location: G/9
Average Gradient: .72
SBR: 6.5
IDmax - 1.66
DR = .1.4
0.8 + 0.08 = IDmin 0.25
B+F = Dmin 0.17
2.4 2.1 1.8 1.5 1.2 0.9 0.6 0.3 0.0
Negative Range and Densities
3.0 2.7 2.4 2.1 1.8 1.5 1.2 0.9 0.6 0.3 0.0
Emin - 2.19
LogE - 1.95
Emax - .24

FIGURE 11.4 A Typical Individual Film Curve for Platinum/Palladium Paper Exposed at an Approximately Normal (6.5) SBR. Note that the average gradient is .72. This film was processed with D-76 undiluted.

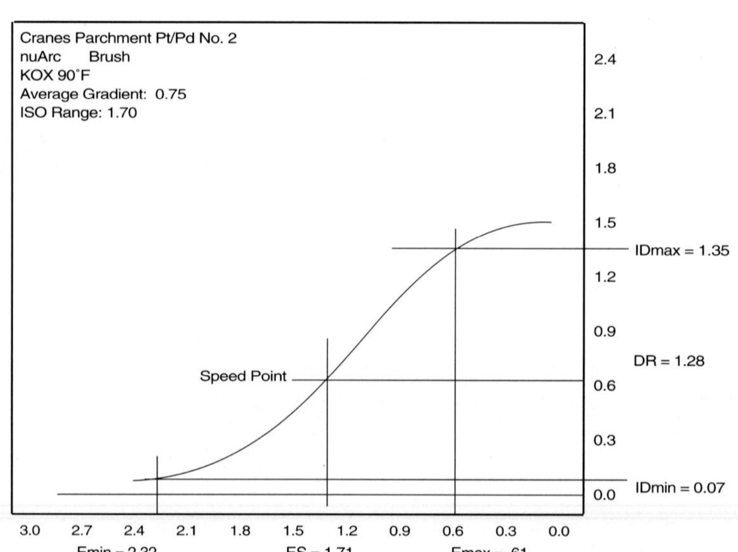

FIGURE 11.5 A Platinum/Palladium Curve for a High-Contrast Negative

(Figure 11.6). While the *Dmin* of 0.10 may appear to be infinitesimal, it is readily visible to the eye. It is sufficiently above the reflective density of paper white to be annoying in many images. Because of the effect of fog, only an ES of 1.75 could be reached.

A Platinum/Palladium Curve for a Low-Contrast Negative

A negative with a DR of 1.0 to 1.1 represents the least usable contrast for the contrast mixtures typically employed. Figure 11.7 represents a mixture of all ferric oxalate B. In this case, a negative with a density range of 1.09 (1.1) is indicated. Because of the amount of restrainer used, there will be an increase in printing time, as well as granularity.

When the Negative Has Inadequate Contrast

When the DR of a negative is still inadequate even after intensification, such as with Selenium toning, it is possible to further shorten the paper scale by an increment of 0.1 to 0.15 by doubling the amount of potassium chlorate in the sensitizer from 0.6 to 1.2%. We refer to this contrast mix-

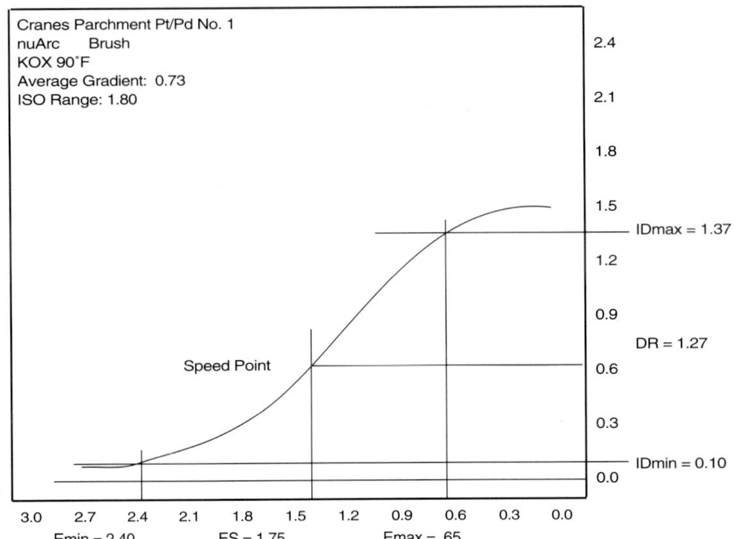

FIGURE 11.6 Fog from Elimination of Restrainer by Using Only Ferric Oxalate Solution A

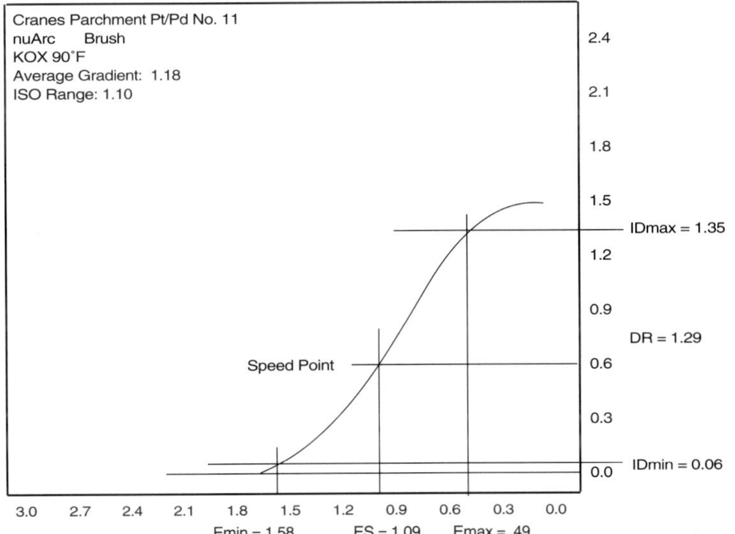

FIGURE 11.7 A Platinum/Palladium Negative for a Low-Contrast Negative.

ture as 13+. The resultant granularity will be enhanced. Note that the ES is now 0.97 (0.95) (Figure 11.8).

The Family of Platinum/Palladium Curves

By adjusting the amounts of ferric oxalate solutions A and B, thirteen paper grades can be obtained. (See the *Standard Negative Contrast Ranges* in Chapter 7, "Calibration.") When the resultant curves are plotted simultaneously, a *family of curves* is obtained (Figure 11.9). When these are analyzed under appropriate conditions, it can be found that for Pt/Pd paper, exposure scales from 1.1 to 1.70 can be obtained. Using these methods, the changes in printing speed related to the amount of restrainer used can also be calculated. Read on!

The Palladium Print

The Family of Palladium Curves

When comparing the Family of Curves produced by pure palladium to that of Pt/Pd (Figure 11.10), some of the features discussed in Chapter 1, "Platinum and Palladium," can be visualized.

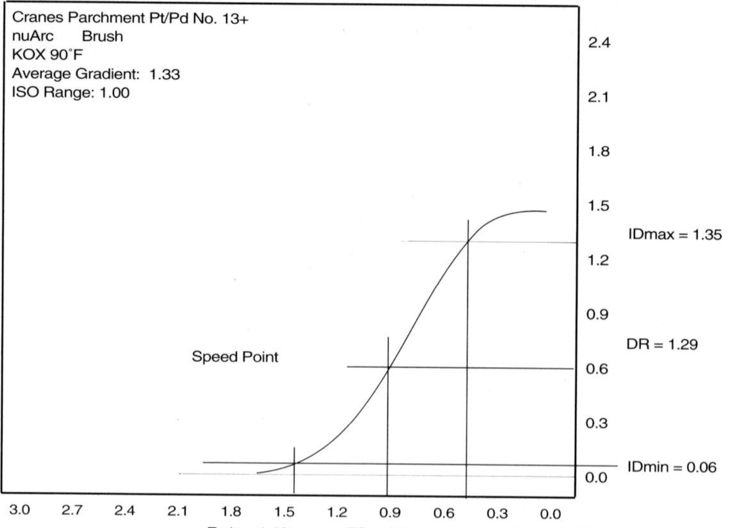

FIGURE 11.8 A Platinum/Palladium Curve No. 13+ Obtained with Ferric Oxalate Solution B Containing Double the Concentration of Potassium Chlorate (1.2% instead of 0.6%).

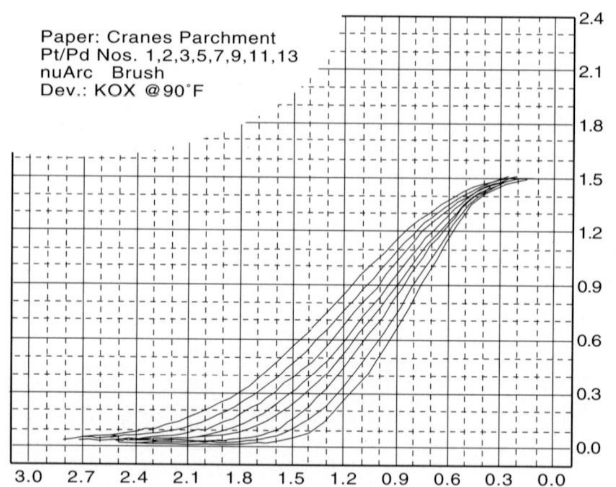

FIGURE 11.9 A Family of Platinum/Palladium Curves

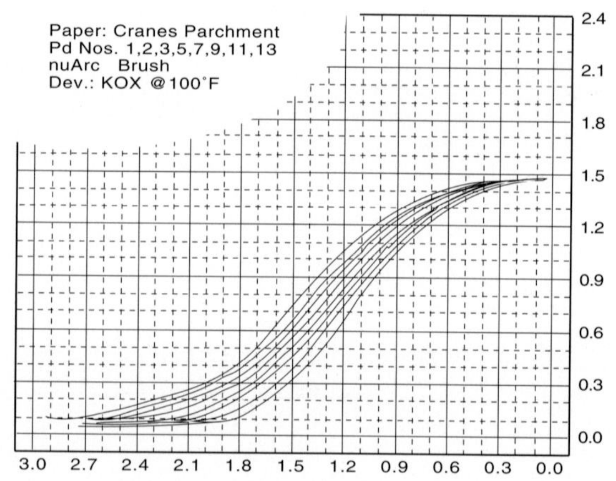

FIGURE 11.10 A Family of Palladium Curves

Note that, although the vertical placements are approximately the same as Pt/Pd, the curves are spread over a greater horizontal distance, indicating the need for a negative of even greater density range. The toe portions indicate a more gradual elevation than with Pt/Pd. Translated to practical terms, we see that with palladium, the distribution of textured whites is more broadly dispersed.

The tests for the family of palladium curves were done using ferric oxalate B containing the same 0.6% concentration of potassium chlorate as with the Pt/Pd curves.[3]

[3] Bostick and Sullivan market a special sensitizer B (No. 2 Pd) with double the restrainer (1.2%) for use with palladium. With this, the exposure scales approximate those of Pt/Pd used with the 0.6% (No. 2 Pt). When printing with pure palladium, however, I prefer to use the ferric oxalate B with 0.6% restrainer. With the resultant expansion of the exposure scale, a more contrasty negative can be used. A longer scale negative allows a ferric oxalate mixture containing less restrainer to be utilized, resulting in a print of smoother tones. The toe is accentuated to the point where the textured whites continue for several stops of exposure. These properties, added to the exquisite hue of the pure palladium print, make it unique among the photographic printing processes.

A Palladium Curve for a Normal Contrast Negative

For more information we can analyze a single curve produced by a mixture of 50% each of ferric oxalate A and B, with an equal amount of palladium salt (Figure 11.11). Note the gradual toe. Also, with this mixture for a medium contrast negative, the ES is 1.59 (1.60). Compare this to the 1.4 ES found with a similar mixture for Pt/Pd. Therefore, the construction of an "ideal" negative for a middle "normal" contrast mixture depends also upon the combination of metal salts to be used. Also, to a lesser extent, the type of paper and developer must be factored in.

A Palladium Curve for a Low-Contrast Negative

The use of less restrainer with palladium has its disadvantages. Even with high-contrast mixtures, the palladium negative must still exhibit considerable density range. One can see from Figure 11.12 that with the most contrasty mixture (No. 13) with only ferric

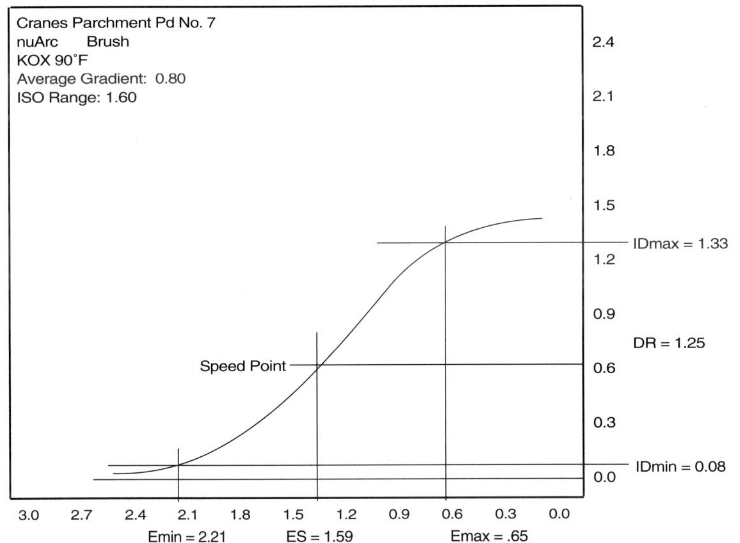

FIGURE 11.11 A Palladium Curve for a Normal Contrast Negative. Ferric oxalate B with 0.6% potassium chlorate was used.

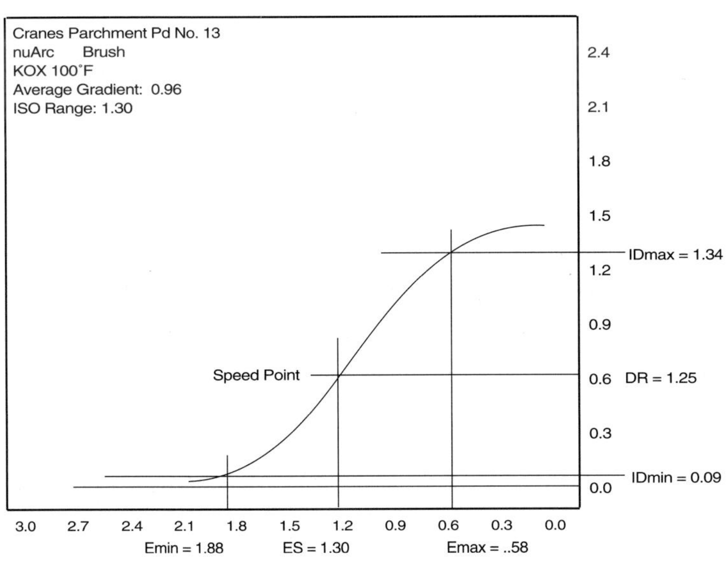

FIGURE 11.12 A Palladium Curve for a Low-Contrast Negative. Ferric oxalate with 0.6% potassium chlorate was used.

oxalate B, a negative with an density range of 1.30 is needed for a full-range print!

A Palladium Curve for a High-Contrast Negative

Figure 11.13 has been kept for last for the purpose of demonstrating, graphically, the remarkable properties of a pure palladium print. Note particularly the rise of the curve from the toe to the mid-portion. This may easily be visualized as print tones undergoing an almost endless transition from barely textured white to the upper midtones of the print. It is from negatives such as these that the uniqueness of the palladium printing process is unsurpassed. (See the book cover and Plates Intro.1, 3.2, 11.1, and B.1.) Note that this No. 2 palladium mixture calls for a negative with a 1.9 ES.

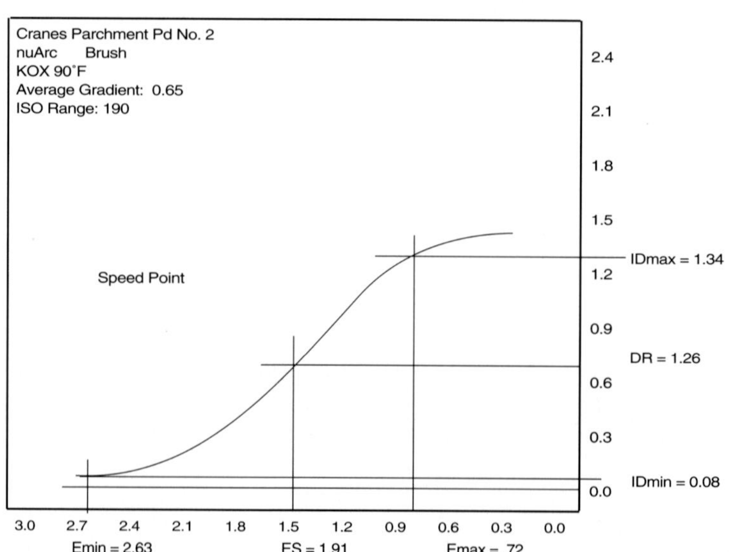

FIGURE 11.13 A Palladium Curve for a High-Contrast Negative. Ferric oxalate with 0.6% potassium chlorate was used.

CHAPTER 12

Using the Print Curves

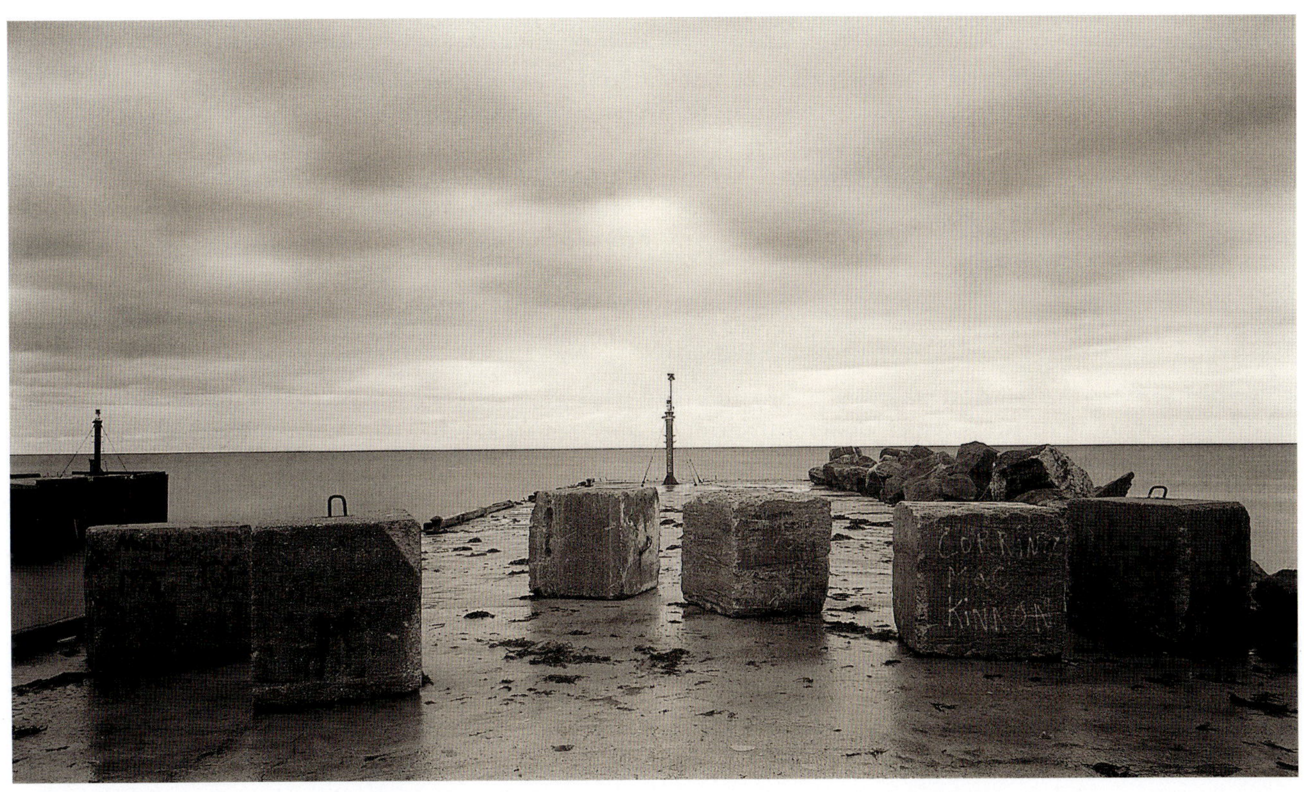

PLATE 12.1 Bay St. Lawrence. 1997 12 × 20 inch Pt/Pd

In choosing the contrast mixture for a particular negative, many platinum and palladium printers will use guides similar to those represented in the *Standard Negative Contrast Ranges* provided in Chapter 7, "Calibration," analyze a concurrently printed step tablet, or simply resort to trial and error. It is, however, possible to customize your own work, incorporating your coating technique, paper, light source, and developer.

While the curves generated by the Plotter Program® (see Chapter 11, "The Film and Paper Curves") are illuminating, more useful information can be obtained from a detailed analysis of the information provided in a graphic representation of platinum and palladium paper characteristics. In the earlier portions of this text, I showed that a reflection densitometer was not necessary for basic calibration. At this point, one will be of value. However, once your technique is fine-tuned, you will no longer need one. So, unless you intend to extensively study these matters, it is best to arrange for the temporary use of a reflection densitometer by borrowing or renting (a print shop is a good source). *For practical adaptation of the material in this section, the continued use of a transmission densitometer is essential.*

Refining the Standards

When compared to the standard enlargement procedure used in the printing of silver paper, contact printing from a set light source allows the elimination of two variables. The distance of the light source to the paper (the height of the enlarger head) and the aperture of the enlarging lens do not need to be factored in to any data used in calibration.

Since the light intensity is constant, the only issues we must consider are the shadow values and contrast mixture.

Shadow Values

The time of paper exposure is determined by the transmission density of the "Zone III" textured shadow areas of the negative. In the making of the print, these values are translated to the darkest portions of the image. We now understand that these are arbitrarily defined at 90% of maximum paper black. During the analysis of the step tablet prints in Chapter 7, "Calibration," we identified those values by the eye. Now, with 90% increment values accurately determined by a reflection densitometer, and matched to a known shadow density that produced it, we can use this standard to calculate printing times for those negatives where the shadow readings match that standard. For negatives where the shadow values deviate to less or more than that standard, further calculations are possible to determine printing time.

When calibrating the light source, a standard was approximated for a 50% (No. 7) mixture of ferric oxalate A and B with a particular metal salt combination, at an exposure of 10 minutes or 400 units with a nuArc. That standard must now be assessed with more accuracy with a reflection densitometer.

NOTE: For assistance in these exercises, refer to the depiction of step tablet values in "Calibrating the Light Source" in Chapter 7, "Calibration."

During the light source calibration, it was recommended that the 90% black should be produced by the Nr. 5[1] (0.65 density) step of the tablet. Now, this should become a requirement.

Using the reflection densitometer, the light-to-print distance for a No. 7 contrast mixture at 10 minutes (400 units), should now be accurately stabilized to produce a 90% black on the Nr. 5 step.

1. The making of a No. 7 contrast mixture printed step table has been described in Chapter 7, "Calibration" (see Figure 7.6). Read the area of maximum black *(Dmax)*. It should be at the step Nr. 1 or the surrounding area. That reflective density will fall in the 1.40 to 1.50 range. If the coating is not sufficient, another print of the step tablet must be made. It is at this point, that the brush and coating rod could be compared, as well as coating technique. An anemic coating will lead to weak reflective values and mottling of the image.
2. Multiply that Dmax value by 0.9. For example, $1.50 \times 0.9 = 1.35$. A reflective density of 1.35 *(IDmax)* will be the 90% "convincing black" of your prints.
3. Using the reflection densitometer, find the tablet Nr. on the print that most approximates this number. Make minor adjustments in the light-to-print distance until this becomes step Nr. 5. (Again, refer to Chapter 7 for graphic presentation of the effects of printing time and contrast mixture on a step tablet print.)

We now know that with a No. 7 medium mixture of 50% ferric oxalate mixtures A and B, with a particu-

[1] Numbers will be used in reference to both step tablet numbers and contrast mixture numbers. For clarity, the European abbreviation (Nr.) will be used for step tablet numbers and the English (No.) for the contrast mixture.

lar metal salt(s), a shadow value of 0.65, exposed at 10 minutes, will give a 90% print black.

Now we will offend the purists by converting the 0.65 transmission density of the Nr. 5 step to a more manageable 0.60.[2] This will be your *Speed Point.*

Factoring in the Effects of Contrast Control

Up to now, we have been dealing with negatives that will print on a Pt/Pd No. 7, 50% mixture of ferric oxalate A and B. They therefore have the optimum density range of 1.4.

For negatives deviating from that, we must alter the mixture of A and B, either adding or subtracting the restrainer found in the No. 7 mixture. *This will change printing speed*, compounding upon the properties of shadow values to determine printing time. Less restrainer, as found in mixture No. 3, results in less printing time than the No. 7 mixture. More restrainer, as with mixture No.13, comparatively adds more printing time. This can be observed in the step tablet prints in "Calibrating the Light Source" in Chapter 7 (Figures 7.7 through 7.10).

If the strips were coated well, when laid in order from No. 1[3] to No. 13, the 90% black step will move relative to the contrast mixture, indicating changes in printing speed.

In the strip made from the No. 2 mixture, the 90% black will have occurred at a higher number panel than the strip made with the No. 7 mixture (Figure 7.9). If the No. 7 strip indicated a 90% black at Nr. 5 (0.60 transmission density), the same value on the No. 2 strip may occur on step Nr. 6, a 0.8 transmission density. Therefore, the same 90% black, when printed with a No. 2 mixture, occurred at a *greater* negative density, showing an *increase in printing speed.*

In the No. 13 strip, the opposite is observed (Figure 7.10). Now the 90% black is at a lower number with less transmission density. To produce the 90% black under the same amount of light, it requires that the negative be *less dense. The printing time is slowed.*

In observing strips made from contrast mixtures No. 3 and No. 5, you will note printing speeds between the No. 2 and No. 7 strips. The No. 9 and No. 11 mixtures will show slower speeds to fall between No. 7 and No. 13. The eventual calculations will show approximate linear speed changes from mixtures No. 2 to No. 13, to encompass slightly less than a one-stop increase or decrease in each direction from the No. 7 standard—*a total range of almost two stops.* (Look ahead to Figure 13.1, "The SPEED TRACKER©.")

Analyzing the Print Curve

To analyze and customize our own technique, we must leave the computerized arena and investigate manually drawn curves. Figure 12.1 represents the standard graph used to plot paper densities. Note that the horizontal or *x* axis has been marked with increases in light at 0.3 log intervals, from left to right. The numbers are dropping because they represent decreasing step tablet transmission densities. The vertical or *y* axis is scribed with transmission densities, also in 0.3 log intervals, increasing from the base to the top.

Using reflection densitometer readings from the same strips that were produced during the contrast studies, each contrast mixture can be plotted (Figure 12.2).

Note that except for mixture No. 2, only the odd numbers were used. Here, plotting reflective densities, a Family of Platinum/Palladium Curves has been produced similar to the computer-generated Figure 11.9. Note that here, all of the strips have a maximum black of 1.5. When a horizontal line is drawn at the 90% black, or 1.35 level, the line intersects the film curves at different points.

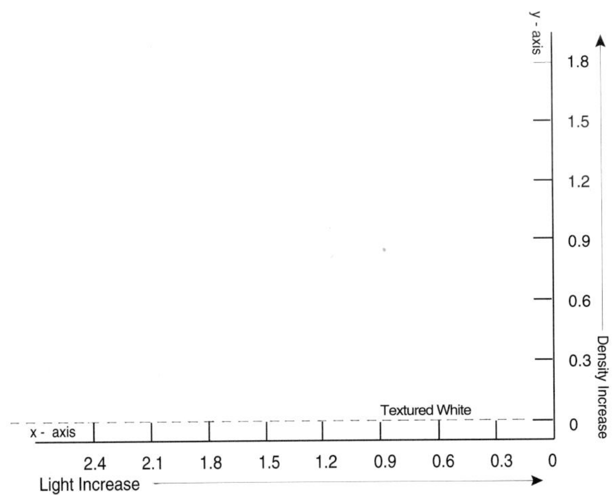

FIGURE 12.1 The Graph Used to Plot Light and Density. As the light increases from left to right along the *x* axis, paper reflective densities increase on the *y* axis.

[2] These techniques are intended to save considerable time and expense in producing a good test print. They will not eliminate the fine-tuning and visual interpretation needed for the final print. Therefore, a deviation of 0.05 is hardly significant.

[3] Normally, we do not analyze the No. 1 contrast mixture strip because of fog.

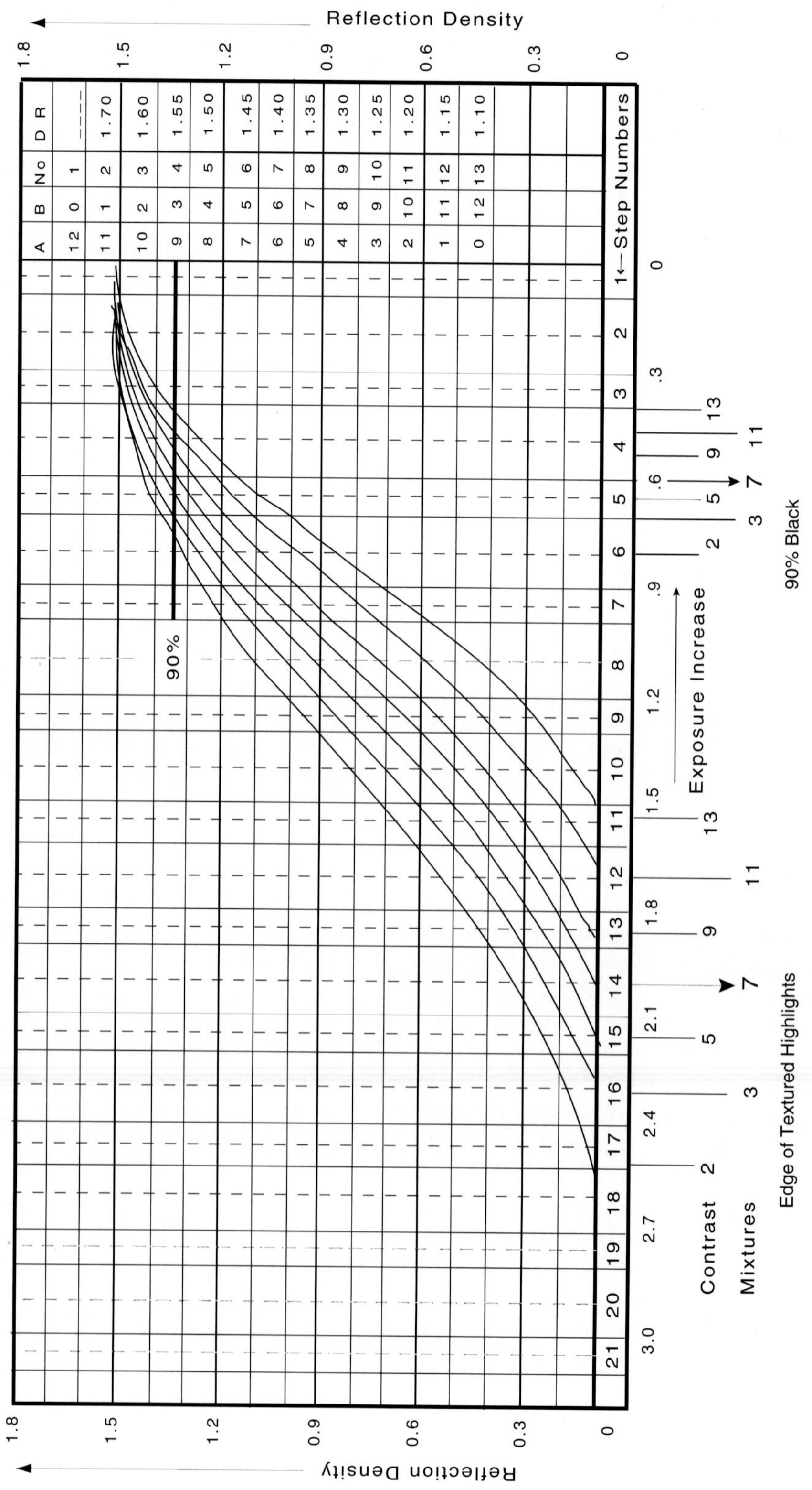

FIGURE 12.2 Family of Platinum/Palladium Curves.
Crane's *Platinotype* Developed in Potassium Oxalate at 90°F.

Graphic Illustrations of Speed Changes Produced by Contrast Mixtures

In Figure 12.3, Three curves are shown intersecting the line for 90% black. The vertical lines projected downward represent the speed changes produced by the different contrast mixtures. By noting where these vertical lines cross the calibrated base of the graph, we can calculate printing speed changes produced by the contrast mixtures. The horizontal dotted line adjacent to the base represents the beginning of textured white.

NOTE: For those not working with photographic sensitometry, the concept of speed changes tracking along the horizontal axis may initially be difficult to grasp. Remember that the numbers on the *x* axis represent light increase, from left to right. The log numbers (0.9, 0.6, 0.3, etc.) are the transmission densities of the step tablet. The lower the number, the more light is allowed to reach the paper. Each contrast mixture film curve, if projected down from where it crosses the 90% line, intersects the step tablet density that caused that 90% black.

The 90% black shown in Figures 12.2 and 12.3 is a *measurable and duplicable* constant. In this case it is reflection density 1.35.

- If a more dense step tablet value caused the same 90% black, the contrast mixture has a *faster Printing Speed.*

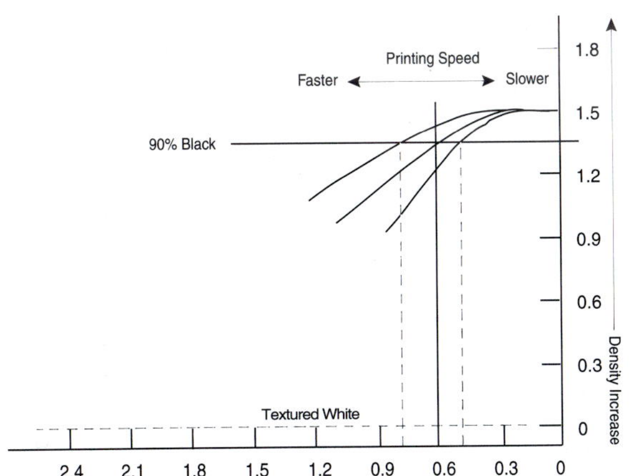

FIGURE 12.3 The Intersection of Platinum/Palladium Curves at 90% black.

- If a less dense step tablet value caused the same 90% black, the contrast mixture has a *slower Printing Speed*

The step tablet densities are also a constant.

- When tracking the vertical lines from where each curve crosses the 90% line to the *x* axis, going from left to right, each 0.3 change represents a *halving* of Printing Speed change or a *doubling* of exposure time.
- When going from right to left, each 0.3 change represents a *doubling* of Printing Speed change or a *halving* of exposure time.

In Figure 12.3, a portion of the No. 7 curve is shown in the center. The solid center vertical line is projected from the point where that curve intersects the 90% black to the horizontal shadow density scale. *The No. 7 mixture represents the standard from which other contrast mixture corrections will be made.*

Note in Figure 12.3 that, to the left, a portion of another curve is shown crossing the 90% black. This is drawn from a contrast mixture of a lower number containing less restrainer. The dotted vertical line crosses the horizontal axis to the left of the solid line produced by the No. 7 mixture. In this case, a *shorter* printing time will be needed than with the No. 7 mixture.

To the right, a portion of a curve produced by a contrast mixture containing more restrainer than the No. 7 mixture is represented. Here the projected dotted line intersects the horizontal base to the right. A *longer* printing time will be needed.

Using the Algorithm

In learning the steps necessary, from the reading of the negative to the calculation of printing time, it is helpful to follow a planned series of steps, or an *algorithm*, until the process becomes more routine (Table 12.1).

1. Using the transmission densitometer, read the highlight and shadow values of the negative.[4] Do the subtraction to determine DR.

4. As I have emphasized textured values in the print, it is also necessary to read the clear and dense portions of the negative where shadow and highlight textures are desired. If the negative has been well made, these are usually the clearest and most dense areas. If either the shadows or highlight areas of the negative are without texture (a frequent occurrence with enlarged second- or third-generation negatives), the print will reflect the same absence of values.

TABLE 12.1 Algorithm for Using Negative Density Readings to Calculate Printing Time

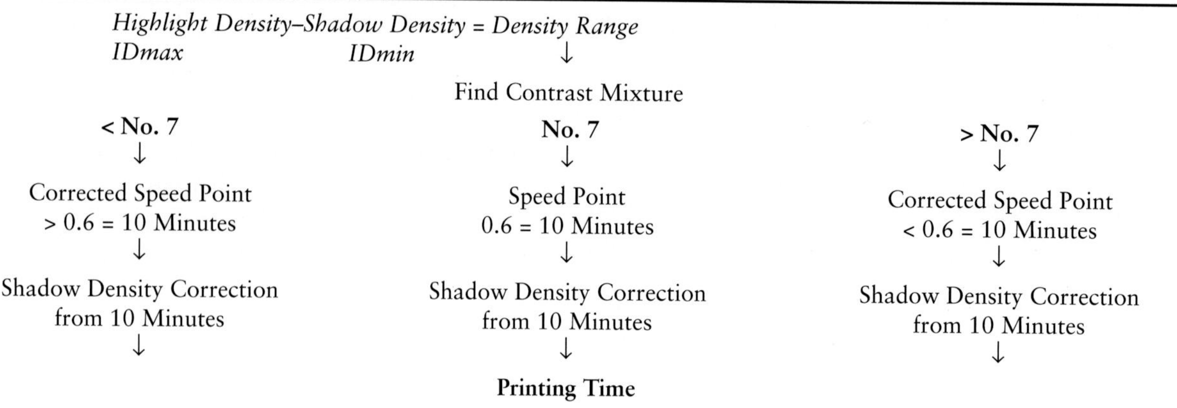

Highlight Density–Shadow Density = Density Range
IDmax *IDmin*
↓
Find Contrast Mixture

< No. 7	No. 7	> No. 7
↓	↓	↓
Corrected Speed Point > 0.6 = 10 Minutes	Speed Point 0.6 = 10 Minutes	Corrected Speed Point < 0.6 = 10 Minutes
↓	↓	↓
Shadow Density Correction from 10 Minutes	Shadow Density Correction from 10 Minutes	Shadow Density Correction from 10 Minutes
↓	↓	↓

Printing Time

2. Determine the contrast mixture. Use your own data or refer to Table 7.2, "Standard Negative Contrast Ranges," in Chapter 7, "Calibration."

3. Find the appropriate curve in Figure 12.2 (Pt/Pd) or Figure 12.18 (Pd).

4. For contrast mixture No. 7, project a vertical line from the 90% black to the horizontal axis. It should cross at 0.6, your Speed Point.[5]

5. For contrast mixtures Nos. 2 to 6, see the left side of the algorithm. Note that a *Corrected Speed Point* will be needed. Find the curve for that contrast mixture and project a vertical line from the 90% black to the horizontal axis. It will cross somewhere between 0.8 and 0.6. That density is your Corrected Speed Point.

6. For contrast mixtures Nos. 8 to 13, see the right side of the algorithm. Note that a *Corrected Speed Point* will also be needed. Find the curve for that contrast mixture, and project a vertical line from the 90% black to the horizontal axis. It will cross somewhere between 0.6 and 0.4. That density is your Corrected Speed Point.

7. Using either your Speed Point or Corrected Speed Point, do the shadow densities correction using the actual shadow value of your negative. From this, working from the 10-minute printing time standard,[6] you will determine your printing time. This will be discussed in detail, and examples given, in Figures 12.4 to 12.17.

[5] If, for some reason, you choose not to calibrate at this point, use the step tablet density that gave you a 90% black at 10 minutes printing time.

[6] If you standardized at a printing time other than 10 minutes, you must calculate from that time. It is strongly suggested that the nuArc be standardized at 400 units. The nuArc and other plate burners allow for such adjustments.

Examples of Various Negative Density Values

While going through these exercises, refer to the Family of Curves for your particular metal combination and the algorithm. After a while, you will understand the process. Following that, you will be able to make the first test strip surprisingly close to what you have envisioned for the final image. Only reprinting the test strip for fine-tuning will be necessary. For those who have worked empirically in the past, you will probably be pleasantly surprised by the controls possible for sophistication of imagery.

The Normal Negative

Observe the No. 7 curve in Figure 12.4. If a vertical line is drawn down from its intersection of the 90% black

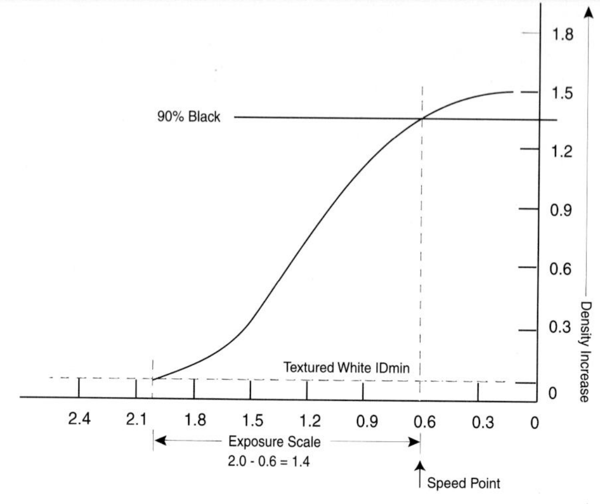

FIGURE 12.4 The No. 7 Platinum/Palladium Curve

line, it will fall at the 0.6 transmission density. If, from that point, the logs are counted until the curve intersects the dotted horizontal line (textured paper white), the number is 2.0, a 1.4 interval from 0.6. The exposure scale (ES) of the mixture is 1.4.

A Normal Negative with a 0.6 Shadow Density

- **Transmission Densities:** 2.0 – 0.6 = 1.4

In Figure 12.4, note the vertical line intersecting the base at 0.6. It is from a No. 7 curve. We know that mixture was used for standardizing the light source; therefore, it can be used as our standard. The 0.6 shadow density represents the *Speed Point.*

After the *IDmax* and *IDmin* transmissions densities are read and recorded, using you own data, or referring to the *Standard Negative Contrast Ranges* charts in Chapter 7, "Calibration," you can determine your contrast mixture. Now you can calculate printing time. In Figure 12.5, the top section of the illustration shows a portion of the Figure 12.2, *Family of Platinum/Palladium Curves*. Note that in Figure 12.5 the densities at the base of the graph match the schematic below it. The intersection of the curve for contrast mixture No. 7 and the 90% black line is projected downward where it meets at a shadow density of 0.6. This is the *Speed Point.*

The light source was distanced to provide that a No. 7 mixture exposed for 10 minutes would produce a 90% black in step Nr. 5 of the step tablet (0.6 transmission density). Therefore, a negative measuring 2.0 – 0.6 = 1.4, will duplicate this curve. Going back to the vertical line, one can deduce that this negative will require the same conditions that produced this graph: 10 minutes or 400 units. No correction for shadow values is needed.

The Negative Shadow Density schematic shown is simply a scrap of paper upon which the densities are recorded. Figures 12.6 to 12.17 will show how this paper scrap can be moved relative to the base of the graph to determine printing time.

Practically, a shadow of 0.6 is too dense, and the indicated printing time is equally too long. It has been indicated that the "ideal" negative should have shadow densities just above the base + fog. Referring to Figure

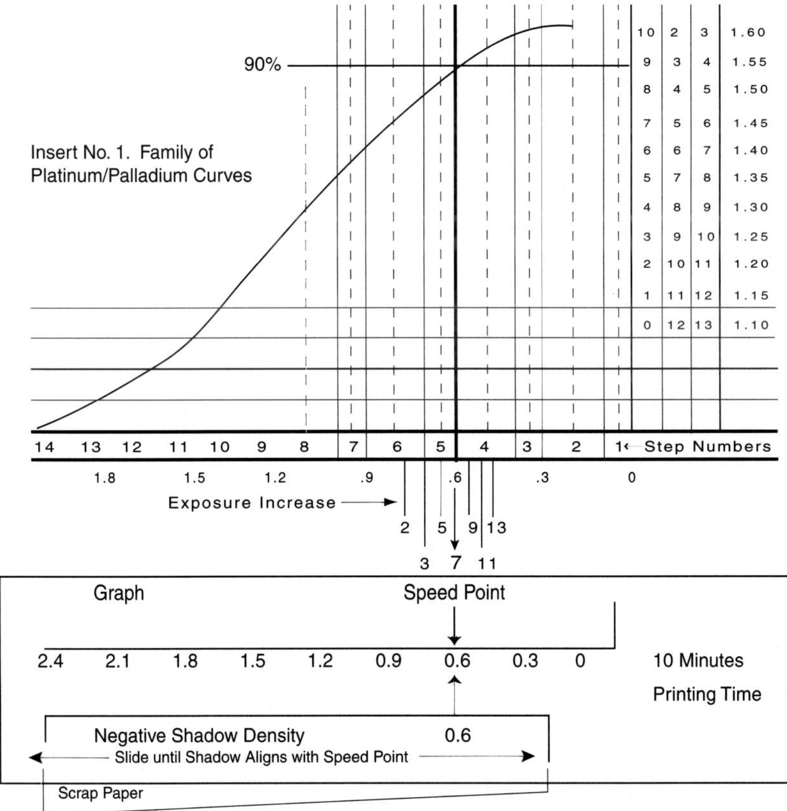

FIGURE 12.5 A Normal Negative with a 0.6 Shadow Density. By manipulating the two schematic presentations, printing times can be calculated.

11.4 in the last chapter, note that the density is approximately 0.3, the desirable shadow density.[7]

The "Ideal" Negative

- **Transmission Densities:** 1.7 – 0.3 = 1.4

An "ideal" negative will also use the No. 7 mixture, but will require a shadow density correction (Figure 12.6). Using the logarithmic calculations presented in Chapter 3, "The Negative," we know that 0.3 is half the density of 0.6. Therefore, the printing time for this negative would be 5 minutes or 200 units, both quite manageable.

The Normal Negative with High Shadow Values

- **Transmission Densities:** 2.3 – 0.9 = 1.4

This negative, while still requiring the No. 7 mixture, will need a shadow value correction that will increase printing time (Figure 12.7).

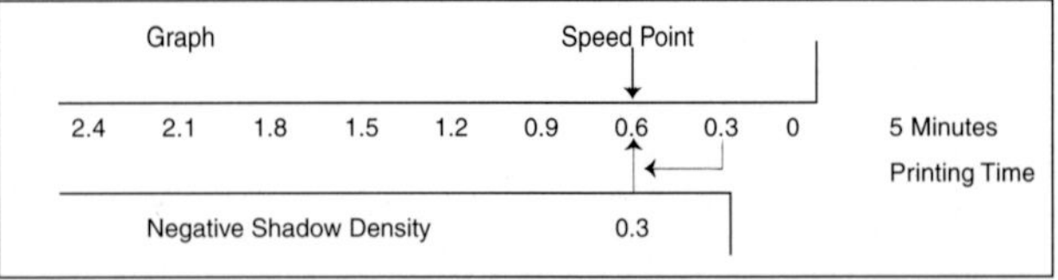

FIGURE 12.6 A Normal Negative with a 0.3 Shadow Density

If a shadow density of 0.9 is read (0.3 + the 0.6 standard), the printing times are doubled to become 20 minutes or 800 units, well approaching impractical levels.

Working with Intermediate Shadow Values

When shadow density variables of 0.1 exist, we can adjust printing times in smaller increments. Instead of halving or doubling the time, times falling in between can be factored.

A Normal Negative with a 0.4 Shadow Density

- **Transmission Densities:** 1.8 – 0.4 = 1.4

This negative still requires the No. 7 mixture (Figure 12.8). It is close to ideal, so it will need only a minor shadow value correction.

Here, a shadow density of 0.4 would fall 1/3 between 5 minutes (0.3) and 10 minutes (0.6), or approximately 6.5 to 7 minutes.[8]

A Normal Negative with a 0.8 Shadow Density

- **Transmission Densities:** 2.2 – 0.8 = 1.4

In this negative, the shadow value will require a considerable increase in printing time (Figure 12.9).

A reading of 0.8 would fall 2/3 between 10 and 20 minutes, or approximately 18 minutes. With the assistance of the schematic aid of a graph, printing intervals of 30 seconds can be calculated.

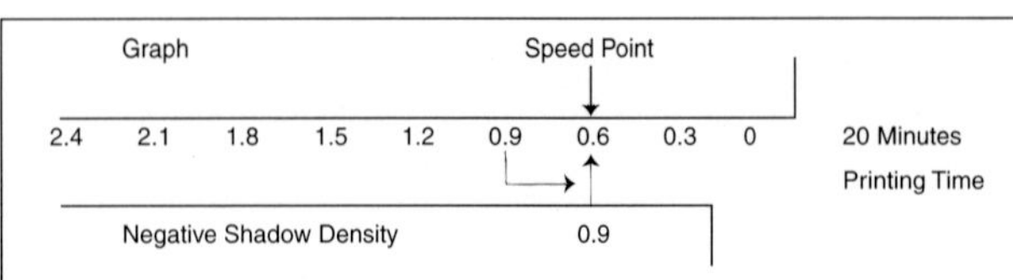

FIGURE 12.7 A Normal Negative with a 0.9 Shadow Density

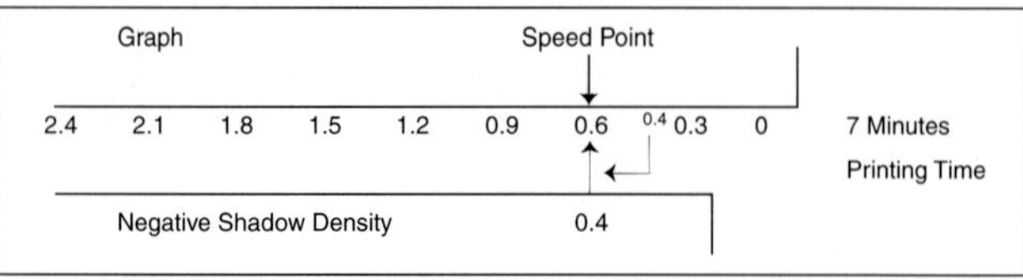

FIGURE 12.8 A Normal Negative with a 0.4 Shadow Density

7. For uniformity in this text, the log transmission density of 0.3 will be used to define an ideal negative shadow density. Some newer films, such as TMX and TMY, will produce effective shadow densities lower than 0.3. Some, such as HP5+, will have values over 0.3. After mastery of this technique, changes can be made to accommodate different films.

8. Some with a background in mathematics will observe that we are dealing with a logarithmic scale, so the calculation of intervals is not entirely correct. To use the logarithmic intervals with more accuracy, a modification of lens aperture openings can be set up and the 1/3 stop values simulated. The method presented is, however, close enough to produce very good test prints.

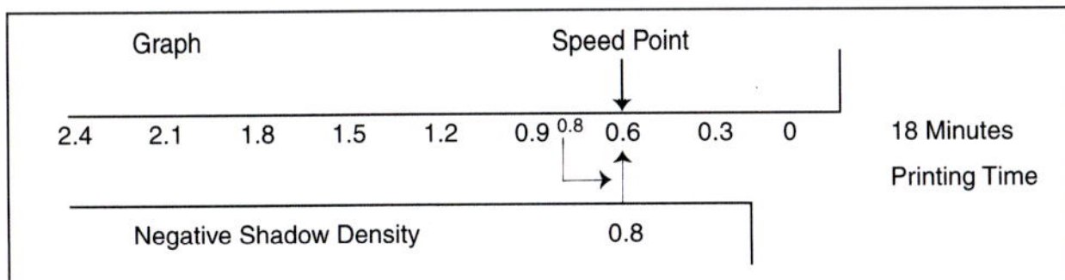

FIGURE 12.9 A Normal Negative with a 0.8 Shadow Density

The High-Contrast Negative

Figure 12.10 represents a curve drawn from a No. 2 Pt/Pd mixture. This time, to determine the exact exposure scale, one must drop a vertical line from where this particular curve crosses the 90% black line. This is the *Corrected Speed Point,* for a No. 2 Contrast Mixture. It is from here that shadow value corrections must be made.

NOTE: To avoid any confusion, realize that, in the following sections, I will refer to medium-, high-, and low-contrast negatives. The paper contrasts to accommodate these negatives will, of course, be medium, low, and high, in that order.

Working at the base, or *x* axis, measure the span from the Corrected Speed Point to where the curve actually intercepts the horizontal line at textured white *(IDmin)*. This is the exposure scale (ES) for this mixture. For example, the No. 2 curve intersects the 90% line at a 0.8 transmission density. At its intersection *IDmin* at 2.5 subtract 0.8 for an ES of 1.7.

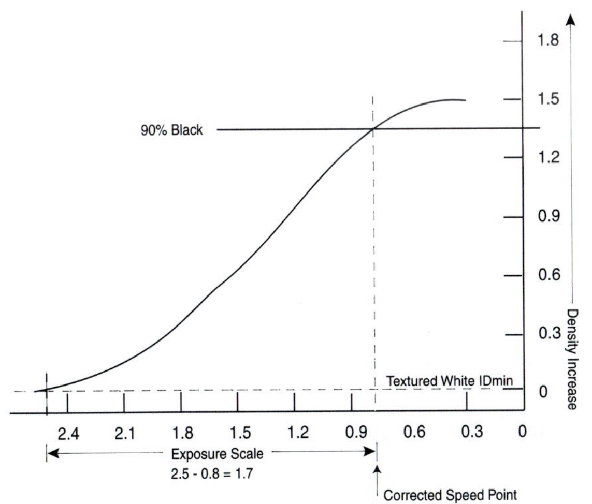

FIGURE 12.10 The No. 2 Platinum/Palladium Curve

A High Contrast Negative with a 0.8 Shadow Density

- **Transmission Densities:** 2.5 – 0.8 = 1.7

Note that the shadow density of the negative represented in Figure 12.10 is 0.8. This is the value at which the vertical line from the 90% black crosses the horizontal axis. *This negative duplicates the print made using the step tablet at the No. 2 mixture at 10 minutes*. Therefore, the printing time is the same: 10 minutes (Figure 12.11).

This is the first practical example of how lower-contrast mixtures increase printing speed. In comparison, a No. 7 contrast mixture, with the same 0.8 shadow density, would yield an approximate 18-minute printing time. As you will see later, a *low*-contrast negative with a 0.8 shadow value calling for a No. 13 mixture would require a 35-minute printing time!

A High Contrast Negative with a 0.5 Shadow Density

- **Transmission Densities:** 2.2 – 0.5 = 1.7

If the shadow density of a high-contrast negative is 0.5, the final printing time is calculated by using the negative shadow value. For example, if, after projecting from the 90% line, the shadow density is 0.5, the printing time is 5 minutes (0.8 – 0.5 = 0.3, or one stop) (Figure 12.12).

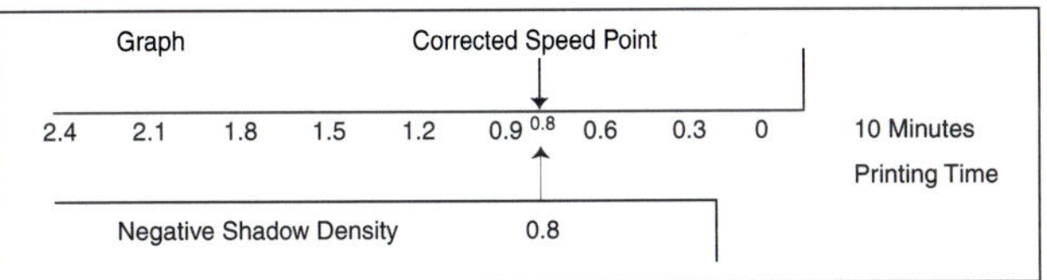

FIGURE 12.11 A High-Contrast Negative with a 0.8 Shadow Density

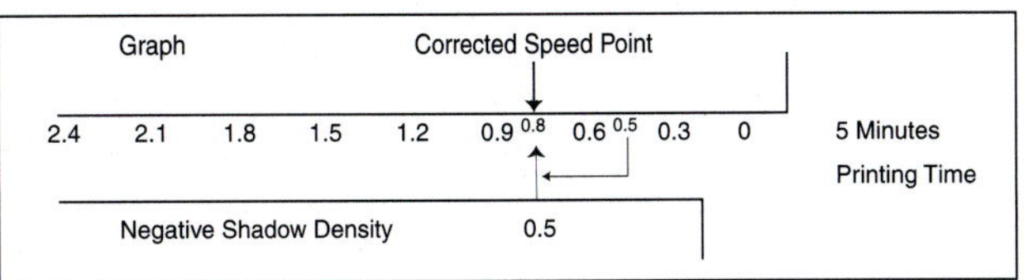

FIGURE 12.12 A High-Contrast Negative with a 0.5 Shadow Density

A High Contrast Negative with A 0.3 Shadow Density

- TRANSMISSION DENSITIES: 2.0 – 0.3 = 1.7

A shadow value of 0.3 requires that the time be calculated in segments, since it is indeed a logarithmic scale, and each one-stop segment must be handled as a unit (Figure 12.13). To start, find that 0.5 would be 50% of 0.8 or 5 minutes. Now find 0.2 on the horizontal axis. This would indicate a printing time of half of 5 minutes, or 2.5 minutes. The amount 0.3 falls one-third the way from 2.5 to 5 minutes, or a printing time of approximately 3 minutes, not an unusual time for low-contrast mixtures.

With a nuArc printer calibrated at 400 units, the calculations would be:

400 units ⟶ 200 units •⟶ 100 units
• is at 1/3 between 100 and 200 = 135 units

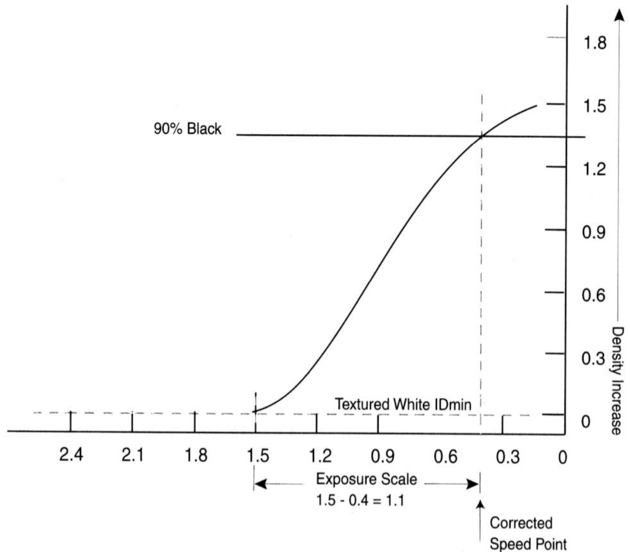

FIGURE 12.14 THE NO. 13 PLATINUM/PALLADIUM CURVE

THE LOW-CONTRAST NEGATIVE

To analyze the other extreme, the No. 13 curve, find it in Figure 12.2. It will intersect the 90% line to the right of the No. 7 curve. Drop a vertical line. It should fall at the 0.4 transmission density, indicating that it is 2/3 stops *slower* than the No. 7 mixture (0.6). This means that an appropriate negative with a shadow density of 0.4 will produce a 90% black at a printing time of 10 minutes. This is the *Corrected Speed Point* for the No. 13 contrast mixture. Also, note that at the base the exposure scale is 1.1 (Figure 12.14).

A Low-Contrast Negative with a 0.4 Shadow Density

TRANSMISSION DENSITIES: 1.5 – 0.4 = 1.1

Since the Corrected Speed Point and Negative Shadow Density coincide, no correction is needed. The printing time is 10 minutes (Figure 12.15).

A Low-Contrast Negative with a 0.6 Shadow Density

- TRANSMISSION DENSITIES: 1.7 – 0.6 = 1.1

As often is the case with less contrasty negatives, if times must be adjusted for shadow density, they will be longer than 10 minutes (Figure 12.16). A shadow density of 0.6 is 2/3 the distance from 0.4, the Corrected Speed Point for this No. 13 mixture, and 0.7, one stop more. If that were the case, the printing time would be 20 minutes. Our printing time would be less, at approximately 18 minutes.

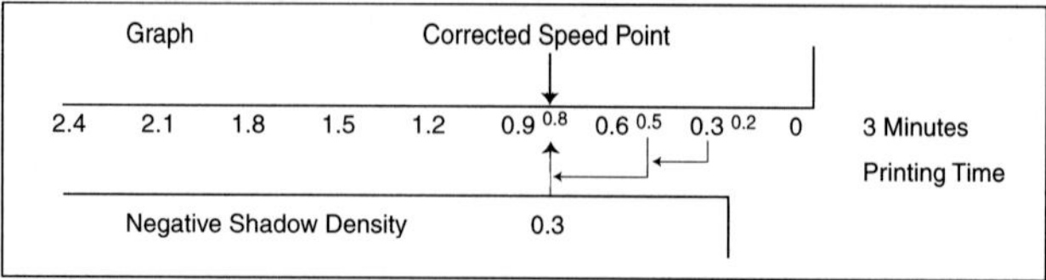

FIGURE 12.13 A HIGH-CONTRAST NEGATIVE WITH A 0.3 SHADOW DENSITY

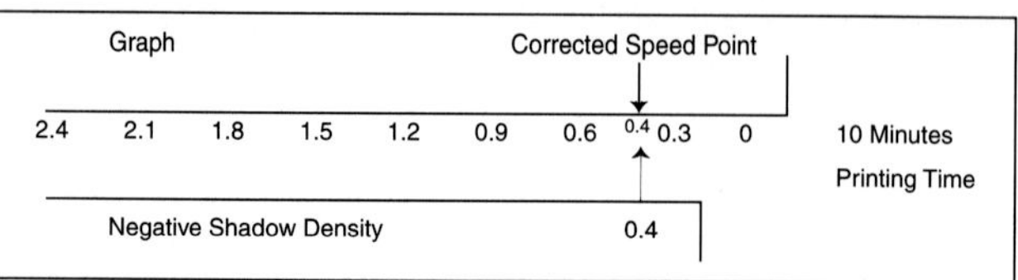

FIGURE 12.15 A LOW-CONTRAST NEGATIVE WITH A 0.4 SHADOW DENSITY

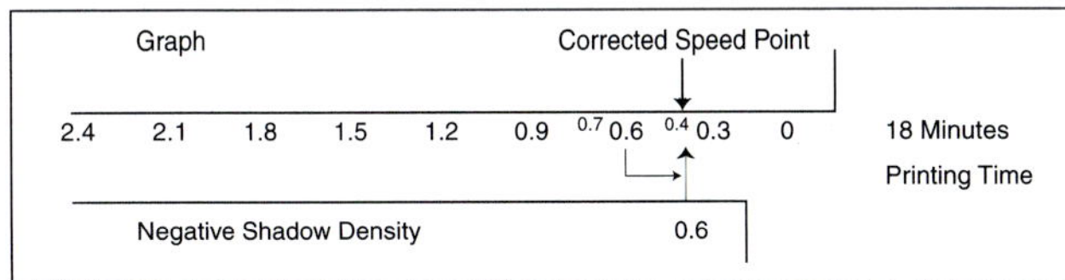

FIGURE 12.16 A Low-Contrast Negative with a 0.6 Shadow Density

---

A Low-Contrast Negative with a 0.9 Shadow Density

- **Transmission Densities:** 2.0 – 0.9 = 1.1

It is in this area that things can rapidly get out of control. With a No.13 mixture, a shadow density of 0.9 requires a double correction. From 0.9 to 0.6 doubles the printing time to 20 minutes. Going to 0.3 would be 40 minutes. The corrected speed point is 1/3 stop short of that. The printing time is 35 minutes!

NOTE: At some point, reciprocity failure will come to haunt you—another good reason for controlling shadow densities.

When adjusting for contrast, recognize the following.

Intermediate Contrast Mixtures

Using the above principles and referring to the *Standard Negative Contrast Ranges* in Chapter 7, "Calibration," and Figure 12.2, the printing times can be calculated for all contrast mixtures. For the even-numbered mixtures that are not shown in Figure 12.2, simply position a point between the two nearest curves. Where each contrast mixture crosses the 90% black line, the point at which a vertical line intersects the horizontal axis establishes the *Corrected Speed Point* for that mixture. It is from there that corrections are made for shadow density.

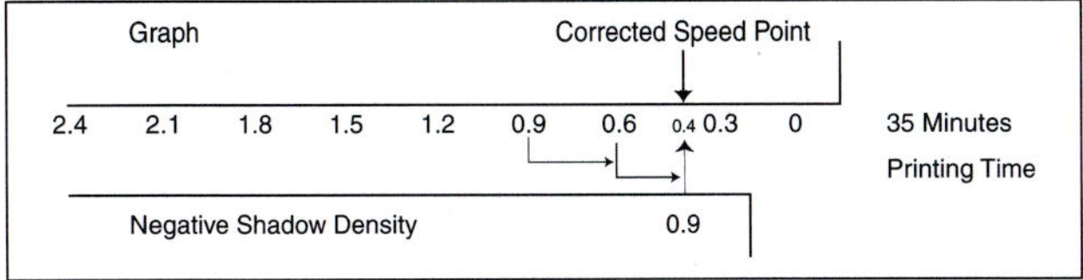

FIGURE 12.17 A Low-Contrast Negative with a 0.9 Shadow Density

Being Practical

The Speed Point and the Corrected Speed Point

We have engaged in some minutia to convey the principles of printing time calculations. If you have indeed stabilized your light source to print a Nr. 5 step in the 90% black, it may not be necessary to construct your own graphs. We have found that regardless of differences in technique, the properties of materials are quite consistent. If, for example, your tests match the curves in this text, the Speed Point and Corrected Speed Points for each contrast mixture will remain a constant. You can interpolate this published material with your own work. If, in the future, the controls go astray, you know that some quality control is in order. In most cases it will be that the light source intensity is drifting or that a particular paper has changed. *Metal salts and fresh sensitizers purchased from a reputable supply house are quite stable and are rarely responsible for any deviation of controls.* Note that some paper developers differ considerably from the potassium oxalate that was used to establish this data.

Papers

The material presented here will be applicable, with minor adjustments, for most papers. If, however, you choose to use one of the thicker art papers, or double coat, you may need to recalibrate your light source for that particular paper. See Chapter 5, "Paper."

Palladium

As demonstrated with the computer-generated curve, you will notice the extended toes and tonal ranges with pure palladium. The speed changes related to contrast mixture are quite similar to those observed with Pt/Pd, but because of the greater density ranges of palladium mixtures, the speed changes may be more pronounced, particularly with the low-contrast mixtures. It is important that, regardless of the material used, you verify your own Speed Point.

In Figure 12.18, note that, except for the greater exposure scales, and more of a horizontal spread in the curves, the Palladium Family of Curves is quite similar to the Platinum/Palladium Family of Curves. The Speed Point and Corrected Speed Points for various contrast mixtures are the same. If you work in palladium, make your own printed step tablet and calibrate your UV

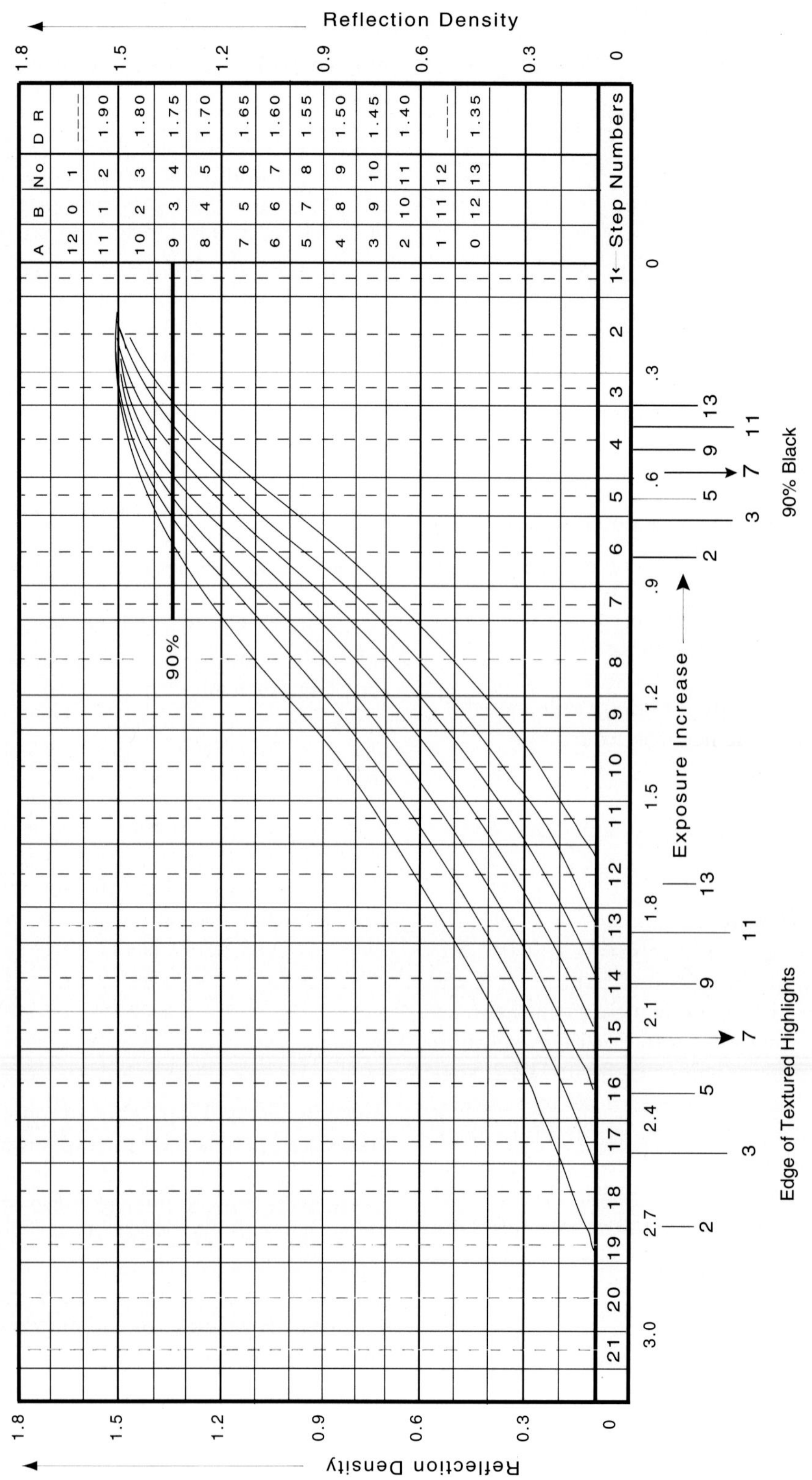

FIGURE 12.18 Family of Palladium Curves

light source at 10 minutes (or 400 nuArc units). If the data is the same, use the exercises in this chapter.[9]

USING PORTIONS OF THE PAPER CURVE

See Plate 12.2. This "high-key" print was made allowing the tonal values to fall primarily between Zones V and IX. The minimal vertical line on the telephone pole falls in Zone IV and gives a *convincing black* reference point.

USING INTERMEDIATE TONAL VALUES

Up to now, we have utilized the paper curves to calculate a *full tonal range print*, a print which exhibits a total scale of possible tonal values. One of the advantages of working from curves, however, is that a print need not be placed to encompass both the absolute shadow or highlight values.

A perfect example of deviating from this practice is the creation of a high-key print: one that contains textured highlights, but stops short of exhibiting the darker registers. As one might conclude, if only a portion of the curve is used, the negative need not have the total density range called for at a particular contrast mixture. Or, a contrast mixture may be chosen that exceeds the DR of the negative, allowing the use of only a portion of the curve.[10]

In Figure 12.19, a negative with a 1.1 density range would normally call for a No. 13 contrast mixture. By positioning it toward the high end of the curve (to the left, therefore, decreasing exposure), we have kept the highlights near paper white. Note, however, that the blacks now fall in the low midrange of the paper scale at a reflected density of 0.8 (Zone IV).

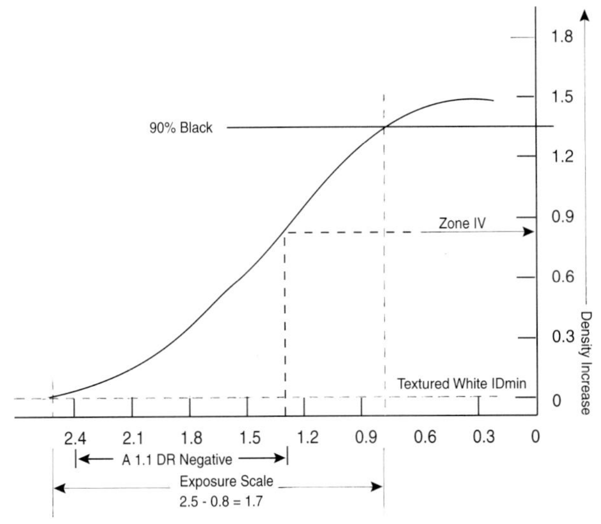

FIGURE 12.19 USING A PORTION OF THE CURVE

TO USE A PORTION OF THE CURVE

1. Read the negative on the transmission densitometer. Record the highlight and shadow densities. Perform the subtraction to determine the density range. Using your own data or that in the *Standard Negative Contrast Ranges*, note the particular contrast mixture called for.

2. Place a scrap of paper at the base of the curve graph (Figures 12.2 or 12.18). Refer to Figure 12.19 for guidance. Mark the points on the paper where the textured highlights and shadows fall. Sliding the scrap paper along the base, fit it to the curve indicated by the contrast mixture. The left portion should match where the curve intercepted the line for paper white. The right side of the paper will lie at the point where a vertical drawn from the curve interception with 90% black would fall. If the shadow value written on the paper is matched with the density written on the x axis at this point, a full tonal range print would result.

3. Now, sliding to the left and right, see how the paper markings fit in the other curves. For example, if you are planning a high-key print, find a curve to the left, one that calls for more contrast in the negative. You may find that your paper markings will incorporate only the toe and mid portions of the curve. You can visualize your print by imagining the "Zones" that might be displayed (Plate 12.2). Also note the book cover's illustration: *Salmon River* has been printed emphasizing high values to accentuate the sun and its halo. The dock, while appearing black, falls in the Zone IV to V areas.

4. If you are satisfied, note the new contrast mixture, and comparing, as before, your shadow value with the density indicated on the graph, compute your new printing time. (Note that, since you are not entering the

[9] Some printers have reported palladium to have a slower printing time than Pt/Pd. This observation is based on the use of an identical negative. Palladium requires a negative of more contrast than Pt/Pd. If the same negative were to be used for both metal combinations, palladium would require *more sensitizer,* thus slowing the printing speed.

[10] One of the joys of teaching workshops is to find a negative, from a talented student, that has been made for silver and, therefore, has a short DR. When such a negative (usually a portrait or nude), is placed in the upper registers of a palladium curve, the result, many times, is exquisite.

Zone III areas, you need not drop the vertical line from the 90% black intersection.) As you are going left from the "full tonal range print," and therefore lighter, your new printing times should be *less* than those calculated in mixture No. 2.

Conversely, the same procedures can be used to plan a darker, more somber image, using the darker tones and eliminating the higher values. In this case, the pencil markings would be shifted to the right portions of the curve, calling for *more* printing time.

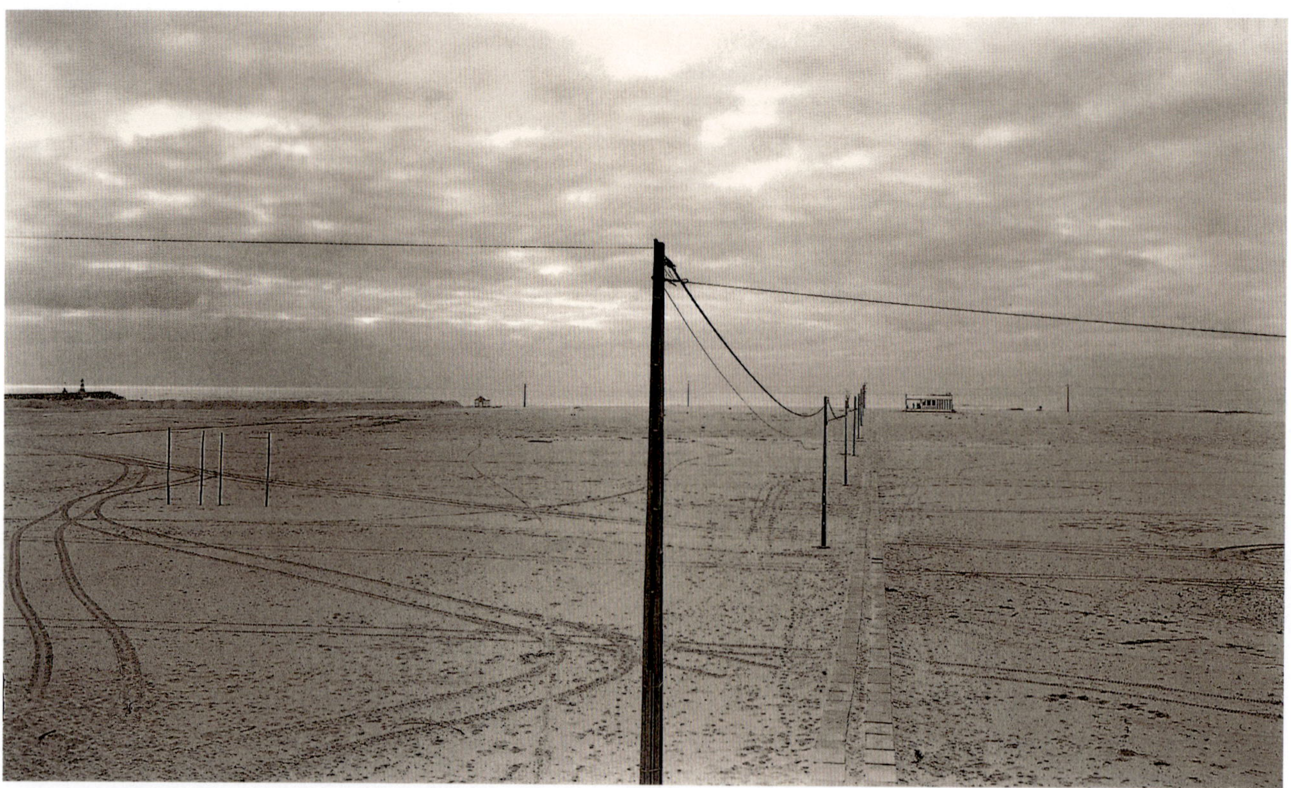

PLATE 12.2 Figueira da Foz, Portugal. 1990 12 × 20 inch Pt/Pd. This "high-key" print covers Zones IV to VIII. The small black area of the pole is seen as *convincing black.*

CHAPTER 13

The SPEED TRACKER

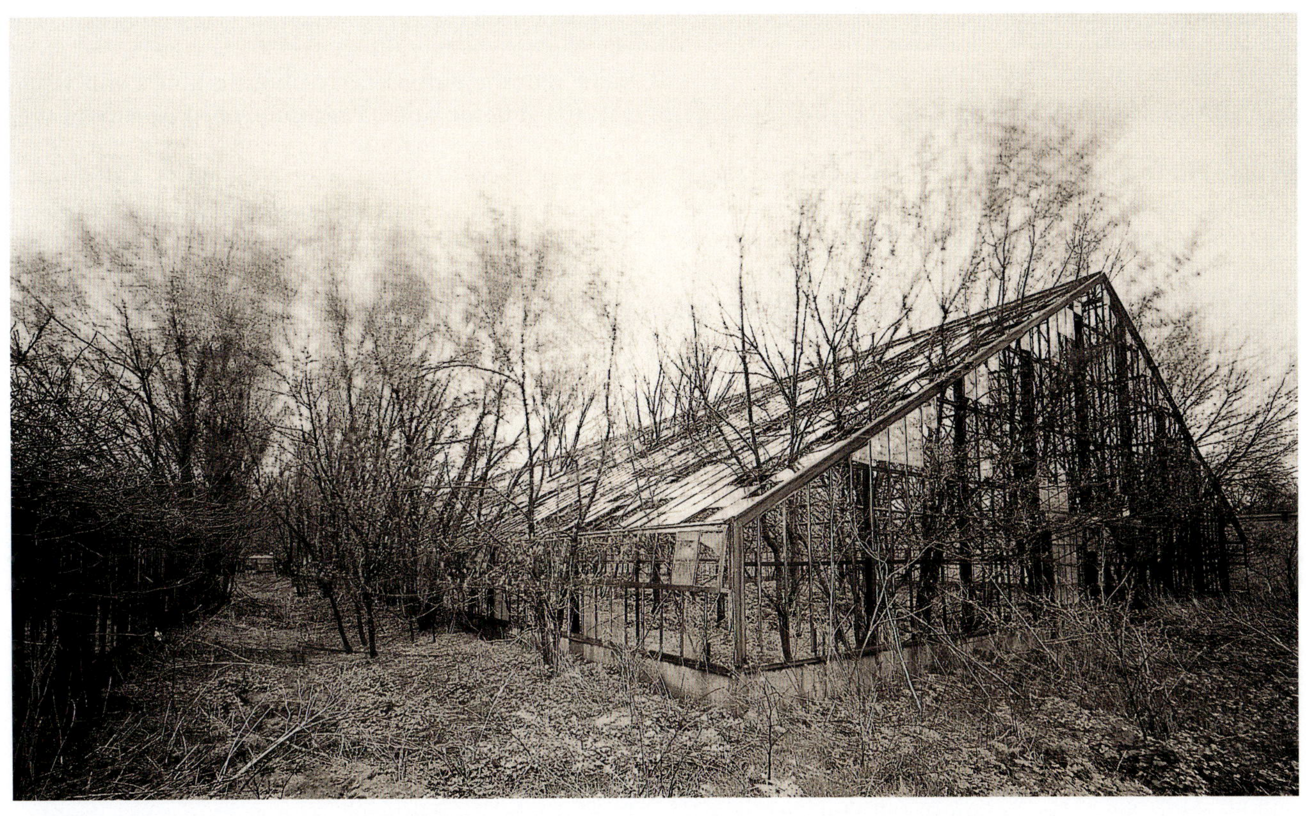

PLATE 13.1 Wyant Farm II, Tyndall, Ohio. 1996 12 × 20 Pd

The two variables of contrast mixture and shadow density follow predictable, near linear progressions. It is possible to dispense with the curves and use a graph of my design that would incorporate both variables: the SPEED TRACKER© Dick Arentz. Note that with this method, however, selective interpretation of curve portions is far more difficult.

The printing time with a fixed light source, and constant chemicals and paper, is related to both shadow density at 90% print black *(IDmax)* and to contrast mixture. Interestingly, the speed changes with contrast mixtures are somewhat uniform, regardless of paper, developer, or metal used. It is possible, therefore, to construct a "generic" curve or bar for contrast mixtures that can be adapted to your standard printing time (Figure 13.1). *You must have a transmission densitometer to use this method.*

Standard Printing Time

In the SPEED TRACKER, the heavy black vertical midline intersecting the diagonal bar represents your printing time to obtain a 90% black with a step tablet, using a No. 7 mixture and your light source, chemicals, and paper. The point at which the vertical line intersects the base is your *Speed Point*. You must establish a *Standard Printing Time* that will be assigned to that line. The SPEED TRACKER graph indicates a 10-minute or nuArc 400-unit time. If your time is different, simply substitute it at the 10-minute mark and alter the remaining printing times. If you have a nuArc printer that is working properly, no corrections will be necessary.

Your Speed Point

You will need a shadow density value that will produce that 90% black at your *Standard Printing Time*. It ideally should be a transmission density of 0.6 (Nr. 5 on the step tablet).[1] From this, shadow density corrections will be made. Since few negatives will fit your test values of a 0.6 shadow density at a No. 7 contrast mixture, two corrections may be needed: contrast mixture and shadow density. Refer to the algorithm in Table 12.1 in Chapter 12, "Using the Print Curves," for a review of the sequences.

Contrast Mixture Corrections

In examining the SPEED TRACKER graph, note the diagonal bar that will be your *Contrast Mixture Bar.* Contrast mixtures No. 1 to No. 13 are on the vertical axis at the right. The Contrast Mixture Bar will be used to "track" speed changes caused by using different contrast mixtures.

Shadow Density Corrections

You will need correction when the shadow densities of the negative to be printed vary from your Speed Point value. For the purposes of demonstration, I will assign the Speed Point value a recommended density of 0.6. The dots on the Shadow Density Bar at the horizontal axis of the SPEED TRACKER represent printing speed changes in 0.1 density increments related to the useful shadow density of your negative.

Always work in 0.3 units from your initial printing time; each unit represents one half or twice that time. That way, 0.1 intervals are easier to calculate. Going left, each 0.3 change indicates a decrease by half from your standard printing time. Going right, each 0.3 change indicates a doubling of your standard printing time. Changes of 0.1 are calculated in increments, each representing approximate 1/3 intervals between one half and your full standard printing time. This is made easier through the use of a semilogarithmic graph. After you have made the shadow density correction, simply look to the upper numbers to find your actual printing time.

Using the SPEED TRACKER

Read the densities of your negative to be printed with a transmission densitometer. Make the highest reading where you want the limit of textured white to appear on the print (Zone VIII). Place your shadow reading in textured shadows (Zone III). Do the necessary subtraction to obtain the density range of your negative.

Some Practice

Before you plan your negative, we will now use the SPEED TRACKER with some hypothetical negatives.

[1] If your printing apparatus makes it impossible to standardize at a 10-minute printing time, choose a time that is easily divisible by at least two factors. If you choose a time longer than 10 minutes, printing times for high shadow values may become unwieldy. In any case, place the 90% black on the Nr. 5 step to ensure optimum printer performance.

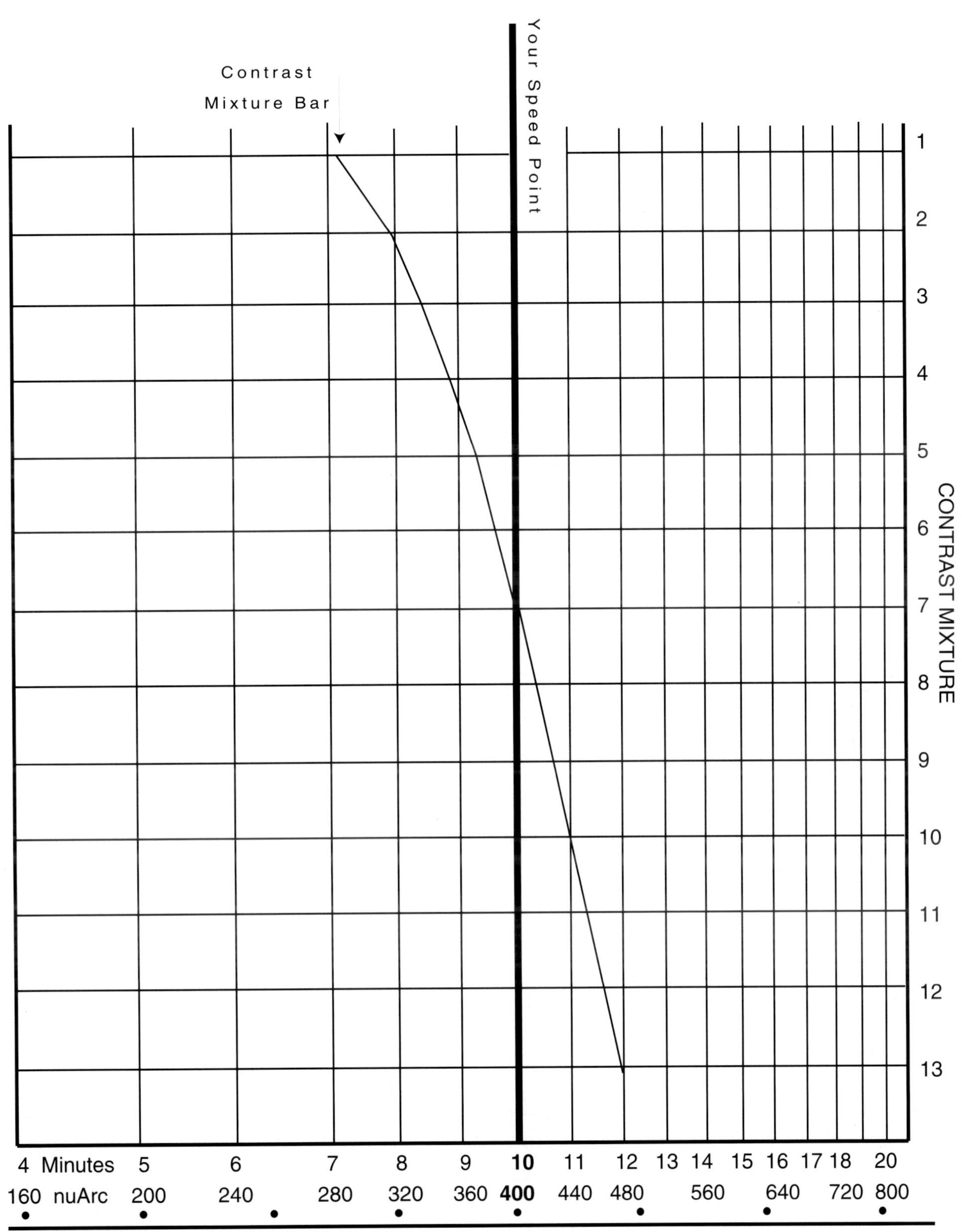

The SHADOW DENSITY BAR. Each dot indicates a 0.1 shadow density correction.

FIGURE 13.1 The SPEED TRACKER©

Assume that your Speed Point is 0.6 and your Standard Printing time is 10 minutes. Also assume that your contrast mixtures correspond to those in the *Standard Negative Contrast Ranges*. We will round off the DR to the nearest 0.1. Obviously, you must use your own figures with the SPEED TRACKER, particularly your Speed Point.

Normal Negatives

A 1.4 Density Range Indicating a No. 7 Contrast Mixture

- Transmission Densities: 2.0 – .6 = 1.4

Track horizontally on the mixture No. 7 line to the diagonal Contrast Mixture Bar. Since that bar intersects the vertical midline at this point, follow that midline to the baseline. As the 0.6 shadow density of your negative duplicates your Speed Point, no shadow correction is needed. Your printing time is 10 minutes or 400 nuArc units.

- Transmission Densities: 1.7 – .3 = 1.4

Track horizontally on the mixture No. 7 line to the diagonal Contrast Mixture Bar (Figure 13.2). Since that bar intersects the vertical midline at this point, follow that midline to the Shadow Density Bar. You must now make a correction for shadow density. Your standard printing time is for a 0.6 shadow density. This negative has 1/2 that density (0.6 – 0.3 = 0.3 or 1/2). At the Shadow Density Bar go left a distance of three dots (0.3). Look up. Find your printing time of 1/2 of 10 minutes = 5 minutes or 200 nuArc units.

- Transmission Densities: 1.6 – .2 = 1.4

Track the No. 7 line to the left and drop to the Shadow Density Bar as with the previous example. This time go four dots to the left (0.6 – 0.2 = 4 dots). Look up. Your printing time is 4 minutes or 160 nuArc units.

- Transmission Densities: 2.2 – .8 = 1.4

This time track to the midline, drop to the Shadow Density Bar and go right a distance of two dots (0.6 + 0.2 = 0.8). Your printing time is slightly less than 16 minutes, or 600 nuArc units.

High-Contrast Negatives

A 1.7 Density Range Indicating a No. 2 Contrast Mixture

- Transmission Densities: 2.3 – .6 = 1.7

Since your standard printing time is set at a shadow density of 0.6, you will need only one correction: that related to change in contrast grade.[2] A No. 2 mixture has less restrainer; therefore, printing times will be faster. The diagonal bar represents your Contrast Mixture Bar. *The slope of that bar corrects printing time for all contrast mixtures at your Speed Point of 0.6.* With a

[2] Unlike the exercise using the family of curves in Chapter 12, "Using the Print Curves," you need not designate a Corrected Speed Point. The Contrast Mixture Bar does that for you. You still must do a shadow density correction when indicated.

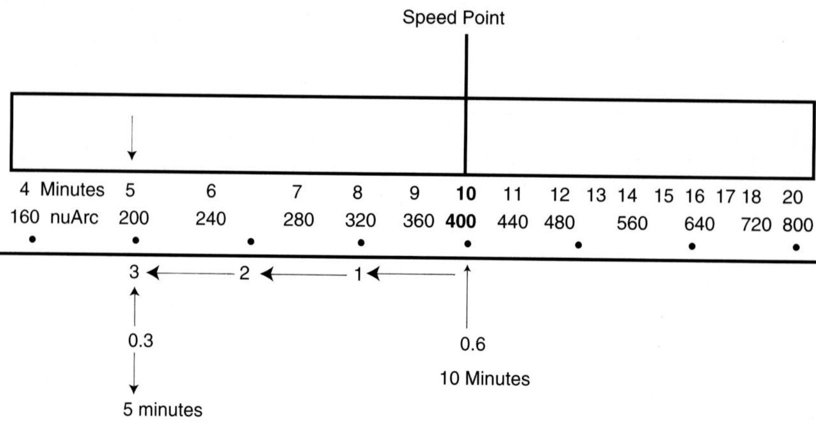

FIGURE 13.2 SPEED TRACKER Corrections for No. 7 Contrast Mixture with a 0.3 Shadow Density

shadow density of 0.6, simply find the bar intersection along the No. 2 horizontal line and drop to the baseline. No shadow density correction is needed. Look up. Your printing time is 8 minutes or 320 nuArc units (Figure 13.3).

- Transmission Densities: 2.0 – .3 = 1.7

Two corrections will be needed: for contrast grade and shadow density. First, contact the Contrast Mixture Bar along the No. 2 line and drop to the baseline. At the Shadow Density Bar, count three dot intervals[3] more to the left (0.6 – 0.3 = 0.3). Look up for a printing time of 4 minutes or 160 nuArc units (Figure 13.4).

[3] When the numbers do not fall directly at the dots, find the relative spacing between two dots and count from there.

- Transmission Densities: 2.5 – .8 = 1.7

Again, two corrections will be needed. As before, drop from the intersection of the No. 2 line and the Contrast Mixture Bar to the Shadow Density Bar. Move two dot intervals to the *right* (0.6 + 0.2 = 0.8). Your printing time is 12 1/3 minutes, or 500 nuArc units.

Low-Contrast Negatives

A 1.2 Density Range Indicating a No. 11 Contrast Mixture

- Transmission Densities: 1.80 – .6 = 1.2

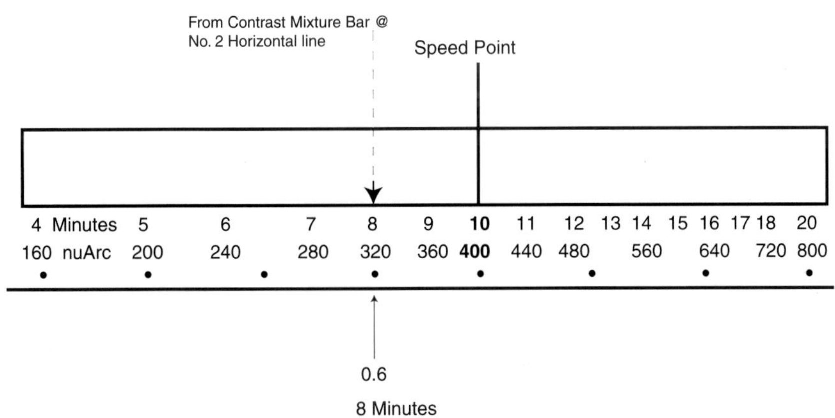

FIGURE 13.3 SPEED TRACKER
Corrections for a No. 2 Contrast Mixture with a 0.6 Shadow Density

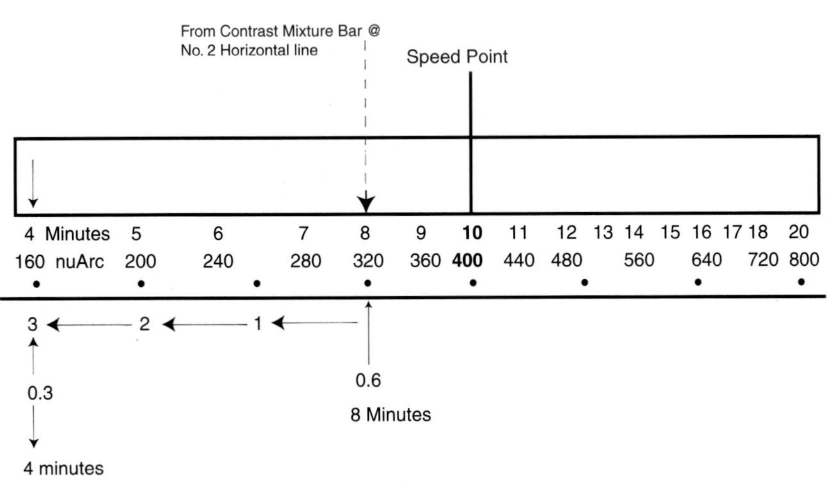

FIGURE 13.4 SPEED TRACKER
Corrections for a No. 2 Contrast Mixture with a 0.3 Shadow Density

Track the No. 11 line to your Contrast Mixture Bar. Drop to the base. No shadow density correction is needed. Your printing time is 11 1/3 minutes or approximately 450 nuArc units.

- **Transmission Densities:** 1.6 – .4 = 1.2

Track the No. 11 line to the Contrast Mixture Bar. Drop to the Shadow Density Bar. Move two dot intervals to the left (0.6 – 0.4 = 0.2) (Figure 13.5). Your printing time is 7 1/4 minutes, or 300 nuArc units.

A 1.1 Density Range Indicating a No. 13 Contrast Mixture

- **Transmission Densities:** 2.0 – .9 = 1.1

Track the No. 13 line to your Contrast Mixture Bar. Drop to the Shadow Density Bar. Project three dot intervals to the right. You are now off of the graph and into reciprocity problems. You have a bulletproof negative. Factoring in reciprocity failure, your printing time is probably well over 30 minutes. *This is graphic evidence of why negative control is important, particularly at the shadow values.*

All other negatives within reason can be used with the SPEED TRACKER. Simply work out the density values, choose your contrast, and use the methods described to calculate printing time.

Some Practical Considerations

The diagonal Contrast Mixture Bar is constant for most situations. Even when changing between Pt/Pd and Pd is possible, it allows you to plan your print with minor variations. Under unusual conditions, such as extreme humidity or absorbent paper, the effects of contrast mixtures on printing speed may be unpredictable, making the SPEED TRACKER difficult to use.

Changing paper may alter your Speed Point. Most heavier papers will lower it. If you get so slow as to lose your standard printing time, corrections may have to be made: either increase your standard printing time or decrease the print-to-light distance. The nuArc, like most plate burners, allows for adjustment of the light sensor. It is also possible to speed the sensitizer a bit by increasing the oxalic acid, but fogging may become a problem.

Although we discuss numbers and fractions, remember that photography is a relatively inexact science. The SPEED TRACKER is not intended for precision; it will give you printing times within 10%—enough to start fine-tuning with test strips for esthetic print values.

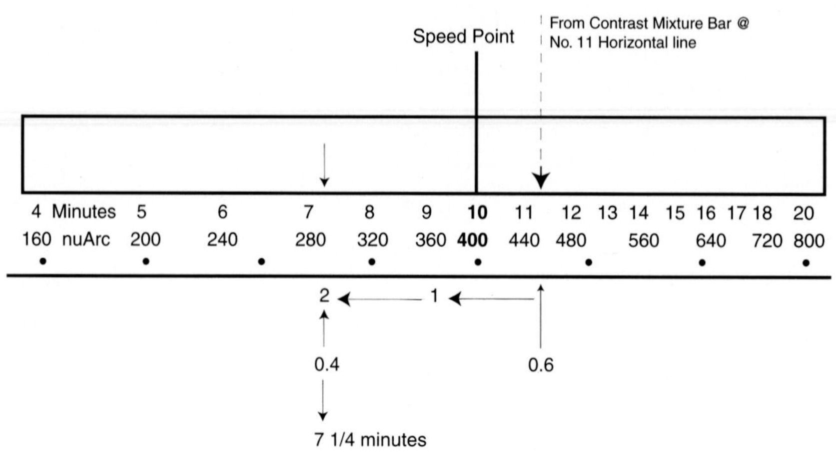

FIGURE 13.5 SPEED TRACKER corrections for a No. 11 Contrast Mixture with a 0.4 Shadow Density

Appendix A

The Large Negative

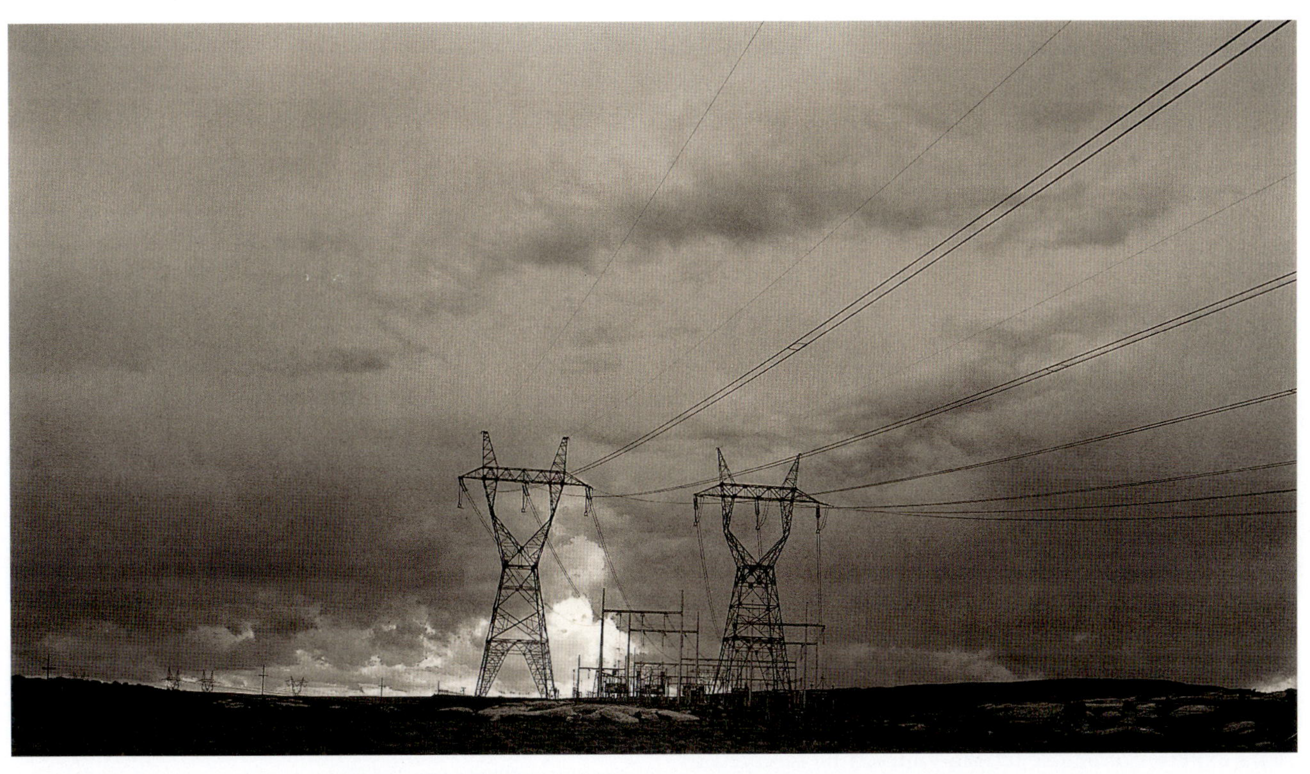

PLATE A.1 Power Lines, Cameron, AZ. 1994 12 × 20 inch Pt/Pd

In practicing platinum and palladium printing, you will eventually determine which format is most applicable for your work. Given that platinum/palladium is, by necessity, a contact printing process, three choices of negative construction are available:

- The original negative exposed directly in the camera
- Photomechanical methods to enlarge negatives
- Computer-generated enlarged negatives

The Camera-Exposed Negative

To directly expose the negative in the camera, the actual size of the image reproduced must be taken into account. While effective prints can be made from medium format cameras, including 120 roll film, many photographers will find the large format view camera to be most ideal. In addition to the increased image size and authenticity, sheet film allows for individual processing.

Camera Size

In considering the format of a first view camera, my personal recommendation for Pt/Pd printing would be to skip the 4 × 5 inch format in favor of 5 × 7. Most 4 × 5 cameras sold are actually 5 × 7 sizes with a reducing back. The 5 × 7 format is a cousin to the English "*half frame*" used by early photographers to produce many of the platinum prints we see in museum collections. If 5 × 7 is found to be impractical, or if you wish also to make silver gelatin prints by the more ubiquitous 4 × 5 enlarger, all 5 × 7 cameras can be fitted with a 4 × 5 reducing back.

Since practically all difficulties in working with larger cameras are exponentially related to the size of the format, I would also recommend at least a few years experience before letting yourself be tempted to move to 8 × 10 or the "*Ultra-Large*" cameras. It would be better to spend the extra money on a transmission densitometer. Most likely, once you form an attachment to the half-frame, you may not want to discard it (Figure A.1).

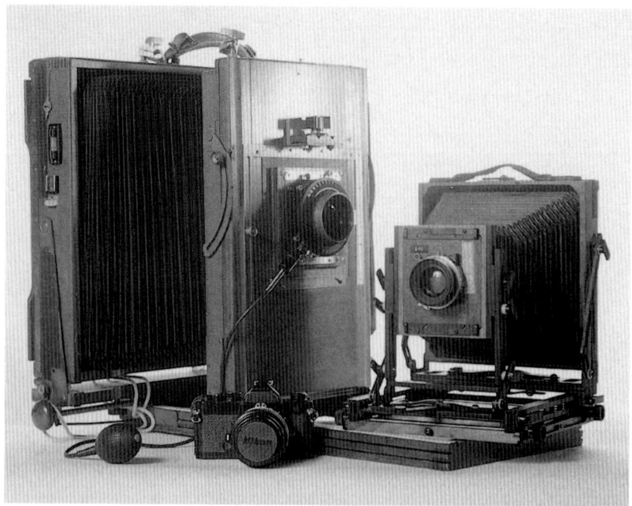

FIGURE A.1 The 5 × 7 and 12 × 20 Inch Cameras (A 35 mm camera is included for scale.)

The Ultra-Large Format

For those who have a strong back and a weak mind, as I do, and who might have an interest in the ultra-large format, a brief description follows. Most cameras of this nature are related to the standard sizes of the *Banquet* cameras used seventy-five to one hundred years ago. Due to the low resolution of camera and enlarging lenses of that time, when large groups of people were photographed (at a banquet, for example), their features were not recognizable in the final enlarged print. Therefore, a negative was needed that was large enough to be contact-printed at the size desired. It was also preferable that it be formatted to accommodate the usual grouping of the subjects. Consequently, the long rectangles of the banquet camera format were developed that persist to this day. They are: 7 × 17, 8 × 20, 12 × 20, and to a lesser extent, 14 × 17 inches. Many original examples made by Korona and Folmer Schwing still exist and are used today. Several manufacturers will make a new camera on special order (see "Sources"). Film holders[1] can also be ordered. Film is available at special order quantities. (See Appendix B, "Some Film/Developer Combinations for Selective Processing of Platinum.")

[1] Note that the Korona and Folmer Schwing cameras and their descendants do not take the same type of film holders. With Folmer Schwing, the light trap is a slot; with Korona it is a positive ridge. Better yet, your camera back should be at hand when the film holders are made, or vice versa. Never take any view camera in the field without first giving it the "flashlight test," wherein a flashlight is placed in the camera, with holders inserted. After two minutes in a totally dark environment, a bad fit as well as other light leaks can be detected by the slits of light escaping from the camera. At the same time, the light traps can be checked by removing the dark slide.

Processing the Large Negative

Large sheet film negatives can be processed individually or in small sets of no more than six. A number of choices are available:

- Tray
- Rotary processing:
  - Drum (JOBO®)
  - BTZS tube development
- Film holder/open tank
- Daylight plastic tanks

Recently, rotary systems of development (and print processing) have gained in popularity. There are considerable advantages:

- It is primarily a closed system, minimizing skin or respiratory contact with chemicals.
- Although film must be loaded in the dark, processing is done in normal room light.
- Smaller amounts of solutions are used.
- Since processing is done in a water bath, precise temperature control is possible.
- As the entire surface of film is in equal contact with developer, mottling or uneven development is less likely.
- Sheets of film do not contact each other, reducing the chances for scratches.
- Multiple sheets of film can be processed utilizing larger tanks.

Nevertheless, tray processing is still practiced by the majority of large format photographers, and is unlikely to be displaced in the near future:

- It is simple and dependable.
- It is less expensive. A mechanized rotary system can cost over $1,000.00.[2]
- Tray processing can more easily be done in alternative spaces, such as a kitchen or bathroom.
- Trays take less storage space.
- Although ultra-large film can be rotary processed, the monstrous size and expense of the drums and tubes make it impractical. Also, uneven development in sizes greater than 11 × 14 has been reported.

2. In matters of size and expense, BTZS Tubes are compact and relatively inexpensive. They are an economical alternative to the mechanized rotary processors. See Darkroom Innovations (DI) in "Sources."

Tray Processing

Since the majority of readers will, at least initially, tray process, I will present this procedure first. This is my choice, partly because it is most amenable to my ultra-large format photography. In experienced hands, there is little chance of uneven development or scratching.

For tray development, the use of latex gloves is recommended. Regardless of any opinions about the relative toxicity of photographic chemicals, it is best that hands not be immersed in any solution constantly for multiple periods of 20 to 30 minutes. Also, gloves give an added advantage of shielding the softened emulsion surfaces from fingernails and rough skin particles. When you are choosing latex gloves, first determine whether or not you have an allergy to latex. It is quite common. Most disposable gloves come lubricated, either with powder or silicon. Each brand differs. Look for gloves lightly covered with silicon. Too much silicon will grease the hands to the point that wet film cannot be held securely.

Surprisingly, little information is available in the literature adequately covering this most basic of photographic procedures. Therefore, I present the following as my recommended method:

1. Prepare trays of developer, stop bath, and fixer. To prevent the uneven development of edges by splash back, choose trays at least one size larger than will accommodate the film. Darkroom modifications such as space heaters, coolers, or water baths may be utilized if the area is subject to air temperature changes. If a presoak[3] is desired, add an additional tray of distilled water that is the same temperature as the developer. Set the clock for the indicated development time.

NOTE: A mechanical tray agitation system is made by Edwards Engineering. *(Source: EE)*

NOTE: If the pungent odor of the acetic acid stop bath is bothersome, other alternatives exist. See Anchell's *Darkroom Cookbook*, or purchase the TS-4 stop bath from Photographers' Formulary or Clayton's "odor-free" stop bath and fixer from a photographic supplier.

2. Lay out the film holders and put on the gloves before turning off the light. I use cotton gloves whenever handing film. In this case, it is advisable to place

3. If more than one sheet is included in a tray, a presoak in distilled water will lessen the chances of film adhering in the developer. It also facilitates even absorption of developer into the film emulsion.

cotton gloves temporarily over the latex gloves until just before the film is immersed. You can remove the cotton gloves with your teeth.

3. If more than one sheet is to be processed, hold the film as a deck of cards. Immerse one at a time, emulsion side up, either in developer or presoak, allowing each to become somewhat moistened. Set the clock and immediately separate the film.

NOTE: I do not prefer to have more than two sheets stacked at a time. If more sheets are to be processed, choose a tray that will hold either two, four, or six sheets of film spread across the bottom. Purchase two-inch suction cups used for window decorations from a party store. Be sure they have a small hole at the nib. Remove the metal hook and cut a wooden cotton applicator midpoint in the shaft. Insert the wooden end in the hole opposite the suction area with the cotton end protruding. Moisten the suction cups and place them to serve as dividers in the tray. When solution is added, a single sheet of film is placed in each "compartment." If properly done, the film should move freely without touching. The cotton tips prevent scratching of the base side of the film. Similar dividers can be placed in the trays for stop, fix, and wash. This method is particularly useful for developing two sheets of 7 × 17 film placed side by side in the same tray.

NOTE: Another option is a manufactured tray: The "Shlosher," a dipping mechanism based on the fast-food process of deep frying food. The negatives are placed in separated compartments and "dipped" into the developing solutions.

4. During the first minute, agitate vigorously with constant jarring to dislodge air bubbles. Following this, the cycle can be slowed. After two or three minutes, allow the film to remain still for 30-second periods. At each interval, lift the film from the tray and drain for at least two seconds. Agitate for the first five seconds following reimmersion. Halfway through the development period, rotate each sheet 180° for the remaining time.

NOTE: Landscape photographers may wish to consider the following: Whether oriented horizontally or vertically, the notch is always in the area occupied by the sky. When touching the film, use the opposite corner. Any fingerprints of abrasions will most likely end up in the foreground.

5. When the developing time is up, drain and transfer immediately to the stop bath. If the developer is to be reused with replenisher, take care not to introduce stop bath into the developer tray.

6. Follow the manufacturer's instructions for fixing, Hypo Clearing Agent, or Hypo Eliminator and wash.

7. After the wash cycle, rinse vigorously and place the film in distilled water into which the recommended amount of Photo-flo® has been added. Sponge both surfaces in the soak, as well as after it is hung to dry.

Drum Processing

The advantages of a drum (JOBO®) processor have been listed. Although for many purposes, it may be the preferred method, it is hardly an absolute necessity for the hobbyist. The actual unit is bulky, but light enough to be stored when not in use. Individual drums must be purchased based on film or print size.

Detailed instructions come with purchase. For processing sheet film while working in the dark, the negatives are inserted into individual compartments in a cylindrical drum. Drum designs allow for single or multiple films to be processed simultaneously. Following placement of the cap, processing is done in room light. Solutions are injected into and drained from the drum, which is constantly revolving in a temperature-controlled water bath, by means of a lift mechanism with a built-in funnel. Washing and drying are done by conventional means.

BTZS Tubes

Originated by Phil Davis, BTZS Tubes are now marketed as BTZS® Film Tubes by Darkroom Innovations. They come is sizes from 4 × 5 to 8 × 10, as well as odd sizes of 4 × 10, 7 × 17, 8 × 20, and 12 × 20 (Figure A.2).

Instructions come with the tubes and are well detailed in *Beyond the Zone System* by Phil Davis.[4]

[4] About BTZS: Phil Davis published the first edition of *Beyond the Zone System* in 1981. A fourth edition is now available from Focal Press (see "Bibliography"). A number of his inventions are now being marketed by Darkroom Innovations, along with scheduled workshops:

- Plotter Program®. A computerized program for plotting and analyzing film and paper data for personalized metering and development techniques.
- Portable computer programs for practical use of personalized data in the field, either with PC6 or Palm Pilot® computers. The PowerDial" is a fabricated, noncomputerized guide to film exposure in the field.
- BTZS development tubes containing detailed instructions. Their use is also completely discussed in *Beyond the Zone System* (Davis, 1998).

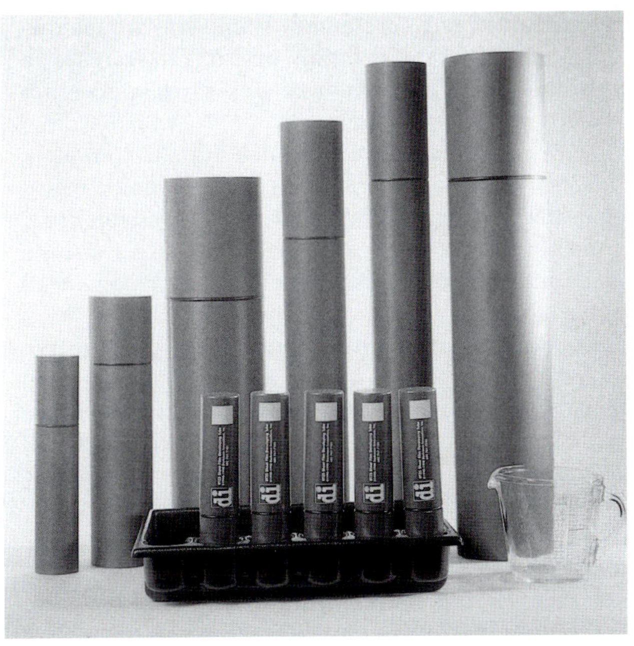

FIGURE A.2 The BTZS Tubes. The 4 × 5 tubes are shown in the foreground with a special tray for their use. Rear, from left to right, are the 5 × 7, 8 × 10, 11 × 14, 7 × 17, 8 × 20, and 12 × 20 sizes.

The original "tubes" were PVC pipe with a seal at one end and a removable cap at the other. Now, they are commercially manufactured to last a lifetime (and most likely, that of your heirs).

1. Working in a lighted wet space, a measured amount of developer is placed in a threaded cap, which is placed upwards in a water bath of a predetermined temperature. The 4 × 5 sizes come with a customized tray, containing receptacles to hold the caps in the water bath.

2. In a dark space, the film is rolled and placed lengthwise into the tube, emulsion side to the interior. Another dry threaded cap is placed on the end.

3. In the wet space, the sealed tubes are rolled in a tray of temperature-controlled water (usually 70 or 75°F) until they obtain that temperature.

4. Turning off the lights, holding the tube cap side down, the cap is removed and replaced by the cap containing the developer. *The new cap is still oriented down, so no developer has yet entered the tube.*

5. With lights on, at the indicated clock time, the tube (or tubes) is rapidly shaken and "log-rolled" in the tray of water bath constantly for the predetermined developing time.

6. When the developing time is up, *without turning off the lights*, the cap is *quickly* removed, the developer is discarded, and the tube is immersed in a tray of stop bath.

7. The film is removed and transferred for traditional tray fixing, clearing, and washing.

Film Hanger/Open Tank

The use of film hangers is well described in Kodak's *Professional Black and White Films.* Some problems inherent with tank development should be considered. The tanks take a significant amount of solution: one gallon for 4 × 5 or 5 × 7 sizes. The perforated sides of the holders are notorious for producing uneven scalloping at the edges of the negative. Unless one is equipped with a nitrogen burst system, they should be used with care.

Daylight Plastic Tanks

I absolutely do *not* recommend daylight plastic tanks. The disadvantages listed for tank development are multiplied to unmanageable levels.

Negative Enlargement

Procedures are possible to create a duplicate negative that not only can be customized for a desired format, but can also be changed in contrast as required for Pt/Pd printing. Two basic processes are available to transform a smaller negative to one that will determine the actual size of the platinum or palladium print:

- Photomechanical
  - Using Direct Positive Film
  - Using an Interpositive
- Computerization
  - Using a Specialty Bureau
  - Using your own Computer

Each has its advantages and disadvantages, which I will discuss with a brief outline of the basic techniques. The details are beyond the scope of this text. More complete descriptions are found in "Bibliography."

NOTE: A Bit of Advice: The processes for negative enlargement are difficult and time-consuming. There may be a tendency, particularly with computerization, to design the negative for more than its intended purpose. Unlike most computer art, the digitized negative is simply a means to an end. The proof is in the print. Regardless of the energy and skill expended to produce a negative, if it yields a sterile print, it is useless.

Photomechanical Enlargement

To do your own photomechanical enlargement you need an enlarger, as well as basic darkroom equipment for processing sheet film. A transmission densitometer is extremely helpful. Direct positive film, or the orthochromic films used to produce an interpositive, are extremely fragile. Scratches will be magnified. Dust is a serious problem. Dust particles at each interface will be transferred to the next. In the initial stages of enlargement, both scratches and dust will be enlarged, frequently producing black defects on the final print.

It is possible, through experience, to change contrast to produce a final negative more suitable to platinum, as well as doing selective manipulation of the negative through dodging and burning in.

Supplies

Anti-static solution (see "Sources")

Cotton gloves and negative dusting brush

Developer, stop bath, and fixer

Enlarger and a high-quality lens suitable for the original negative size

Kodak No. 1A red light or No. 1 safelight filter over a 15-watt bulb

Mat-black construction paper and drafting tape

Processing trays at least one size larger than the copy negative. Use those with flat, nonribbed bottoms.

Tongs, clock, timer, thermometer, film washer

Humidifier for raising darkroom humidity[5]

Hygrometer[5]

Transmission Densitometer[5]

If you plan to use the photomechanical methods of enlargement beyond a few experiments, I strongly recommend that you use a step tablet. When control is required, step tablets will become indispensable. See the discussions of the step tablet in Chapter 7, "Calibration."

Direct Positive

The use of direct positive duplicating film is the simplest, but has also been the least satisfactory of the possible methods I have presented. While you are making duplicate negatives, it is highly desirous to recreate an acceptable film curve. The one-step process does not allow the necessary controls.

With the introduction of Kodak SO-132 to replace SO-339, the situation has improved. Kodak Professional B/W Duplicating Film SO-132 is available from suppliers in 4 × 5 and 8 × 10 sizes. For larger sizes, a minimum order is necessary (usually, 40 boxes of 10 sheets).

For an initiation into the process of negative enlargement, direct positive is a good place to start, particularly if you are working from a miniature negative. When you graduate to the interpositive method, the materials and techniques are essentially the same. If you wish to continue platinum printing, you can purchase a large camera, or explore the use of an interpositive or computer.

If this is a new endeavor, start small until you have mastered the Pt/Pd process. Materials are expensive. You can learn as much from a 4 × 5 negative as with an 8 × 10 or 11 × 14 enlargement.

With photomechanical processes, it is best for the beginner to construct a "Ringaround" (see Kodak's *Professional Black and White Films*). Films are subjected to various degrees of exposure, and development times are arranged in blocks of nine until the ideal combination is found. It is during this process that a transmission densitometer is helpful.

1. If possible, use a humidifier to raise the darkroom humidity to at least 50%. This will help to control the dust. Use an anti-static solution on all glass surfaces. Blow off negatives, or use a negative cleaning brush. Handle with cotton gloves.

2. The enlarger must be light tight. Check in total darkness with the lens cap on. Use black tape to cover any light leaks. Place the negative in the enlarger carrier *emulsion side up* (Table A.1). It is extremely important at this point that a negative representative of your catalogue of negatives be used. It should have textured shadow areas just above base + fog and unblocked highlights. Insert a sheet of black paper between the easel base and film. (This is to prevent reflected light from reexposing the film.)

3. Working under a safelight at least four feet removed from the sensitized material, set size and focus on a piece of sample film placed over the mat paper. Use a small piece to include shadow and highlight values of the original negative. Mark the paper to orient the negative to be exposed.

[5] Optional

4. Prepare solutions. See step 6 for recommended developers. For practice, the copy negative used for focusing can be exposed in room light and developed under safelight. When dried, it can be used to check base + fog. Remember, direct copy film reacts to light in the reverse of photographic paper: more exposure causes it to become less dense (Table A.1).

5. Set the enlarger lens at the largest aperture. If possible, an APO lens at f/2.8 or f/4 would be best. Orient a strip of copy film *emulsion side up* on the easel (Table A.1). The notches should be on the upper right. Partly cover the film with a sheet of black opaque cardboard or red printers' Rubylith material. Using the enlarger timer, make exposure of 5 or more minutes in 40-second increments by sliding the material.

6. Dektol 1:1 at 2 minutes has been recommended in the literature, but Norma Smith has suggested that with film developers, times are long enough for development by inspection under a red No. 1A filter. D-76 1:1 development times are in the range of 10 minutes. XTOL can be used straight or 1:2, depending on the contrast of the original negative. Unitol 1:28 is also a possible choice.

7. Fix, lightly wash, and speed dry. Redo the process until a time or f/stop is reached to produce a clear area in the copy negative approximating base + fog. Slightly *less* exposure time should be proper for the beginning of shadow texture in the enlarged duplicate negative. More development causes the highlight areas of the negative to become more dense (Table A.1).

8. Using that exposure time as normal, make three test strips each at 1/2, normal, and 2X (double).

9. Develop one each at 1/2, normal, and 2X (double) the developing time. More development causes the highlights to be *more* dense (Table A.1). Clear, wash, and dry.

10. This will be the start of a Ringaround. It should be repeated until the ideal copy negative lies in the center of the square of arranged negatives. It is here that a transmission densitometer is valuable. Otherwise, look at some good platinum negatives from a friend or instructor. Using the principles discussed in Chapter 3, "The Negative," you can use the "visual comparison densitometer" (the black card with a small hole for viewing) to identify and match the known values in a step tablet. Make some test prints on platinum or palladium paper. Be sure to identify *textured* shadows and highlights in the copy negative. Clear shadows or blocked highlights are useless.

11. When the exposure and developing time is determined, orient a full sheet of copy film emulsion side up on the easel and secure the corners with drafting tape. (A glass negative proofing apparatus can be used if there is difficulty making the copy film lie flat, but it will add two more surfaces to collect dust particles.) Expose and process.

Now for the bad news. This test is only good for the densitometric characteristics of the original negative that you used. For different negatives, adjustments must be made (Table A.1). Use the Ringaround that you constructed.

The level of base + fog may be too high for reasonable Pt/Pd printing times. It is possible to minimize them with a bath of Farmer's Reducer.

Kodak R-4a Farmer's Cutting Reducer

Stock Solution A		
Potassium ferricyanide	275 grains	18.75 gms.
Distilled water to make	8 oz.	250.0 ml
Stock Solution B		
Sodium thiosulfate	8 oz.	240.0 gms
Distilled water to make	32 oz.	1.0 liter

Soak negative in distilled water for 5 minutes. Mix solutions immediately before use. Mix 1 part Stock Solution A, 4 parts Stock Solution B, and 32 parts distilled water. Place the mixture and negative in a tray,

TABLE A.1 Exposure and Development of Direct Copy Film

Exposure and Development of Direct Copy Film	
Enlarger: Emulsion Side Up	↓ Exposure ⇒ Shadows ↑
	↑ Exposure ⇒ Shadows ↓
Easel: Emulsion Side Up	↓ Development ⇒ Highlights ↓
	↑ Development ⇒ Highlights ↑

and agitate constantly for 20 seconds. Rinse it and examine. Only the shadow areas should be affected. A discarded negative with good shadow values can be soaked in an adjacent tray and used for comparison. When finished, discard the used solution and wash for 10 minutes. For exposure to UV light, the negative should be made more permanent by selenium toning; however, use it at a 1:30 dilution to avoid changing the contrast. Rewash and hang to dry.

At the time of publication, another direct positive method of film enlargement utilizing reversal processing of lithographic film has appeared in the literature. (Lawless, Liam. "Enlarged Negatives by Reversal." *World Journal of Post-Factory Photography* vol.1, issue 2. Oct 1998: pp. 41-44. Editor@post-factory.org)

USING AN INTERPOSITIVE

Despite the evolution of computerization, the negative-interpositive (diapositive) negative method is still used by many commercial custom platinum printers to make the stunning platinum and palladium prints exhibited by leading portrait and fashion photographers.

Using an interpositive adds the distinct disadvantage of two more surfaces to collect dust and scratches, as well as an extra processing cycle. But many advantages exist when compared to direct positive film.

- The copy or lithograph film used is available in sizes up to 20 × 24 inches.
- Unlike direct positive film, many more film choices exist for experimentation in the interpositive process.
- It is easier to "construct" a desired film curve.
- Since the final negative is made by "in camera" methods, it can be tailored using familiar exposure/development techniques.
- Working on the intermediate positive, some dodging and burning is possible from the more familiar standpoint of working with negative film.
- Copy film is orthochromic, so basically the same equipment and safelights apply as for direct positive film.

Richard Lohmann, a master platinum printer, perfected the following procedure before his graduation to digital processing. It is presented here with his kind permission.

Some debate exists over the stage at which the enlargement is made. Here, the enlargement is made during the processing of the interpositive, with the final negative made by contact printing. If you have a 4 × 5 enlarger, you can reduce your film costs by making the interpositive at that size. You can make the final negative by projection. Also, you can use the basic 4 × 5 BTZS tubes while perfecting the positive. If you make a commitment to this method, you can purchase larger BTZS tubes to develop the final negative.

1. Mix the solutions. Kodak developer HC110, dilution B (1 part stock : 7 parts water) is recommended. Dektol 1:10 or Ilford multigrade paper developer may be used at 1:5 to 1:8
2. Kodak Professional Copy Film 4125 has an ISO of 12. The enlarging time and f/stop must be calibrated to accommodate this. The use of an incident meter or a spot meter on a white card is recommended for recording of data. This time, the negative is placed *emulsion side down* in the carrier (Table A.2). Assuming an f/16 aperture,[6] make exposures of 1, 2, and 4 seconds on a strip of copy film.
3. Develop for 4 minutes in Kodak HC110, dilution B (Table A.2). Fix and dry.
4. The process up to this point is similar to printing on silver paper. Expose for the highlights and develop for the shadows (Table A.2). However, the interpositive image should predominately occupy the midportion of the film curve. This calls for slight overexposure and underdevelopment. Shadows should be generously textured. Highlights should not represent the full capacity of the copy film, but be subdued. The image should be softer than one would expect from a finished positive.

[6] Sullivan and Weese recommend that the optimum aperture be used. This is usually two stops less than maximum. To reduce the intensity of the light source, raise the enlarger head, and use filters and color head adjustments. See Sullivan and Weese, *The New Platinum Print.* They also present a method of photomechanical enlargement using the step tablet in the book.

TABLE A.2 THE TWO-STAGE NEGATIVE-DIAPOSITIVE-NEGATIVE PROCESS

Two Stage Negative-Diapositive-Negative Process		
Stage 1	Diapositive ⇒ Emulsion to Emulsion	Expose for Highlights ⇒ Develop for Shadows
Stage 2	Negative ⇒ Emulsion to Emulsion	Expose for Shadows ⇒ Develop for Highlights

If using a densitometer, you could use highlight values of 0.5 and shadow values of 1.35 to stay in the straight line portion of the film curve. A fuller range negative will be made at the next step. Continue to adjust exposure for soft highlights. Control shadows by development. If satisfactory contrast cannot be obtained, go to HC110, dilution A (1 part stock : 3 parts water). If the interpositive is too contrasty, go to dilution E (1:11). Here, constructing a Ringaround will not be quite as useful, since the value of the interpositive can only be determined when the final negative is made.

5. When a satisfactory interpositive is made, it must be projected or contact-printed to an additional sheet of copy film using the enlarger as a light source. If film flatness is a problem, use a contact printing frame or two sheets of heavy glass to hold the copy film for projection. If contact-printing is to be done, this method can be used to sandwich the developed positive and unexposed film. Orient the films *emulsion to emulsion* (Table A.2).

6. Now, basic tenets of exposing for the shadows and developing for the highlights apply. Here, one exposes for shadows and develops for highlights, just as with an in-camera negative. A step tablet can be included and used as discussed for print evaluation in Chapter 8, "The Platinum and Palladium Print." Since the final negative will be expanded into platinum or palladium range, HC110 dilution A is recommended. If that does not provide enough energy, use Kodak developer D11 mixed 1:1 with water.

NOTE: For the sensitometrically inclined, Phil Davis discusses the use of TMX film with precise controls by incorporating the Plotter Program® (*Darkroom Techniques* Magazine, vol. 13, no. 1. Jan/Feb 1992: pp. 46-53).

7. The final and most important step is: record, record, record. Measure and record every bit of data. Another negative with the same characteristics as the first can be duplicated with less effort. Different negatives will demand different data. Eventually, a "bank" of negative types will be accumulated.

Other Films

One choice of film, Kodak Fine Grain Positive film 7302, is similar to silver emulsion paper and equally blue sensitive. It is also developed in Dektol 1:1. Good quality ortho films such as Arista Ortho Lith Film, Agfa n31p, Kodak Commercial 4127, Fuji HCL Camera Film, or Ilford Line Film can also be used.

The Computerized Negative

Perhaps the most significant change since the 1990 edition of this book has been the advent of the computerized image. It is not my intent to debate the relative merits or pitfalls of the computer-manipulated image. Historically, as in the field of photography, artists (and hackers) have followed technology. While many magnificent achievements have already been demonstrated with computers, that same technology can also be identified with the endless noninspirational product hype found on television and the printed page. As with most endeavors of this nature, substance will eventually come to be separated from cleverness. For the Pt/Pd negative, computerized technology has offered an opportunity to produce enlargements relatively free from the limitations of the processes previously described. In the computerized "internegative," the density range can be programmed. Film curves can be approximated. Pixels of "grain," particularly on hand-coated platinum and palladium paper, are essentially invisible to the naked eye. Blemishes can be wiped away.

One might imagine that the large camera will soon become obsolete. That is not the case. My camera-maker friends have never been busier. Why? Like all technology, computerization is a tool to be used or misused. In the traditional practice of "straight" monochrome photography, and in historical processes in particular, working off the computer monitor cannot replace the creativity involved in choosing a subject and then composing it to the actual print size on the ground glass.

In platinum printing, if great care is taken in scanning a medium or large-format negative (2 1/4, 4 × 5, or 5 × 7), and if care is also taken to duplicate the film curve during the computer manipulations, the final print can come exceeding close to one done from an original negative. Nevertheless, with the present technology, there would be a difference, perhaps only discernible to those practiced in viewing photographs. They would not necessarily see the distinctions in line sharpness or pixels versus grain, but they would be able to sense the intangible differences between a computer-generated and camera-generated image.

For the practitioner of the manipulated image, either in the studio or afterward, Photoshop® offers limitless opportunities. When manipulating the platinum image, the type and degree of manipulation practiced is up to the discretion of the individual, and his or her vision of the contemporary usage of this historic process.

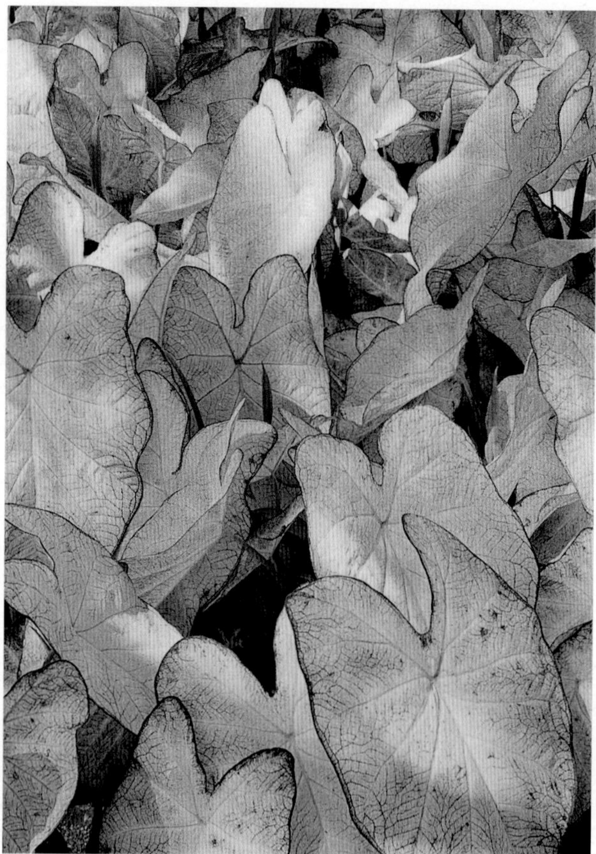

PLATE A.2 Elephant Ears #3, San Antonio, TX. 1983 7 × 10 inches Pt/Pd. This print, measuring 7 × 10 inches, was made from a computerized 5 × 7 original negative.

Computer Service Bureaus

At least two services exist to computerize your negative to a larger size (see "Sources"). You must be specific regarding the density range you desire and the film curve to be duplicated.

Doing Your Own

For doing your own computer-generated negative, four basic forms of equipment are needed:

- *A Scanner:* A way to get your images into the computer (via flatbed scanner, film scanner, Kodak Photo CD, digital camera, etc.).
- *A Computer:* Access to a computer of reasonable speed with considerable Random Access Memory (at least 64 RAM) that can run Photoshop®.
- *A Monitor:* One that is capable of calibration.
- *A Disk:* A way to physically transport large files to a service bureau (Zip®, Jaz®, SyQuest®, or another high-capacity disk that is compatible with the service bureau's hardware).
- *An Image Setter:* From this, a digitally processed "negative" is made, with the image composed not of grains of silver but *pixels*.

The high-quality drum scanners and image setters needed for this process are too expensive for all but the most affluent. Therefore, a *service bureau* is needed. You must contact the service bureau and familiarize them with your requirements. In simplified terms, your negative will be scanned with digital information placed onto a disc (Zip®, Jaz®, SyQuest®) for transportation to your computer. After you manipulate the image in Photoshop®, the image is broken down to a bit map and redelivered to the bureau. From this, they will produce your negative on an image setter.

The entire process is far more complicated and beyond the scope of this text. Fortunately, two experts have emerged on the Web for assistance. Each will provide the information necessary for you to get started:

Dan Burkholder: http://www.danburkholder.com

David Fokos: http://www.bostick-sullivan.com

Dan Burkholder has published a text with accompanying software called *Making Digital Negatives for Contact Printing*, which I highly recommend. Richard Sullivan, a former computer programmer, has written a lucid explanation of the technology in "Digital Platinum," a section of *The New Platinum Print* (Sullivan and Weese, 1998).

If you are accustomed to printing from a conventional negative, using a computerized negative may take some adjustment. The base + fog and minimum shadow densities may call for a considerably reduced printing time. Subtle shadow details are hard to capture and may disappear during dry down. Your first tries may generate the initial excitement experienced with any new process. However, when studying printed images, many photographers may notice a degree of artificiality not initially perceived in the computer-generated negative. Then, depending on the parameters you set for your work, adjustments and multiple examples of the negative will probably follow.

If one chooses to be true to the medium, prints made from original negatives will most likely establish the standards to be met. At this point, as with any process, computerization will require the necessary practice before any proficiency is attained.

Appendix B

Some Film/Developer Combinations to Produce a Platinum/ Palladium Negative

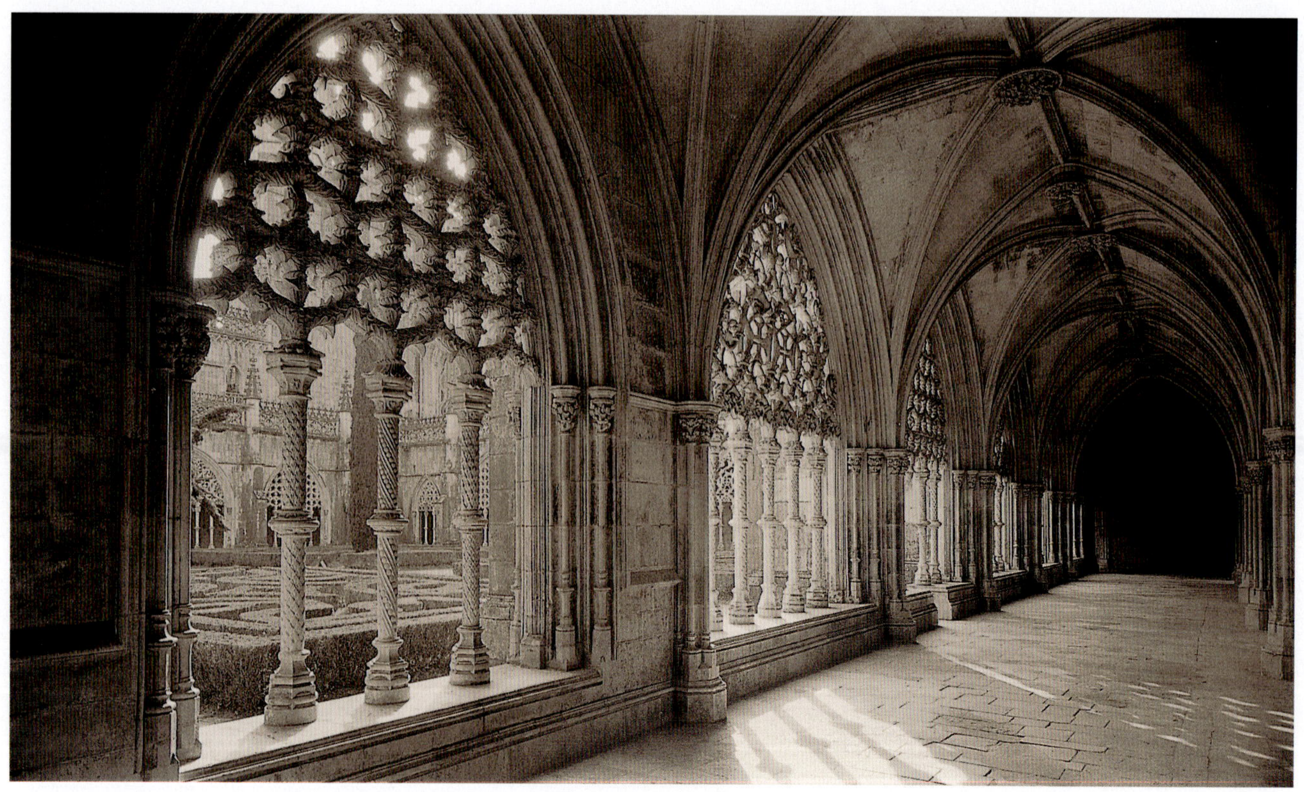

PLATE B.1 Cloisters, Batalha, Portugal. 1990 12 × 20 Pd. From the brightly-lit courtyard to the darkest portion of the interior, a subject brightness range of 12 (N-3) was recorded. TXT was developed 8 minutes in D-76 1:3.

Based on my personal experience, and studies from Phil Davis' Plotter Program®, I recommend the following film/developer combinations as a starting point to be further refined by testing and work in the studio and field.[1]

In the making of platinum or palladium negatives, the choice of the film/developer is largely dependent upon the characteristics found in the *Family of Curves* produced by each combination.

NOTE: The *Family of Curves* expresses the differences in EFS (Effective Film Speed) and the slope of the curve (average gradient) when the film is subjected to varying times and concentrations of development. This is discussed more thoroughly in Part Two, "Sensitometry for the Platinum/Palladium Process" of this book

A platinum or palladium negative must be given considerably more development to reach the steepness of curve necessary to produce sufficient contrast. With many film/developer combinations, a limit is reached, a *Gamma Infinity*, where more time or concentration of developer does not increase the slope, but simply raises shadow and highlight densities equally. This is found in many fine-grain films and compensating type developers, neither of which is suitable for a platinum or palladium negative.

The combinations I have chosen here include films of ISO between 100 and 400 that have been developed in solutions of sufficient "energy" to produce a family of curves applicable to our process. In many cases, two or more dilutions of developer are given to cover the extremes of subject brightness range (SBR). *The numbers only serve as a starting point and will require modification based on your personal practices of metering and development techniques.* Later, you may discover other combinations that are more suitable to your needs.

Generally, those with medium-format cameras (2 1/4 to 4 × 5 inches) can use the slower speed films. For cameras 5 × 7 and larger, due to the smaller apertures required for depth-of-field focus, the 320 to 400 ISO films may be more appropriate.

At the time of the publication of this book, the users of ultra-large format will find their choices limited only to three films. Moreover, while rotary development techniques are gaining in popularity, their uses for film sizes from 7 × 17 on up are impractical. For this reason, developing times for TXT, FP4 plus, and HP5 plus are given for tray development.

Choosing a Film

T-MAX Films: TMX, TMY

- Available in all sizes up to 8 × 10
- Very stable EFS and little reciprocity failure
- Straight curve with little dip in shadow values (belly)
- Quite sensitive to inaccuracies in development times
- Red dye must be removed during clearing process
- Medium rise in base + fog (B+F) with higher development
- Family of curves very responsive to development changes
- TMY (ISO 400) developed in D-76 1:1 may be the most appropriate film/developer combination for Pt/Pd photography

Delta 100/400

- 100 is available in only 4 × 5 and 8 × 10 sizes
- 400 is available in all sizes up to 8 × 10. Not very responsive to more then N+1 development
- Relatively stable EFS and moderate reciprocity failure
- Medium rise in B+F from higher development
- Straight curve with little dip in shadow values

FP4 plus

- Available in all sizes
- Relatively stable EFS and moderate reciprocity failure
- Medium rise in B+F from higher development
- Straight curve with little dip in shadow values
- Low ISO (125) makes it problematic for ultra-large format

HP5 plus

- Available in all sizes
- Straight curve with little dip in shadow values
- Relatively stable EFS and moderate reciprocity failure
- *Considerable* rise in B+F from higher development (between 0.2 and 0.3)
- Expansion development over SBR 5.6 (N+1) is difficult

[1] Note that negatives in the 1.4 density range or higher are also required for the nonsilver processes of Cyanotype, Kallitype, Carbon, Bromoil, and others. The information contained in this section can be readily adapted for those processes.

TXT

- Available in all sizes
- Considerable dip in shadow values (belly) causing extreme EFS changes
- Considerable reciprocity failure
- Little increase in B+F with over development.
- Distinct rise in highlight portions of the curves compliments the extended toe of the platinum and palladium print
- Family of curves very responsive to development changes

NOTE: Despite the drawbacks, TXT is my choice for my 7 × 17 and 12 × 20 cameras. The changes in EFS and reciprocity failure are easily calculated in the field using BTZS® computer programs or the PowerDial® available from Darkroom Innovations.

Eight Film/Developer Combinations

TABLE B.1 Eight Film/Dveloper and Temperature Combinations

Tube/JOBO Development		*Constant Agitation*	
Film	*ISO*	*Developer*	*Temperature*
TMX	100	T-MAX RS	70°F
DELTA 100	100	XTOL	75°F
FP4 PLUS	125	XTOL	75°F
TMY	400	T-MAX RS	70°F
TMY	400	D-76	70°F
Tray Development		*Intermittent Agitation*	
Film	*ISO*	*Developer*	*Temperature*
FP4 PLUS	125	D-76	70°F
HP5 PLUS	400	D-76	70°F
TXT	320	D-76	70°F

Effective Film/Developer Combinations for Selective Processing of Platinum and Palladium Negatives

The following data is based on my personal experience and is analyzed from Plotter Program® data. Special thanks to Phil Davis, Keith Schreiber, and Darkroom Innovations.

DR = density range	DR (LogE) = 1.40
SBR = subject brightness range	EFS = effective film speed

- For those using the Zone System, see Chapter 3, "The Negative," for correlations with SBR readings.
- Film/developer combinations are listed for two methods of processing:

  Tube or JOBO®—constant agitation at 70 and/or 75°F.

  Tray—intermittent agitation at 70°F.
- Generally, the choice of tray or tube/JOBO is based on personal preference, laboratory space, and negative size. If one set of data is to be used for the other method, tray to tube/JOBO processors or vice versa, the following should be factored in. Constant agitation and/or higher temperatures used with tube/JOBO result in shorter development times. To convert from tray to tube/JOBO, subtract 15 to 20% from the development times. For the reverse, add 10 to 15%. These conversion factors are only approximate. For accurate development times, analysis of the average gradients of specific films, developers, and methods are necessary. This is outside the scope of this text (Davis, 1998).
- Note that in many cases, it is desirable to change dilutions rather than time. For tray development, times are best kept over 5 minutes, so higher dilutions may be necessary with high SBRs. With drums or tubes, development times of 3 to 4 minutes are possible.
- When you dilute more than the recommended concentration of developer in a tray, add more solution to keep the same amount of active ingredient available.
- Note that for Pt/Pd negatives, an "N+2" development may only be obtained by special processing: heating of developer, high energy developer, or Selenium toning.
- Effective film speed (EFS) is calculated to the nearest 1/3 stop value.
- For palladium negatives (DR 1.6), add approximately 20% more development time.

Data

Tube/JOBO Development

TABLE B.2 TMX and T-MAX RS

Film: TMX		*Developer: T-MAX RS*	*Temperature: 70°F*		
Sheet Film			*Tube Development Constant Agitation Time in Minutes*		
ZONE DEV	*SBR*	*EFS*	*CONCENTRATION*		
			1:4	*1:7*	*1:9*
N	7	100	7.7	11	15.5
	6	100	9.5	15	—
N+1	5.6	125	10	—	—
	5	125	18	—	—
N+1 1/2	4.2	125	20	—	—
	8	100	6	5.5	8
N-1	8.6	100	5	—	7
	9	100	4	—	6.5
N-2	10.5	80	—	—	4.5
	11	80	—	—	4
N-3	12	64	—	—	—
	13	64	—	—	—

TABLE B.3 Delta 100 and XTOL

Film: Delta 100		*Developer: XTOL*	*Temperature: 75°F*
Sheet Film			*Tube Development Constant Agitation Time in Minutes*
ZONE DEV	*SBR*	*EFS*	*CONCENTRATION*
			1.1
N	7	100	8
	6	100	10
N+1	5.6	100	11
	5	100	13
N+1 1/2	4.2	125	18
	8	80	6.5
N-1	8.6	80	6
	9	80	5
N-2	10.5	80	4

TABLE B.4 FP4 PLUS AND XTOL

Film: FP4 PLUS		*Developer: XTOL*	*Temperature: 75°F*		
Sheet Film			*Tube Development Constant Agitation Time in Minutes*		
ZONE DEV	*SBR*	*EFS*	CONCENTRATION		
			STR	*1:1*	*1:2*
N	7	125	—	7.5	9
	6	125	—	10	12
N+1	5.6	125	8	11	14
	5	125	12	13.5	17
N+1 1/2	4.2	125	18	20	—
	8	100	—	5.5	8
N-1	8.6	100	—	—	7
	9	100	—	—	6.5
N-2	10.5	100	—	—	4.5
	11	80	—	—	4

TABLE B.5 TMY AND T-MAX RS

Film: TMY		*Developer: T-MAX RS*	*Temperature: 70°F*		
Sheet Film			*Tube Development Constant Agitation Time in Minutes*		
ZONE DEV	*SBR*	*EFS*	CONCENTRATION		
			1:4	*1:7*	*1:9*
N	7	400	7	8	16
	6	400	9	10.5	—
N+1	5.6	400	10	12	—
	5	500	15	16	—
N+1 1/2	4.2	500	20	—	—
	8	320	5.5	6.5	12
N-1	8.6	320	4.5	6	10.5
	9	250	4	5.3	10
N-2	10.5	250	—	4	7.5
	11	250	—	—	7
N-3	12	250	—	—	6
	13	250	—	—	4.5

TABLE B.6 TMY and D-76

Film: TMY		*Developer: D-76*		*Temperature: 70°F*
Sheet Film			*Tube Development Constant Agitation Time in Minutes*	
ZONE DEV	*SBR*	*EFS*	*CONCENTRATION*	
			STR	*1:1*
N	7	400	8.5	10
	6	400	10	12
N+1	5.6	400	11	13.5
	5	500	14	16
N+1 1/2	4.2	500	18	20
	8	320	7.3	8.5
N-1	8.6	320	6.8	8
	9	320	6.3	7.5
N-2	10.5	320	5	6.5
	11	320	—	6
N-3	12	320	—	5

Tray Development

TABLE B.7 FP4 PLUS and D-76

Film: FP4 PLUS		*Developer: D-76*		*Temperature: 70°F*	
Sheet Film			*Tray Development Intermittent Agitation Time in Minutes*		
ZONE DEV	*SBR*	*EFS*	*CONCENTRATION*		
			STR	*1:1*	*1:3*
N	7	125	—	12	
	6	125	—	12.5	
N+1	5.6	125	12	16	
	5	125	16	20	
N+1 1/2	4.2	125	20+	—	
	8	100		10	
N-1	8.6	80		9	
	9	80		7.5	
N-2	10.5	80		6	9
	11	64		—	8
N-3	12	64		—	7
	13	50		—	5

TABLE B.8 HP5 PLUS AND D-76

Film: HP5 PLUS		*Developer: D-76*		*Temperature: 70°F*
Sheet Film			*Tray Development Intermittent Agitation Time in Minutes*	
ZONE DEV	*SBR*	*EFS*	*CONCENTRATION*	
			STR	*1.1*
N	7	400	8	16
	6	400	10	—
N+1	5.6	450	11	—
	5	500	16	—
	8	320	—	11
N-1	8.6	320	—	10
	9	250	—	9
N-2	10.5	250	—	8
	11	200	—	7.5
N-3	12	200	—	7
	13	200	—	6

TABLE B.9 TXT AND D-76

Film: TXT		*Developer: D-76*		*Temperature: 70°F*	
Sheet Film			*Tray Development Intermittent Agitation Time in Minutes*		
ZONE DEV	*SBR*	*EFS*	*CONCENTRATION*		
			STR	*1:1*	*1:3*
N	7	250	—	14	—
	6	320	—	20	—
N+1	5.6	400	18	—	—
	5	600	20	—	—
N+1 1/2	4.2	800	20 @ 85°F	—	—
	8	160	—	12	—
N-1	8.6	125	—	11	—
	9	125	—	10	—
N-2	10.5	80	—	9	—
	11	64	—	7	10
N-3	12	50	—	5	8
	13	40	—	—	6.5
N-4	14	25	—	—	5

Appendix C

Principles of the Development and Clearing Processes

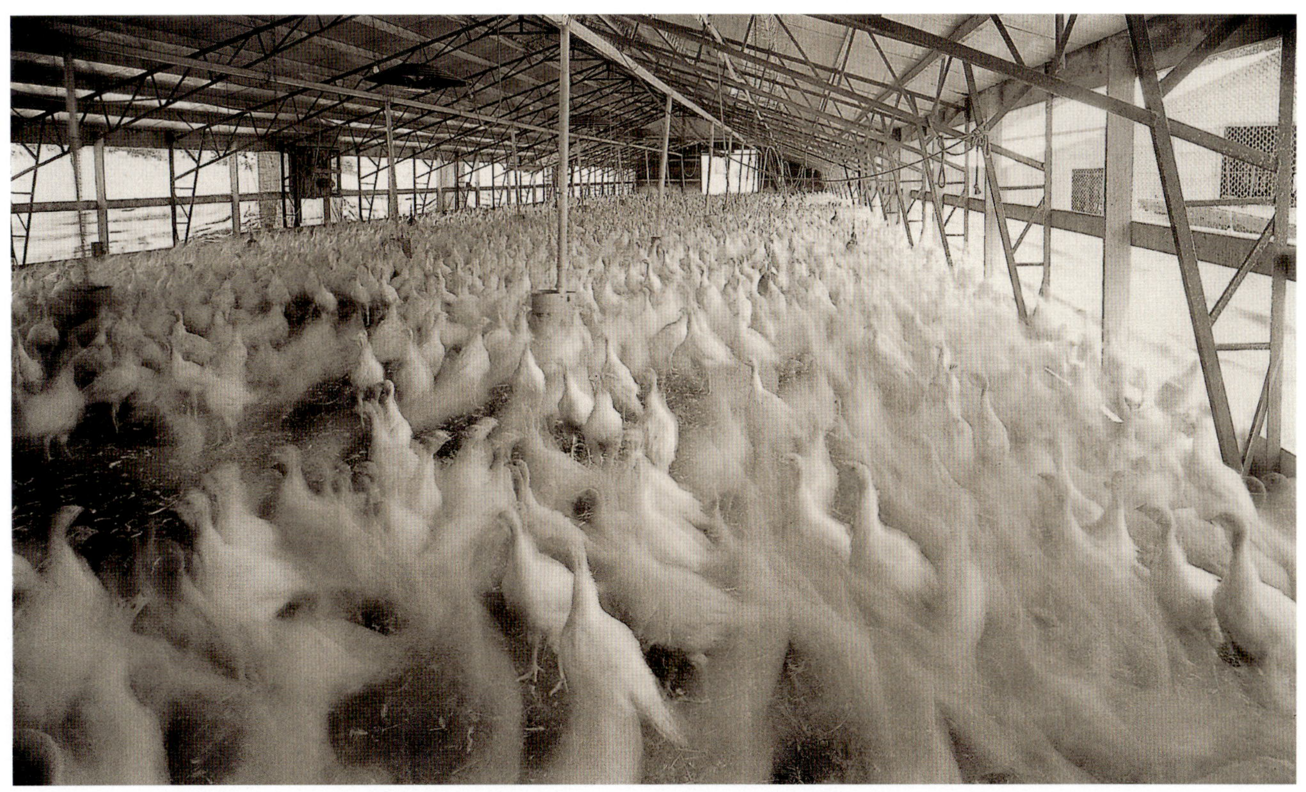

PLATE C.1 Gabbard Farm, Arkansas. 1988 12 × 20 inch Pt/Pd

THE OXIDATION-REDUCTION REACTION

As with many types of photographic printmaking, including the silver gelatin process, the platinum/palladium image is dependent upon the *reduction* of electrically charged metal salts to the uncharged metallic state. In this *oxidation-reduction* or *redox* reaction, there is a change in the *oxidation number* of one or more elements. The oxidation number, or oxidation state, is determined by the transfer of negatively charged *electrons*.

> *Oxidation* is the loss of electrons, or an increase in the oxidation number.
>
> *Reduction* is the gain of electrons, or a decrease in the oxidation number.

Chemical equations must be electrically balanced. If one or more elements are reduced, other elements must be equally oxidized. In the case of the reduction of silver, the silver salt Ag^+ is reduced by the addition of one negatively charged electron to metallic Ag°. In the process, the developer is oxidized.

The platinum/palladium process is only a bit more complicated. The metallic salts contain more than two elements, but the principle is the same. In the case of platinum, three elements comprise the salt: potassium (K^+), platinum (Pt^{2+}), and chloride (Cl^-). The compound is called potassium chloroplatinite and is depicted as K_2PtCl_4.

The palladium salt contains sodium (Na^+) in place of the potassium and is termed sodium tetrachloropalladate, or Na_2PdCl_4.

The platinum or palladium process uses another salt, or *sensitizer*, as part of the coating to facilitate the reduction process. Iron is one of many compounds to exist in more than one positive oxidation state:

Ferric	Fe^{3+}
Ferrous	Fe^{2+}

The *sensitizer* salt, ferric oxalate, or $Fe_2\,(C_2O_4)_3$ contains iron (Fe) in a state that easily accepts an electron to change to the ferrous state, or ferrous oxalate, $Fe\,(C_2O_4)$. This reduction occurs slowly with time, or is rapidly expedited by ultraviolet light in the 200 to 400 nanometer range. (See "The Ultraviolet Light Source" in Chapter 2, "Setting Up a Laboratory.") Since the process is directly related to the amount of exposure to UV light, the photographic negative serves as a vehicle to selectively filter the light to create an image. After exposure to UV light, the converted iron salts can be observed as a yellowish *printing out* image.

$$\underset{\text{Ferric oxalate } (Fe^{3+})}{Fe_2\,(C_2O_4)_3} \xrightarrow[\text{time}]{\text{UV light or}} \underset{\text{Ferrous oxalate } (Fe^{2+})}{Fe\,(C_2O_4)}$$

Note that, as time is also a factor to facilitate reduction, outdated mixtures of ferric oxalate will contain excessive amounts of the ferrous salt. If used, the ferrous oxalate will cause a diffuse amount of the metal salt to be precipitated as *fog*. For this reason, it is best to use only fresh ferric oxalate.

In a second reaction, this reduced form of iron (ferrous) is then *oxidized* to ferric oxalate, which serves as a *reducing agent* for the platinum or palladium salts. In the process of reverting to the ferric state, it gives off an electron.

This can be expressed with *Berkeley's Formula*.

BERKELEY'S FORMULA

$$\underset{\text{Ferrous oxalate}}{6\,Fe(C_2O_4)} + \underset{\text{Potassium chloroplatinite}}{3\,K_2PtCl_4} \longrightarrow \underset{\text{Ferric oxalate}}{2\,Fe_2(C_2O_4)_3} + \underset{\text{Ferric chloride}}{2\,(FeCl_3)} + \underset{\text{Potassium chloride}}{6\,KCl} + \underset{\text{Metallic platinum}}{3\,Pt^\circ}$$

A developer facilitates the process, causing the platinum (and palladium) in the coating to convert to pure metal. Much of this process is one of *hydration*, as the addition of moisture facilitates the clumping of metal particles on and within the paper. The relative insolubility of ferrous oxalate, while in the developer, attaches to the metal salt until the process of reduction is complete. In the ferric state, then, it is highly soluble (Schaefer, 1998).

Platinum and palladium are referred to as "noble" metals: as metallic elements, they are highly resistant to combining with any other chemical element or compound. The archival permanence of the platinum and palladium print is due to this phenomenon.

THE OXIDIZER

Oxidizing agents gain electrons, thereby oxidizing elements by acquiring their electrons. One of the most common is hydrogen peroxide (H_2O_2), which is capable of accepting an electron to be reduced to H_2O. To balance this process, the extra oxygen atoms (O) are converted to naturally occurring oxygen gas (O_2). Compounds of chlorate and dichromate have the same effect of strongly attracting electrons.

Oxidation

$$2H_2O_2 \longrightarrow 2H_2O + O_2$$

When an oxidizer is introduced into the photographic chemicals, the effect will be to arrest the process of reduction. In photographic paper, two reactions are observable. The printing speed of the photographic paper is slowed. Also, since the blocking of the reduction of the metallic salt is related to the concentration reacted upon, the slowing of the reaction is not linear, but causes a disproportionate slowing of reduction in the shadow and highlight areas. The net effect is that of shortening the latitude, or the exposure scale of the paper. When an oxidizer is used photographically, it is referred to as a *restrainer.*

Contrast control for the platinum or palladium print can be achieved in a number of ways. An oxidizer (restrainer) can be introduced to allow for contrast control, either into one of the sensitizing ingredients used in coating the paper or in the developer. The ferric-ferrous equation can be used to demonstrate the effect of a small amount of hydrogen peroxide to reoxidize a portion of the ferrous oxalate.

Reduction

UV light
(Reduction)

$$Fe_2\,(C_2O_4)_3 \longrightarrow Fe\,(C_2O_4)$$

Ferric oxalate (Fe^{3+}) ⟵ Ferrous oxalate (Fe^{2+})

H_2O_2
(Oxidation)

Clearing

While the platinum and palladium metals are permanent, the salts remaining after reduction are not. They will continue to react with one another and impurities in the environment. They must, therefore, be removed. The clearing agents used in the platinum/palladium process are either dilute acids or EDTA/sulfite compounds. Both facilitate the removal of the metal and iron salts from the paper. When in solution, these salts can be eliminated by successive clearing baths and washing. Inadequate removal of the salts results in stain.

Under most conditions, the clearing bath must remain acidic to keep the iron salts in the soluble oxalate state. If the clearing agent (or developer) is allowed to become alkaline, insoluble iron hydroxide may form, which resists further attempts at removal. The traditional dilute acid baths and hypo clearing agents (because of the presence of acidifying sodium metabisulfite) accomplish this purpose.

Nevertheless, an alkaline clearing bath may be used if EDTA is employed. EDTA is a powerful chelating agent that dissolves the iron salts from the paper without the necessity of an acidic solution. It is commonly used with sodium sulfite.

Appendix D

The Ammonium-Based Processes

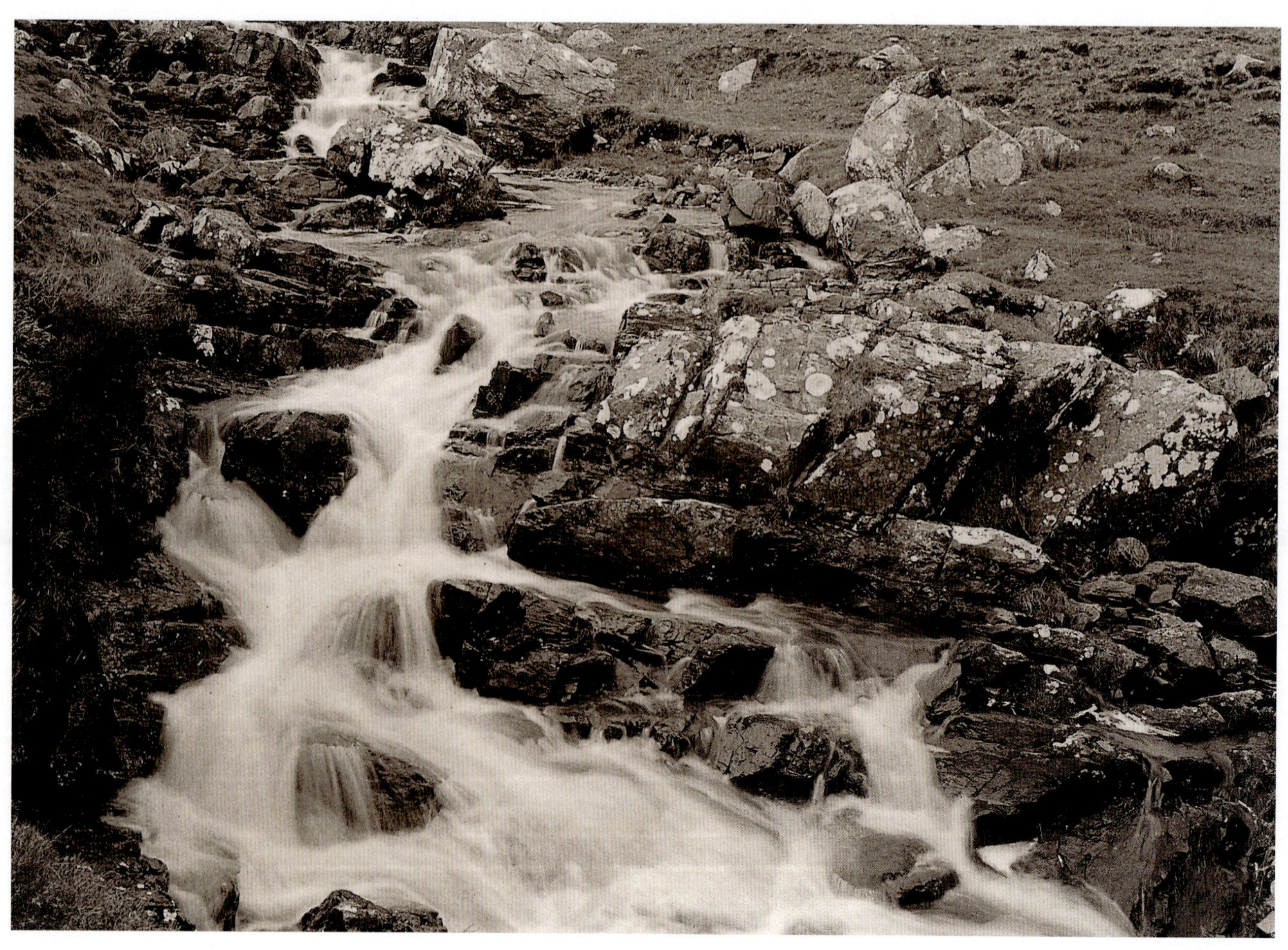

PLATE D.1 Connemara, Ireland. 1995 5 × 7 inch Ziatype

With the ammonium-based processes, ammonium salts of platinum and palladium and the ferric ammonium oxalate (ammonium trisoxalatoferrate III) sensitizer are used. Rather than requiring the development of, essentially, a latent image, as we have discussed in previous chapters, the Malde/Ware system and the Ziatype are *printing out* processes. In the traditional process, as we have seen, the reduced platinum and palladium metals cannot encounter one another in the dry state: an aqueous solution is required before they can form the metallic particles of the platinum or palladium print. In the printing out processes, moisture is provided by the hygroscopic action of the ammonium salts in the coated paper to facilitate an image before and *in place of* development. Development is, therefore, a final addition of moisture and the beginning of the clearing process.

The key to both ammonium-based processes is the placement of the coated paper into an environment of controlled humidity before exposure to the negative. By modifying the relative humidity of the paper, and the proportions of platinum and palladium, tones ranging from blue-black to sepia brown can be obtained. Also, some degree of contrast control is possible by varying the relative humidity.

The ammonium-based processes have some advantages over the traditional process.

- It is a printing-out process. With practice, the image can occasionally be assessed during exposure by opening the printing frame. (See Chapter 6, "The First Print.")
- A wider range of tone color is possible. With the Ziatype the tones can be modified with the use of lithium and cesium salts, as well as other additives.
- Many papers that are not suitable for the traditional methods may be found to be more amenable to the ammonium-based processes.
- The chelating agents used for development (EDTA) are less toxic than the oxalates and citrates used in the traditional process. However, as discussed in Chapter 4, "Chemicals," more traditional Pt/Pd chemicals can be as safe with reasonable and prudent use.
- Following clearing in hypo clearing agent and/or EDTA, the print emerges with an alkaline pH.
- The printing-out processes have a self-masking effect that delays the further exposure in the shadow areas while highlights are being brought to the desired tones.

There are still inherent advantages to the traditional method, making it the most popular and frequently practiced form of platinum and palladium printing.

- The monitoring of the humidifying environment may take some practice. In England, where Mike Ware prints, maintaining a constant 65 to 80% relative humidity is not as much of a challenge as in some parts of the United States. Here, however, a humidifying "chamber" must be constructed. For the Ziatype, Sullivan and Weese describe a quite empirical method of drying with a nonheated blower (Sullivan and Weese, 1998).
- As a consequence, while the ammonium-based processes may be adequate for the occasional printer, more reproducible results can be obtained by the use of restrainers to make use of the many paper grades possible with the traditional method.
- Many platinum printers, including the author, consider the attainment of well-exposed shadow and highlight areas only the beginning of a successful print. Considerable modifications, utilizing the precise controls over printing time and contrast, are necessary before the print progresses from the point of "clinical" perfection to an interpretation of our emotions at the time of film exposure. When those specifications are reached, accurate, *reproducible* methods are indispensable to assure that the standard is met over many different printings. Frequently, it is necessary to duplicate images within set parameters, under different seasonal conditions, over periods spanning ten to fifteen years or more.
- The use of sensitometric controls to match negative density ranges accurately to the appropriate paper contrast is difficult with the ammonium-based processes.

Nevertheless, the ammonium-based process have too many distinct attributes for the Pt/Pd printmaker to ignore. It is strongly recommended that if a career or avocation as a platinum printer is contemplated, the Malde/Ware process and the Ziatype be investigated.

I will present outlines of the Malde/Ware and the Ziatype processes as an introduction. *These descriptions are by no means complete.* If your curiosity leads you to the desire to make an actual print, more complete treatises are available from the following sources:

Malde/Ware Method:
  http://pmalde@sewanee.edu (or)
  http://mikeware.demon.co.uk

The Ziatype®:
  http://www.bostick-sullivan.com (or)
  Sullivan and Weese,
  The New Platinum Print

Before you practice the Malde/Ware Method or the Ziatype, I advise you to familiarize yourself with the Hazards and Safety Precautions inherent with the use of any of the chemicals represented. See Chapter 5, "Chemicals," and the material contained in the original Malde/Ware and Ziatype instructions.

Malde/Ware Method

The following is a summarized version of the Malde/Ware, reprinted from his Web site with the kind permission of Professor Mike Ware. The Malde/Ware method utilizes many of the steps described in Chapter 8, "The Platinum and Palladium Print"; however, there are distinct modifications that will be discussed.

The Coating Solutions

Ammonium salts of both the sensitizer and metals are used. Ware refers to the alternate terms of ammonium iron (III) and ammonium ferrioxalate.[1]

Sensitizer

Ferric ammonium oxalate 60% $(NH_4)_3Fe(C_2O_4)_3{\cdot}H_2O$

The Metal Salts

> Ammonium tetrachloroplatinate (II) 25% or ammonium chloroplatinite $(NH_4)_2(PtCl_4)$

Ware gives instructions for mixing. He advises that the solution stand for 24 hours before use.

> Ammonium tetrachloropalladate (II) 20% $(NH_4)_2(PdCl_4)$

[1] The ammonium salts are available in the U.S., from only a few suppliers (FR and QC). See "Sources."

In his Web site, Ware gives instructions for mixing from ammonium chloride $NH_4\,Cl_2$, and palladium (II) chloride $PdCl_2$.

The Malde/Ware method establishes three Relative Humidities (RH%) that, in combination of mixtures of metal salts, determine speed, printing exposure range (logH), extent of development, and color (Table D.1).

- Speed is relative arithmetic, referring to middle tones.
- logH is the Printing Exposure Range, extending from fog + 0.04 to 0.9 Dmax.
- Extent of Development is in logH units (0.3 = 1 stop). 0 indicates total print-out.

NOTE: These parameters will vary with the choice of paper.

The Process

Coating

The coating processes, done with a coating rod, is essentially the same as described in Chapter 8, "The Platinum and Palladium Print." When using straight platinum, it is recommended that the coating solution be allowed to "mature" for two to three hours before using. It is also recommended that in a dry environment the paper be prehumidified to 70 to 80% RH before coating.

Drying

According to Ware,

> After coating, allow the sensitized paper to rest horizontally at room temperature until its surface has dried sufficiently to appear nonreflective to the subdued (tungsten) light. Then dry the sensitized paper for about ten minutes in a warm (40°C, 100°F) air stream, or at room temperature for an hour, preferably in the dark.

TABLE D.1 Characteristics of Platinum-Palladium Sensitizers

Sensitizer	*RH%*	*Speed*	*logH*	*Develops*	*Color*
Platinum	32	1.8	1.2	0.9	warm black
	55	1.7	1.2	0.3	warm black
	80	1.0	1.5	0	neutral
Palladium	32	0.5	2	0.4	Vandyke brown
	55	1.3	1.9	0.2	sepia
	80	2.5	1.8	0	neutral
Pt/Pd 3:1	32	1.2	1.6	0.6	warm black
	55	1.0	2	0	neutral
	80	1.0	2	0	neutral

Humidifying

It is at this point that the ammonium-based systems deviate considerably from the traditional processes. As you can see from Table D.1, relative humidities (RH) of 32, 50, and 80 are variables that can modify printing characteristics. For most purposes, 80% is preferred.

An RH of below 50% will produce only partial print-out. Above 80% RH, the maximum density of the image will tend to weaken because the sensitizer can diffuse too deeply into the paper. Professor Ware indicates that in the British humidity of 70 to 80%, the dried, coated paper can simply be allowed to remain in the dark for one or two hours before exposure.

Most likely, however, a humidifying tank (i.e., a tray with a close-fitting lid, in which the paper may be placed to assume a desired humidity) will be necessary. Directions for construction can be obtained from the Malde/Ware literature. The coated paper is placed face down, over, but not in contact with, a saturated aqueous solution.

The following is recommended for control of humidity:

- Ammonium chloride: which provides an RH of 80% at 20°C (68°F).
- Calcium nitrate tetrahydrate: which provides an RH of 55%.

As noted on Ware's Web site,

> It is important that there should be excess solid salt in contact with its saturated solution, and that the paper should be evenly exposed to the vapor. The time of exposure in the humidifying tank should not be less than half an hour, for the sake of evenness; the upper limit is not critical and can be a few hours.

Another method of humidifying is to use pure water in the tank. For this, the timing of the humidification is critical:

- A time of 5 to 20 minutes is recommended for a warm-toned result.
- A time of 20 to 30 minutes will yield fuller print-out and a colder image tone.

Humidification for more than an hour may lead to weakening of the image density, as well as clearing problems (chemical fogging or an irremovable yellow stain of iron hydroxide), because the paper will absorb an excessive amount of water. Overhumidified paper is also more likely to damage the negative during contact printing.

Exposure

Because of the necessity of assessing the progression of the printing-out image, a contact printing frame with a hinged back is required. See "Contact Printing Frames" in Chapter 2, "Setting Up a Laboratory," and Chapter 6, "The First Print." Under conditions of full print-out (80% RH) the exposure is continued until the image has the desired appearance; do not be concerned about extending the exposure to provide textured highlights; the shadows will not block up, because of the self-masking properties of the printing-out process.

Tray Processing

After exposure, the print is processed in the recommended solutions:

1. Disodium EDTA (5%) (Developer)	5 minutes
2. Rinse in water	30 seconds
3. Kodak Hypo Clearing Agent	15 minutes
4. Rinse in water	30 seconds
5. Tetrasodium EDTA (5%)	15 minutes
6. Wash in running water	Minimum 30 minutes

Finishing

The final steps of printmaking are similar to the techniques discussed in Chapters 6, 7, and 8.

The Ziatype

Richard Sullivan, of Bostick and Sullivan, developed the Ziatype process while exploring the printing-out process described by Giuseppi Pizzighelli in 1880. He made modifications in the process, utilizing the lithium and cesium salts of palladium for tone control. As in the case of the Malde/Ware method, humidification is necessary to provide a printing-out image. But, unlike the Malde/Ware process, restrainers can be added for additional contrast control. The Ziatype is said to have the following advantages for the printing-out images, as well as further attributes.

NOTE: The Ziatype was named for the *Zia*, the ancient Anasazi people's symbol for the sun.

- Greater color control with the use of lithium, cesium, and gold salts.
- A cold, neutral black color with the use of palladium.
- A better *Dmax* without the use of platinum.
- The Ziatype has approximately three times the printing speed as other processes. With the use of

contrast control agents, negatives with contrast indices more appropriate for silver gelatin can be printed without the excessive graining associated with other processes.

A number of Ziatype kits are available from Bostick and Sullivan. The following is the most complete:

Sensitizer: Ferric ammonium oxalate solution No. 1

Metal Salts:

- Lithium palladium Solution No. 3a LiPd
- Cesium palladium Solution No. 3b CsPd

Other Additives: lithium ferric oxalate, sodium ferric oxalate, and sodium tungstate

Contrast Control Ingredient: Ammonium dichromate 20%

Surfactin: Tween 20 10%

Developing and Clearing Agent: EDTA

Toning Agent: Gold chloride 5%

Some considerations: The Ziatype uses the same methodology as the traditional and Malde/Ware processes. However, it is more sensitive to light, so reduced illumination is needed for coating. The coating rod is preferred. Negatives of density ranges up to DR or CI 2.0 can be used.

Coating

The coating is done as with the other methods. The use of a coating rod is recommended.

Print Color

Print color ranges from cool black to sepia. The extreme tones of purple, green blue, to red are possible with additives. Colors are controlled by varying the proportions of a myriad of metal salts, sensitizers, and restrainer. This process is featured in Sullivan and Weese, *The New Platinum Print*, as well as on their Web site, therefore it would be redundant to go into any more detail.

Humidification

Like the Malde/Ware process, it is a printing-out process, depending on the properties of ammonium to hydrate and form a vehicle for the laying down of metal. Unlike the Malde/Ware process, it is not necessary to vary humidity for effect.

Ziatype Impressions

With this sketch introducing the many variables in the Ziatype, you no doubt can see the potential complexity of the process. To explore this process further, it is essential that you consult more thorough and extensive guides—in addition to practicing considerable experimentation. As Carl Weese indicated in his article for the July/August 1997 issue of *Photo Techniques*, most workers will establish a set pattern for their preferable practice of this extraordinary process. After two days in the Sullivan lab in 1997, I returned home with prints exhibiting a range of color tones that I would never have thought possible from the use of pure palladium.

Appendix E

Sizing of Paper

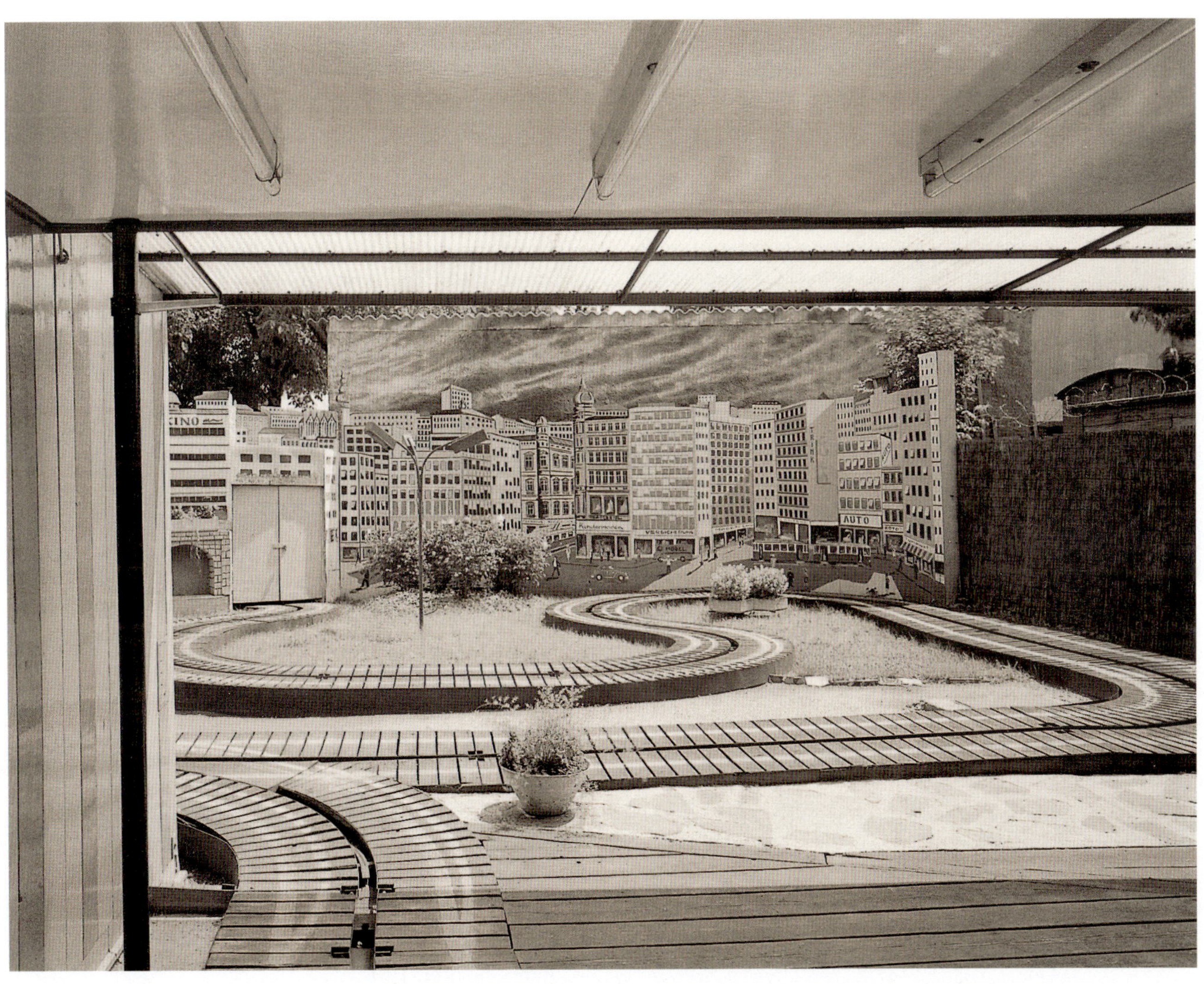

PLATE E.1 Prater, Vienna, Austria. 1983 8 × 10 inch Pt/Pd. At the time this print was made, suitable papers for Pt/Pd printing were problematic. The paper was, therefore, sized with gelatin.

Gelatin Sizing (Formaldehyde Free)

By James Hajicek, Arizona State University

Supplies

Chrome potassium sulfate (chrome alum)
Hot plate
Knox unflavored gelatin
Line and clothespins
Plateglass
Plexiglas or PVC rod
Pyrex beaker, 1 qt.
Stirring rod
Thermometer
Tray one size greater than paper

Many nineteenth-century printing processes require the use of well-sized paper. Sizing paper helps keep the light sensitive coating on the surface of the paper (rather than sinking too deep into the paper fibers); stabilizes the paper dimensionally (eliminating problems of registration, which is especially important with multiple printing); and eliminates many staining problems that can occur with some processes. Different processes require different degrees of sizing. Many papers are manufactured with some sizing material in them, but often it is not enough to correct the above listed problems.

1. Presoak your paper at least 15 minutes in tap water that is as hot as you can stand to touch. Make sure that the water remains hot throughout the time it is being used. Use constant agitation. If you are doing several sheets at one time, move the bottom sheet to the top, continuing this process throughout the required time. Eliminate any air bubbles on the surface of the paper, and make sure all areas of your paper are evenly wet. Hang to dry by two corners. This is basically a stage of preshrinking your paper before the application of the size.

2. When dry, mark the back of your paper with a small × or your initials in a lower corner. Dissolve 30 grams of Knox unflavored gelatin in 1,000 ml of distilled water. The water should not be hotter than room temperature. Stir gently for 15 minutes as the gelatin absorbs the water. Slowly heat this solution to a temperature of at least 125°F. Hotter is better, but do not exceed a temperature that you can stand to the touch.

While this is being heated, mix 2.5 grams of chromium potassium sulfate (chrome alum) in 60 ml of distilled water. Heat this solution, then very carefully and slowly pour it into the gelatin while stirring constantly. If the chrome alum in not close to the temperature of the gelatin, or you pour it in too fast without stirring, the gelatin will lump and you will have to begin all over again. Pour the gelatin/chrome alum mixture into a clean tray that will easily accommodate the size of your paper. It is helpful to have that tray inside a larger tray into which you can pour extremely hot water, in order to keep your gelatin mixture from becoming too cold during the process of sizing. Soak your paper in the sizing (gelatin/chrome alum), again moving the sheet on the bottom to the top and so on, for at least 10 minutes.

Make sure that no air bubbles are on the surface of the paper and the gelatin has been evenly absorbed into the paper. Take one sheet from the gelatin and place against an inclined plane of 1/4 inch glass that is very clean and free of all dust. Place the sheet so that the back, the side that you have marked with an × is face up. Use a Plexiglas or PVC rod that is at least as long as the shortest dimension of your paper, applying even pressure and forcing the gelatin into the fibers of the paper. Roll the Plexiglas rod under the palms of your hands along the length of the paper. The excess gelatin will slowly run down the glass. Turn the paper over so that the mark is against the glass, and repeat. Hang to dry by two corners.

3. When dry repeat step two. It is best not to try to save the gelatin as it becomes contaminated with dirt. This process may be repeated one more time to ensure a very even and well-sized surface. Always finish with the mark against the glass. This will be the back of the print. For multiple printing of gum bichromates, three coats of size is sometimes used. Sized paper will keep indefinitely. Store in a clean environment.

Starch Sizing

(From Photographers Formulary)

Supplies

Arrowroot starch 20 gm
Brush, small
Hot plate
Masonite board
Pins
Pyrex beaker, 1 qt.
Shaving brush
Stirring rod
Thermometer

Method

1. Add 20 gms. of arrowroot starch to 20 ml of hot water. Stir to the consistency of thick cream.
2. Add 1 qt. of hot water and boil for 5 minutes.
3. Cool to 68°F. Decant solution.
4. Pin paper to the board, and apply sizing solution with the brush until paper is completely wet.
5. Work in solution with shaving brush until it loses its gloss.
6. Allow to dry.

Sources

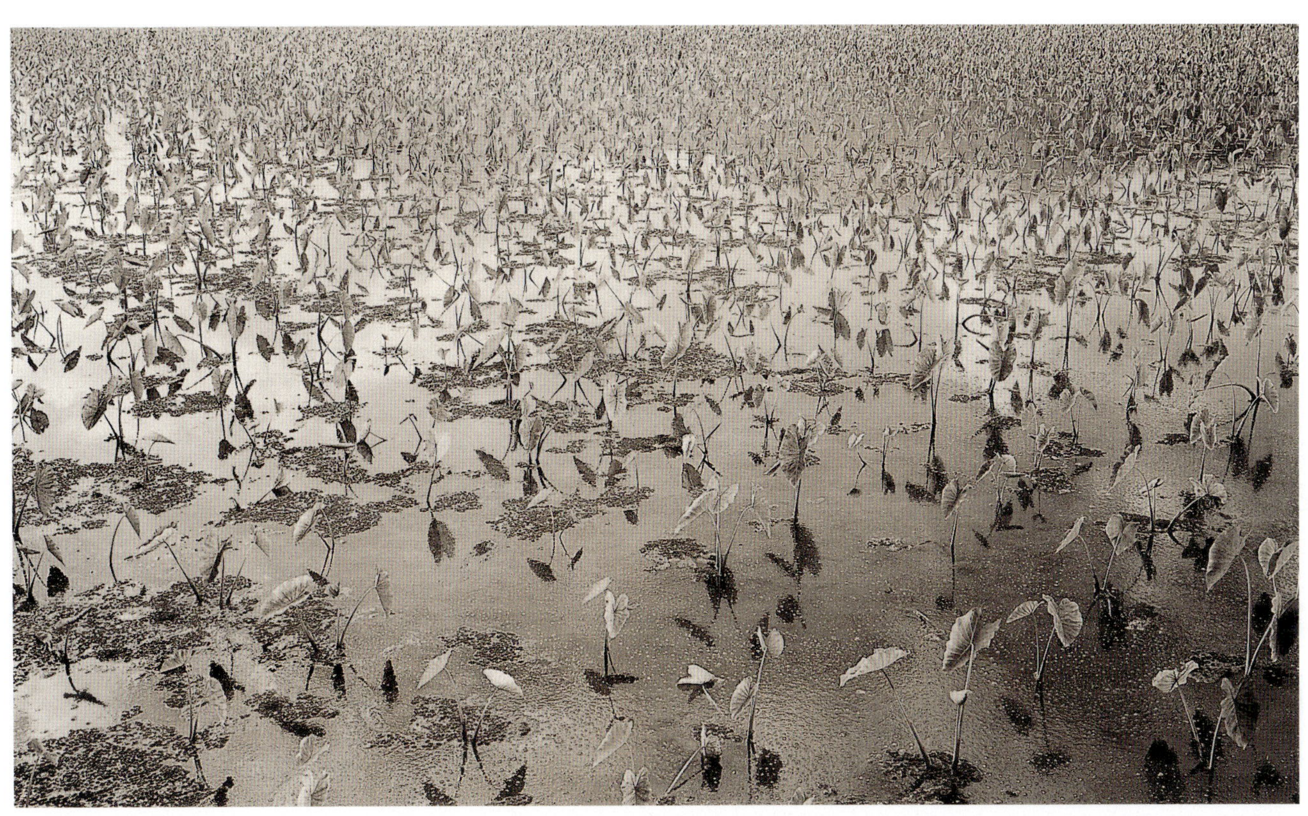

PLATE S.1 Taro, Hanalei, Hawaii. 1987 12 × 20 inch Pd

Antistatic Solutions

MD Modern Solutions. 6370 Copps Ave., Madison, WI 53716
Tel: (800) 288-2023
Fax: (608) 222-2704
http://www.modernsolution.com

Archival Products

GA Gaylord Brothers. P.O. Box 4901, Syracuse, NY 13221-4901
Tel: (800) 448-6160
Fax: (800) 272-3412
http://www.gaylord.com

LI Light Impressions. P.O. Box 940, Rochester, NY 14603-0940
Tel: (800) 828-6216
Fax: (800) 828-5539
http://www.lightimpressionsdirect.com

BTZS Products

DI Darkroom Innovations. P.O. Box 19450, Fountain Hills, AZ 85269
Tel: (602) 767-7105
Fax: (602) 767-7106.
http://www.darkroom-innovations.com
info@darkroom-innovations.com
(Also a source for large format film and densitometers)

Camera Makers

KC K.B. Canham. 2038 East Downing, Mesa, AZ 85213
Tel: (602) 964-8624
Fax: (602) 892-4146

HC Hoffman Camera Company. 19 Grand Ave., Farmingdale, NY 11735
Tel: (516) 694-4470
Fax: (516) 935-0748
hi203019@nassaulibrary.org

PC R.H. Phillips & Sons. P.O.Box 1281, Midland, MI 48641-1281
Tel: (517) 835-7897
Fax: (517) 839-9745

WC Wisner Company. P.O. Box 21, Marion, MA 02738
Tel: (800) 848-0448
Fax: (508) 748-2733
http://www.wisner.com

Chemicals

AC Artcraft Chemicals. Box 583 Schenectady, NY 12301
Tel: (800) 682-1730
Fax: (518) 355-9121
http://www.nfinity.com/~mdmuir/artcraft
jacobson@juno.com

AP Abbey Camera. 1417-25 Melon St., Philadelphia, PA 19130
Tel: (800) 252-2239
Fax: (215) 236-5666
http://www.abbeycamera.com

BL Bryant Laboratory, Inc. 1101 Fifth St., Berkeley, CA 94710
Tel: (800) 367-3141
Fax: (510) 528-2948
http://www.sirius.com/~bry_lab/

BS Bostick & Sullivan. Box 16639, Santa Fe, NM 87506-6639.
Tel: (505) 474-0890
Fax: (505) 474-2857
http://www. bostick-sullivan.com
richsul@roadrunner.com
Orderinfo@earthlink.com
(Paper, printing supplies, printing frames)

FR First Reaction. 37 Depot Rd., Hampton Falls, NH 03844
Tel: (603) 929-3583
Fax: (603) 929-5023
firstrxn@ttlc.com
(Ammonium platinum and palladium salts)

PF Photographer's Formulary. Box 950, Condon, MT 59826
Tel: (800) 922-5255
Fax: (406) 754-2896
http://www.montana.com/formulary
formulary@montana.com

QC Quality Camera Company. 382 Trabert Ave., Atlanta, GA 30309
Tel: (404) 881-8700
Fax: (404) 881-9010
(Ammonium platinum and palladium salts)

Computerization

Film Duplicating Services

EC EverColor. 70 Webster St., Worcester, MA 01603
Tel: (508) 757-2216
Fax: (508) 757-2216
light@evercolor.com

LL Laser Light Photographics. P.O. Box 4365, Shrewsbury, MA 01545
Tel: (508) 799-3996
Fax (508) 799-0695
laslight@aol.com

Resources for Doing it Yourself

DB Dan Burkholder: http://www.danburkholder.com
DF David Fokos: http://www.bostick-sullivan.com

Contact Printing Frames and Film Holders

AWB AWB Enterprises. 33320 Gafford Rd., Wildomar, CA 92595
Tel and Fax: (909) 674-0466
www.cosmoaccess.net/~awbent
awbent@access.net

GB Great Basin Photographic. HC 33 Box 2, Las Vegas, NV 89123
Tel: (702) 363-1900
Fax: (702) 363-1900
http://www.vegas.infi.net/~ginther/indexgbp.html

Densitometers

AP Absolute Photographic Co. 8031 N. Academy Blvd. #401, Colorado Springs, CO 80920.
Tel: (719) 636-0797
Fax: (719) 636-1204
http://www.pcisys.net/mantis
mantis@pcisys.net

ES Eseco Speedmaster. One Eseco Road, Cushing, OK 74023-9912
Tel: (800) 331-5904
Fax: (918) 225-1284
ESECO-speedmaster@worldnet.att.net

Film, Ultra-Large Format

PM Photomark. 2202 E. McDowell, Phoenix, AZ 85006
Tel: (800) 777-6627
Fax: (602) 273-0928
http://www.photomark.com

SC Samy's Camera. 200 S. La Brea Ave., Los Angeles, CA 90036
Tel: (800) 321-4726
Fax: (213) 937-2919.
http://www.samys.com
info@samys.com

Laboratory Equipment

CLS Chem Lab Supplies, 1060 Ortega Way, Unit "C," Placentia, CA 92670
Tel: (714) 630-7902
Fax: (714) 630-3553
http://www.chemlab.com

CPI Calumet Photographic. 890 Supreme Drive, Bensonville, IL 60106
Tel: (800) 225-8638
Fax: (800) 828-5539
http://www.calumetphoto.com

ESc Edmund Scientifics. 101 E. Glouster Pike, Barrington, NJ 08007
Tel: (800) 728-6999
Fax: (609) 547-3292
scientifics@edsci.com

GAS Graphic Arts Supermarket. 727 Venice, Los Angeles, CA 90015
Tel: (213) 749-9569
Fax: (213) 749-9762
(Stouffer's Step Tablets)

TS Tri-Ess Sciences, Inc. 1020 W. Chestnut St., Burbank, CA 91506
Tel: (800) 274-6910
Fax: (818) 848-3521
science@tri-sss.com

VRW VRW Science Products. P.O. Box 1002, S. Plainfield, NJ 07080
Tel: (800) 932-5000
Fax: (908) 757-0313
http://www.vrwsp.com
(Hygrometers)

UV Light Sources

AR Aristo Grid Lamp Products. 35 Lumber Rd., Roslyn, NY 11576
Tel: (516) 484-6141
Fax: (516) 484-6992
http://www.aristogrid.com/

EE Edwards Engineering. 5304 Arrowhead Dr., Lago Vista, TX 78645-5803
Tel and Fax: (512) 267-4274
EEPJON@aol.com
(Also, print dryers)

NA nuArc Company, Inc. 6200 W. Howard St., Niles, IL 60714
Tel: (800) 962- 8883
Fax: (847) 967-9664
http://www.nuarcco.com

PC Palladio Company, P.O.Box 28, Cambridge, MA 02140-0001.
Tel: (800) 628-9618
Fax: (617) 393-0817
palladio@napc.com

PS Psoralight Corp. 2806 William Puller Dr., Columbia, SC 29205
Tel: (800) 331-3534
Fax: (803) 748-9985
(Solar Specs)

Paper

ASW Art Supply Warehouse. 5325 Departure Dr., North Raleigh, NC 27616-1835
Tel: (800) 995-6778
Fax: (919) 878-5075
http://www.aswexpress.com
aswexpress@aol.com

DS Daniel Smith, 4130 First Avenue, S., Seattle, WA 98124-5568
Tel: (800) 426-6740
Fax: (800) 238-4065
http://www.danielsmith.com
dsartmatrl@aol.com

MA Martin Axon. Platinum Press, 20 Maplewood Ln., Madison, CT 06443
Tel: (203) 245-7674

NYC New York Central Art Supply. 62 Third Ave., New York, NY 10003
Tel: (800) 950-6111
Fax: (212) 477-0400

PT Paper Technologies, Inc. 6333 Chalet Dr., Commerce, CA 90040
Tel: (562) 928-5600
Fax: (562) 927-6100
http://www.papertech.com

SS Stationery Store

SK Stephen Kinsella, Inc. P.O. Box 32420, Olivette, MO 63132
Tel: (800) 445-8865
Fax: (314) 991-8090

TR Twinrocker, 100 East Third Street, P.O. Box 413, Brookstone, IN 47923
Tel: (800) 757- 8946
Fax: (765) 563- 8946
http://www.twinrocker.com
twinrock@twinrocker.com

View Camera Restoration and Repair

PA Patrick Alt. 1324 S. Figuera #101, Los Angeles, CA 90015
Tel: (213) 748-3087
Fax: (213) 744-7981
altview@aol.com
(Exposure units and Pt/Pd work stations made to order.)

Bibliography

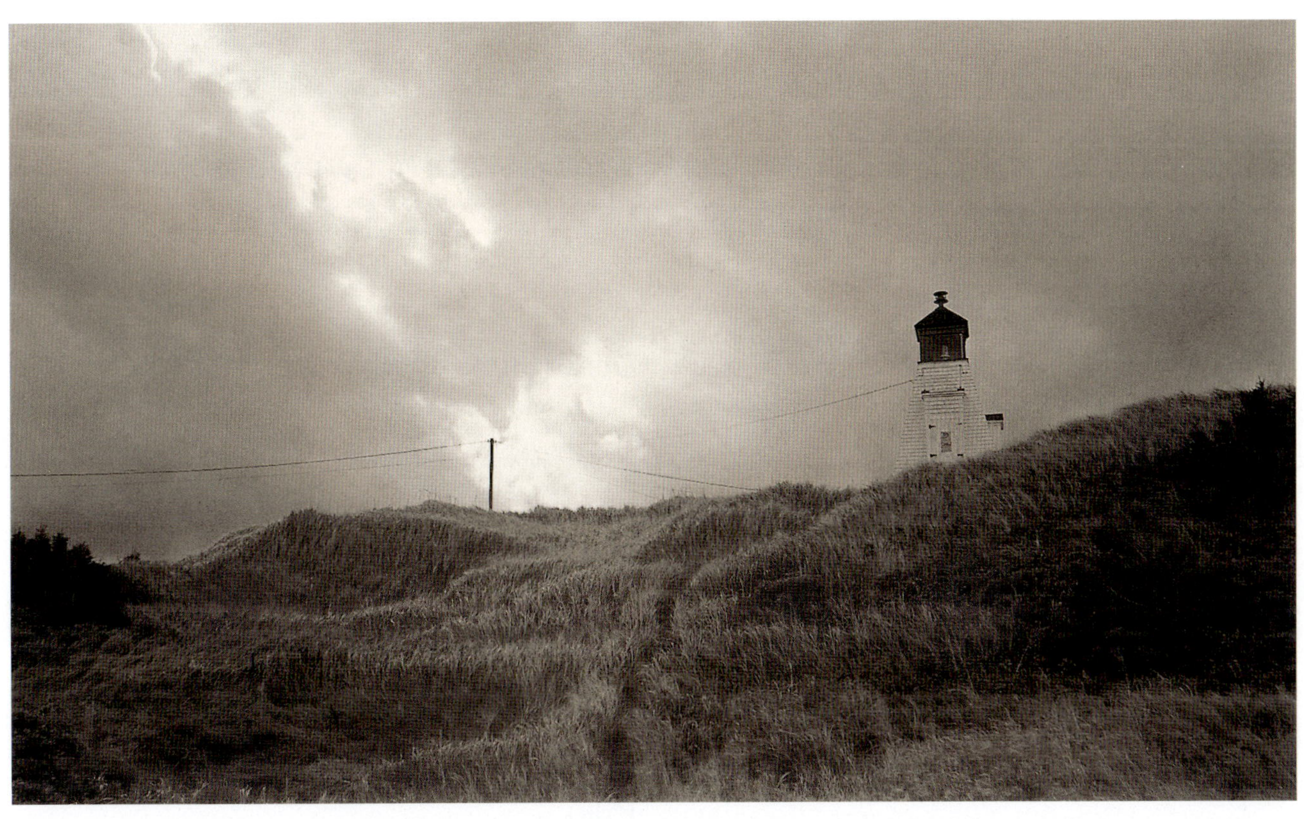

PLATE BIB.1 Margaree, Nova Scotia. 1997 12 x 20 inch Pt/Pd

Historic

Abney, W. *Platinotype: Its Preparation and Manipulation.* London: Sampson, Low Marston, 1895.

Anderson, Paul L. *Technique of Gum-Platinum: The Technique of Pictorial Photography.* NY: J.B. Lippincott, 1939.

Newhall, Beaumont. *The History of Photography.* New York: Museum of Modern Art, 1982.

Pizzighelli, Captain, and Hubl, Baron A. *Platinotype*. London: Harrison and Sons, 1886. Reprinted from *The Photographic Journal.* 1883, pp. 5-59.

Steiglitz, Alfred. *Platinum Printing: The Modern Way in Picture Making.* Rochester, NY: Eastman Kodak, 1905.

Current

Arnow, Jan. *Handbook of Alternative Photographic Processes.* New York: Van Nostrand Reinhold, 1982.

Crawford, William. *The Keepers of the Light.* New York: Morgan and Morgan, 1979.

Farber, Richard. *Historic Photographic Process.* New York: Allworth Press, 1998.

Malde, Pradip, and Ware, Michael. *The Ammonium System: A Contemporary Method for Making Platinum and Palladium Prints.* pmalde@sewannee.edu

Nadeau, Luis. *History and Practice of Platinum Printing.* New Brunswick, Canada: Atelier Luis Nadeau, 1994.

Rexroth, Nancy. *The Platinotype 1977.* Condon, MT: Formulary Press, 1977. (Available from Photographers Formulary.)

Shillea, Thomas J. *Instruction Manual for the Platinum Printing Process.* Philadelphia: Thomas J. Shillea, 1982. (Available from Photographers' Formulary.)

Sullivan, Richard, and Weese, Carl. *The New Platinum Print.* Santa Fe, NM: Working Picture Press, 1998. (www.bostick-sullivan.com)

Chemistry

Anchell, Stephen G. *The Darkroom Cookbook.* Boston: Focal Press, 1994.

Rempel, Siegfried, and Rempel, Wolfgang. *Health Hazards for Photographers.* New York: Lyons and Burford, 1992.

Shaw, Susan, and Rossel, Monica. *Overexposure: Health Hazards in Photography.* St. Paul, MN: Allworth, 1991.

General

Davis, Phil. *Photography.* 7th Ed. Dubuque, IA: Brown and Benchmark, 1995.

Edwards, Betty. *Drawing on the Right Side of the Brain.* Los Angeles: J.P. Tarcher, 1979.

Kodak. *Building a Home Darkroom.* Kodak Publication KW-14. New York: Eastman Kodak, 1996.

Schaefer, John P., ed. *An Ansel Adams Guide. Basic Techniques of Photography, Book Two.* Boston: Little, Brown, 1998.

Simmons, Steve. *Using the View Camera.* New York: Amphoto, 1992.

Stroebel, Leslie. *View Camera Technique.* 6th ed. Boston: Focal Press, 1993.

Sensitometry

Adams, Ansel. *The Negative.* Book 2. Boston: Little, Brown, 1981.

Davis, Phil. *Beyond the Zone System.* 4th ed. Boston: Focal Press, 1998.

Kodak. *Professional Black and White Films.* Kodak Publication F-5. New York: Eastman Kodak, 1998.

Todd, Hollis N., and Zakia, Richard D. *Photographic Sensitometry.* New York: Morgan & Morgan, 1969.

Duplication of Negatives

Kodak. *Copying and Duplicating.* Kodak Publication M-1. New York: Eastman Kodak, 1984.

Digital

Burkholder, Dan. *Making Digital Negatives for Contact Printing.* San Antonio, TX: Bladed Iris Press, 1998. (http://www.danburkholder.com; danphoto@aol.com)

Fokos, David. http://www.bostick-sullivan.com

Pyro

Hutchings, Gordon. *The Book of Pyro.* (1991) Available from: Gordon Hutchings, P.O. Box 2324, Granite Bay, CA 95746.

Paper

Airey, Theresa. *Creative Photo Printmaking.* New York: Amphoto, 1996.

Hunter, Dard. *Paper Making: The History and Technique of an Ancient Craft.* New York: Dover, 1974.

Turner, Silvie. *Which Paper?* New York: Design Books, 1994.

Index